BRIDGE ACROSS THE SKY

The Berlin Blockade and Airlift, 1948–1949

RICHARD COLLIER

BRIDGE THE

The Berlin Blockade

ACROSS
SKY

and Airlift: 1948 - 1949

McGRAW-HILL BOOK COMPANY
New York   St. Louis   San Francisco
Düsseldorf   Mexico

Book design by Kathy Peck.

1234567890   DODO   78321098

Library of Congress Cataloging in Publication Data

Collier, Richard, date
  Bridge across the sky.
  Includes index.
  1. Berlin—Blockade, 1948–1949.   I.   Title.
DD881.C57   943'.155'087   77-17384
ISBN 0-07-011796-9

9-28-78

To
the
men
and women
of
the airlift
and
blockade

Contents

From our lives in the Soviet Union
we have concluded that violence can be withstood
only by firmness. It's the very ideology of
Communism... if you can seize something,
seize it; if you can attack, attack; but if
there's a wall, then go back. Only firmness
will make it possible to withstand the assaults
of Communist totalitarianism . . . you, in 1948,
defended Berlin only by your firmness of spirit—
and there was no world conflict.

ALEXANDER SOLZHENITSYN to the
people of the United States,
Washington, D.C., June 30, 1975

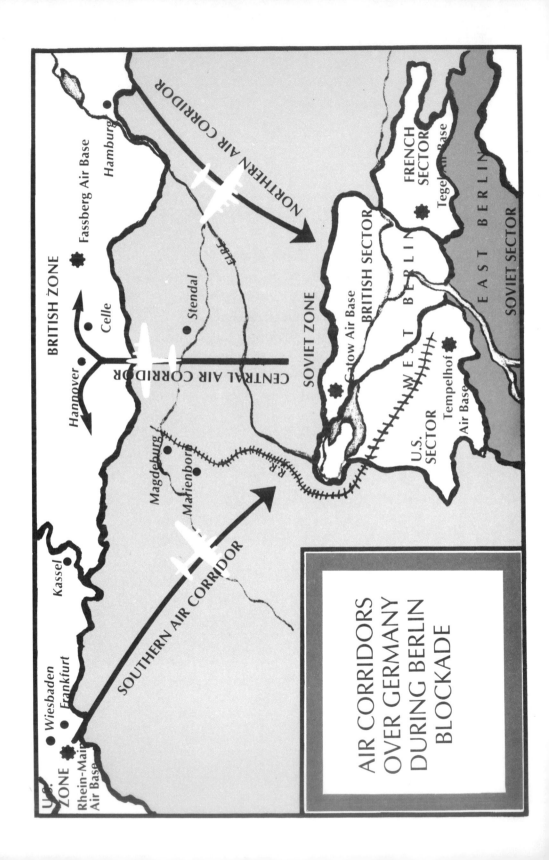

AIR CORRIDORS OVER GERMANY DURING BERLIN BLOCKADE

BRIDGE ACROSS THE SKY

The Berlin Blockade and Airlift, 1948–1949

1

MARCH 20, 1948

At exactly 1:30 P.M., Saturday, March 20, 1948, a royal-blue Fleetwood Cadillac, flying the scarlet rectangular flag of a four-star general on its right bumper, came to a halt in the courtyard of the United States Military Headquarters on Kronprinzenallee, Berlin. Within seconds General Lucius DuBignon Clay, United States Military Governor of Germany and Commander of U.S. Forces in Europe, emerged from the pillared portico of the headquarters building. A twelve-man honor guard, resplendent in khaki, gleaming Sam Browne belts, snow-white gloves, and saffron neckerchiefs, snapped to attention. The general returned their salute, bent and scooped up his Scottie, George, and climbed into his car. To a final flurry of salutes, the Cadillac eased through the white main gates.

The general was on his way to the eighty-second meeting of the Allied Control Council. Ordinarily these were routine sessions in which the four victorious Allies—Britain, France, Russia, and the United States—met to discuss the governing of the four zones of the recently defeated Germany. But Clay's intuition was that trouble lay ahead. How it would come he did

1

not know. Yet every indication, gathered from shreds of intelligence and personal contacts, was that the hour was fast approaching when the Western Allies would be faced with a serious challenge from their wartime comrades, the Russians.

In the three years since World War II ended, he had seen the gulf between Western and Soviet ideology widen to an abyss. One after another the "liberated" countries of Eastern Europe—Poland, Hungary, Romania, Bulgaria, and, most recently, Czechoslovakia—had become Soviet vassal states, and Clay wondered whether Berlin was the next item on Moscow's shopping list. Relations had become so strained that fifteen days earlier Clay had cabled a top-secret message to the Army's Director of Intelligence in Washington: "Within the last few weeks I have felt a subtle change in Soviet attitudes . . . which now gives me a feeling that [war] may come with dramatic suddenness."

The fifty-one-year-old general, known for his courtly manners and bear-trap will, knew all too well the reasons for the mounting Russian hostility. Secretary of State George Marshall's European Recovery Program—the Marshall Plan— which offered food, tractors, and hope to millions of needy Europeans, had been bitterly denounced by the Soviets, who saw it as a direct threat to the abject poverty on which Communism thrived. Suspect, too, were Allied projects designed to rehabilitate Germany's faltering economy: the reform of Germany's grossly inflated currency and the creation of a West German Federal Republic, uniting the three Allied zones of Germany.

Now, as his Cadillac sped toward Control Council headquarters, Clay turned to his political adviser, the State Department's Robert Murphy, to discuss the topic foremost on both their minds: the true intentions of the Russian Military Governor, Marshal Vassily Sokolovsky.

Similar worries flashed through the mind of Lieutenant General Sir Brian Robertson, the British Military Governor, as his silver-gray Rolls-Royce pulled away from his townhouse in the elegant suburb of Grünewald. A quiet, aloof soldier-diplomat, Robertson was not one to show emotion; a raised eyebrow over flashing blue eyes was his usual sign of displeasure. But today, as they headed toward the meeting, Robertson confided to his two companions, political adviser Christopher Steel and economics adviser Duncan Mowat, that he had found Sokolovsky's recent behavior "profoundly disturbing."

Only three months earlier Robertson and his wife, Edith, had entertained Sokolovsky in London, where they both had been convinced that a new understanding had been cemented. From Robertson's box at the Royal Opera House the marshal had reveled in a performance of Puccini's *Turandot* and, later, at a reception at Buckingham Palace, had responded with incredible enthusiasm in a heart-to-heart talk with King George VI. To crown the visit, the Robertsons had given a private dinner party at the Savoy Hotel, where, to Sokolovsky's unbounded delight, the staff, displaying proletarian solidarity, had unexpectedly gone on strike, leaving the guests to serve themselves or go hungry.

But now, at parties or receptions, Sokolovsky's sole acknowledgment of Robertson's presence was a distant bow. It was as though Robertson had offended against some social canon, and it was from such small, yet significant signals that Robertson deduced that trouble lay ahead. As they neared Control Council headquarters, Robertson told Steel soberly: "One foot wrong now and it's World War Three."

The man responsible for the misgivings of the Allied generals, Marshal Vassily Danilovich Sokolovsky, with forty medals—from the Order of Lenin to the Hero of the Soviet Union—in dazzling array across his massive chest, was also en route to the meeting. Soviet Military Headquarters at Babelsberg, known as "The Little Kremlin," was ten miles east of Berlin's center, and it was after 2:00 P.M. when Sokolovsky's 1939 La Salle sped into the broad highway at Potsdamer-Strasse. As usual, the Soviets were fielding a formidable team of dialecticians. Against the three-strong American and British cadres, Sokolovsky was bolstered by no less than five advisers, including his chief political adviser, Vladimir Semeneov, and his deputy, Lieutenant General Mikhail Dratvin.

Few were aware of the two distinct sides of Sokolovsky. To

3

the Allies there was the handsome, imperturbable man, six feet four inches, the genial host and devoted family man, who could quote from Jane Austen's novels and who often joked of the bear that was Berlin's symbol: "I want to skin this bear before I shoot it." The other Sokolovsky, known only to his aides, was often ill at ease: an insomniac who night after night prowled his bedroom, tormented by a World War I leg wound, who spoke by direct phone to Moscow for almost an hour each night, who smoked eighty cigarettes a day and went pitiably to pieces if deprived of tobacco. It was to this Sokolovsky that dispatches came by courier twice monthly from Marshal Alexander Vasilievsky, Chief of Staff of the Red Army's High Command in Moscow—orders in which the problems of Berlin featured ever more prominently.

It was 2:15 P.M. when Clay's limousine swept into the circular driveway of the Allied Control Headquarters at 32 Elszholzstrasse. Descending, the general glanced up at the four sixty-foot flagpoles that towered above the surrounding lawns and beech trees. The blood-red flag that bore the hammer and sickle of the Soviet Union hung to the far right, taking precedence over the Stars and Stripes, the Tricolor, and the Union Jack—a sign that for the month of March Russia was in the chair. Joined by his deputy, Major General George Hays, and his chief of staff, Brigadier General Charles Gailey, Clay mounted the stairs of the headquarters—a 550-room palace that had once been the highest court of Prussia. The ornate second-floor assembly room, flanked by eight marble columns with golden cornices, had once been the scene of warm amity among the Allies. On one memorable night, at a mammoth Russian ball, Clay, Robertson, Sokolovsky, and France's General Joseph-Pierre Koenig had linked arms to sing "The Volga Boat Song," stamping their feet in time with the music. Now it was more often the scene of dissension.

A steady shuffling of feet echoed from the marble stairway as the delegates headed for the assembly chamber. Across the inlaid mahogany floor, a separate table for each delegation formed the four sides of a square. Clay's team faced the French delegation, Robertson's the Russian. Within the square the

4

stenographers were already seated at their speed-writing machines.

In the salon next door waitresses in black-and-white uniforms and white cotton gloves were putting the finishing touches to tables piled high with food. By tradition each chairman offered a banquet at the end of the meeting, and the Russians were lavish hosts. There were mounds of gray-black Beluga caviar, suckling pigs, smoked sturgeon, Strasbourg pâté de foie gras, lobsters, truffled turkey, vodka, and pink Crimean champagne.

At 2:34 P.M., four minutes late, Sokolovsky strode in followed by his advisers. His gray eyes swept the meeting. Then, as he lit the first of a chain of long-stemmed black cigarettes, the delegates relaxed, fumbling for pipes and cigarettes.

No sooner had Sokolovsky called the meeting to order than he demanded that his colleagues consider a resolution, adopted a month earlier in Prague, attacking Western policy in Germany. Koenig was quick to take issue. The matter was being considered by his government; discussion at the Control Council level was entirely out of order. The other Allies demurred on similar grounds.

His eyes flashing with sudden anger, the marshal rapped out, "This only proves once more that the United States, British, and French representatives here no longer consider the Control Council as quadripartite authority in Germany. They regard it as a suitable screen behind which to hide unilateral actions in the Western zones, actions directed against the peace-loving people of Germany."

Clay and Robertson exchanged glances. Never before had Sokolovsky gone so far as to level a deliberate charge of perfidy against his colleagues. The Allies' insistence on the rehabilitation of Germany was obviously rankling Moscow.

Robertson was first to speak: "I wish to protest against the strong language the chairman has used in describing the attitude of his colleagues." He also added that it would be helpful if Control Council members refrained from using meetings for propaganda purposes.

Clay, too, spoke up: "I will not even attempt to reply to these charges. A mere casual examination of the record will show

5

when, where, and by whom the Control Council's efforts to govern Germany have been blocked."

Sokolovsky quickly shifted gears. "I find here no desire to discuss this memorandum, and it is automatically withdrawn," he stated flatly. Then he demanded that the Allied representatives report on any directives they had received at a February meeting in London, where they had met to thrash out Germany's future: the implementation of the Marshall Plan, the creation of a new West Germany with a reformed currency, and the merger of the three Western zones.

The request was out of order, for according to protocol all such directives were confidential. Moreover, as Robertson pointed out, the conversations had been "of a provisional nature," and as yet no governmental decisions had been reached. Clay took pains to explain that notes had been exchanged directly between the United States and Soviet governments with respect to that meeting.

Sokolovsky was adamant. "I insist," he challenged, "on the [Allied] members informing the Control Council what took place in London. What proposals were made? What decisions have been taken on the matters under discussion?" It was as if he were deliberately seeking to bring about a crisis. "In view of the fact that members refuse to give information on the conference in London," he continued vehemently, "I am compelled to make the following statement." He snatched up a typewritten document that had been lying before him and began to read—so rapidly and unintelligibly that the interpreter glanced helplessly around him.

Clay patted his Scottie, George; Robertson, indignant, attempted unsuccessfully to cut in; and Koenig, awaiting the interpreter's version, fell to wool-gathering.

The sudden scraping of chairs on parquet brought them all to attention. Sweeping up his papers, Sokolovsky had risen to his feet: "I see no sense in continuing today's meeting and declare it adjourned." The Soviet delegation rose as one and followed Sokolovsky as he strode from the room.

For minutes the Allies sat rooted to their chairs. Never before had a chairman adjourned a meeting without the approval of his colleagues. Never had he failed to set the date of the next session—or left without inviting the others to join him at the buffet. In every mind the implications were plain: The Allied Control Council was dead.

By late afternoon of March 20 news of the Soviet walk-out had reached every corner of Berlin. Many heard in the way that most news came these days: the 4:00 P.M. newscast by the American radio network in Schöneberg borough. Others heard by word of mouth. Some were angry, some fearful, some wearily resigned.

Few were surprised—and no one less so than Dr. Eugene Schwarz, Chief Public Health Officer for the American sector. Two months earlier Schwarz had predicted this move with near-clinical accuracy. He had been dining with a close friend, a twenty-seven-year-old redhead named Ada Tschechowa. Ada's husband was a gynecologist stationed in the Russian sector and had just delivered a Russian general's wife of a baby boy. At a celebration party that followed, the general and his staff had become ingloriously drunk, and toasts were offered to an objective looming large in the Red Army's summer maneuvers: the early eviction of the Western powers from Berlin.

"I tell it to you for what it's worth, Gene," Ada had cautioned, "but I have a feeling they meant it. They said, 'If those swine aren't out of Berlin by June, we'll close every access that there is.'"

The next day Schwarz reported the incident to his chief, Colonel Frank Howley, Commandant of Berlin's American sector, but Howley was unimpressed. "Write me a memo," he instructed, "and I'll take it to General Clay. But I think it's a lot of bushwah."

Howley had duly passed on the memo, but Clay had dismissed it. "This is nonsense. It would mean war," he had said. For the tensions that would prompt Clay's cable of March 5 were then less in evidence.

Now, as Schwarz heard the news of the Russian walk-out in his office on Königin-Luise Strasse, he smiled cynically. The scenario was developing as Ada Tschechowa had sketched it. It gave him no personal satisfaction, but at least he was prepared. For some weeks now, backing his hunch, he had been making such inordinate demands on the American Medical Supply Department in Frankfurt-am-Main that its director thought he must be preparing either for an epidemic or a siege.

He didn't know what the Russians planned next, but he was sure of one thing: They would in no way steal a march on Dr. Eugene Schwarz.

In his second-floor office at City Hall, an ugly red brick pile deep inside the Soviet sector, another Berlin official got word of the Russian behavior. Fifty-nine-year-old Ernst Reuter, former councillor for traffic and public utilities and current Lord Mayor-elect, needed no Control Council walk-out to bring home the nature of the Kremlin's intentions. For one full year, in 1921, as "Comrade Friesland," Reuter had been general secretary to the KPD, the German Communist Party, until, rebelling against the implacable *diktat* of Moscow, he had quit in disgust. Now, because he knew every lesson in the Soviet primer, Ernst Reuter was No. 1 Berliner on the Russian blacklist.

As far back as February 1947 Reuter had urged the Allies to rebuild Kraftwerk West, the vast 228,000-kilowatt power plant at Spandau, Berlin's westernmost district, a plant the Russians had dismantled before the British took over their sector. Aside from two small auxiliary plants, Reuter had pointed out, almost three-quarters of Berlin's electricity was supplied by Soviet sector power stations, a situation that made the city vulnerable to every Russian whim. Yet the reaction from the Allied *Kommandatura*, the four-power body that administered the city itself, had been a stinging rebuke: Reuter was charged with "creating an indisputable state of panic."

It was not to be Reuter's last run-in with the *Kommandatura*. Four months later, when Reuter was elected *Oberbürgermeister* (Lord Mayor) of Berlin, with 89 out of 108 votes from Berlin's municipal deputies, the four-power governing body had failed to back him, following Russian disapprobation. "Herr Reuter will never be permitted to take office," declared General Alexander Kotikov, the Soviet sector commandant. To the dismay of many, General Clay had gone along with the Russian blackmail in the interests of Allied unity. And though Reuter

8

still served as a Social Democratic councillor, two acting mayors were appointed to serve in his place: Frau Louise Schröder, a frail gray-haired woman, and Dr. Ferdinand Friedensburg, a precise, pedantic Catholic lawyer.

Reuter ordered a new set of cards: "Ernst Reuter, the Elected but Unconfirmed Lord Mayor of Berlin." He was bitter at the Americans' failure to back him, but he bided his time and never ceased to preach of the Communist danger. To one who advised him that a Berlin politician's only course was "to be on a good footing with all four powers" Reuter retorted icily, "It is not my business to act like a terrified rabbit staring at a snake."

Ironically it was Reuter who would prove to be Clay's staunchest supporter in the days ahead. For it was Reuter who, as transport and public-utilities chief in the Twenties, had fathered the vast transport and housing development that had made Berlin Europe's most modern and Americanized metropolis. Now his intimate knowledge of Berlin's beating heart, its railroads, its traffic arteries, its telephone system, was bearing fruit.

Hidden among the Greek and Latin texts that crowded the bookshelves of his Zehlendorf apartment was Berlin in blueprint, scores of large-scale public-utility plans: water, gas, sewage, and streetcar systems. For some months now Reuter and his closest aides had been smuggling them out to the security of West Berlin, ready to turn them over to the Allies when the time came.

Each evening Reuter would spirit out more vital plans—past the doorway police, who, though they perfunctorily inspected his briefcase, found nothing. No one guessed that beneath his shirt and trousers he was shielded against the chill night not by underwear but by warm layers of maps and blueprints.

To Berlin the Control Council crisis was one more burden to be borne on its war-ravaged shoulders. More than 70,000 tons of bombs had rained down on Berlin during the war. Even now the city was cluttered with mounds of gray rubble, stinking of old fires, diesel oil, and wet cement dust. On Sieges Allee, statues of long-dead governors stared blankly across splintered tree trunks. On Unter den Linden, once the city's most

9

fashionable street, the swanky Adlon Hotel was a shell, its cellar restaurant reduced to a menu of cabbage soup and turnips. The burned-out hulk of the Reichstag echoed to the flapping of crows.

As with the city, so with the people. Gone was the sardonic humor that even at the height of the bombing had inspired such graffiti as "Enjoy the war—the peace will be frightful." For most families, milk, sugar, fats, and vegetables were as rare as manna, and many existed solely on boiled roots and nettles. A social worker summed up the mood: "The energies of the people are spent in pursuit of a loaf of bread and a pair of shoes. Hope is alien."

But a greater menace still was the Russian presence. Everywhere there were reminders of the city's island status, 110 miles inside the Soviet zone—the Red flag flying above the shrapnel-pocked gate of the Brandenburger Tor, the spiders' web of checkpoints manned by Russian soldiers. It was the Russians who, when the Allied bombs stopped falling, had rampaged through Berlin, raping and looting with unparalleled ferocity.

No one knew for certain how many had been raped in what Berliners still called "the Russian time"—the fourteen April days of 1945 that marked the battle for the city. Estimates varied from 20,000 to 100,000. To exultant cries of *"Frau, komm!"* women and girls had been dragged from hiding places and served before their horrified husbands and children. Most yielded; those who resisted were hurled from tenement windows with their throats slit.

Russian treatment of Germans in the Soviet sector was still harsh. Only recently hundreds of specialists and scientists had been deported to Moscow to work in an optical plant. Others had been threatened, imprisoned, or hauled off to concentration camps.

Yet, the Allies, after years as comrades in arms, were inclined to view the Russians tolerantly. Their attitude had been born in the heady euphoria of the Teheran and Yalta conferences when Franklin D. Roosevelt had underestimated the Soviet threat. "I think the Russians are perfectly friendly," he told a staff officer in March 1944. "They aren't trying to gobble up the whole of Europe."

At one time Roosevelt had wanted Berlin badly. "The Soviets can take the territory to the east" was all he would concede. But, as arteriosclerosis sapped his energy, his resolution over Berlin waned. At the crucial Yalta conference he took pains to avoid all contentious subjects. The Big Three ratified plans for the division of Germany into zones—French, British, American, Russian—and for the division of Berlin into similar sectors. Berlin was to be in the Soviet zone.

The Allies had no written guarantee of access to Berlin, but there seemed to be no problem. The right to be in Berlin, already accepted by the Russians, apparently guaranteed the right to go there. After lengthy talks with the Soviets, a temporary verbal agreement on access to the city was reached. The Allies were granted a main highway, a rail line and two air corridors, later increased to three.

But it was a tenuous access which was why Clay, Robertson, Koenig, and 6,500 troops were now holding a fragile outpost peopled by three million fearful Berliners deep inside a red sea of Russian power.

For many Berliners the news of the Control Council breakup was but another concern in the daily struggle to survive. Twenty-three-year-old Marlena Eberhardt was typical of thousands for whom survival had become a way of life. Her troubles had begun in earnest on February 13, 1945, the night the Royal Air Force bombed the city of Dresden, where she had been sent by the Wehrmacht to work as a storekeeper's assistant. Marlena had survived the holocaust only by submerging herself in the steaming waters of the Elbe, while all around the city burned with a blue-white phosphorescent light. With it burned the bodies of 150,000 men, women, and children.

It took Marlena more than two months to make her way home to the working-class suburb of Prenzlauer Berg in Berlin. She arrived to find her world in ruins. On April 21 Berlin had become the front line in the final battle for the city. Shells had reduced the family home to the kitchen and one bedroom. Her

11

father's tailor workshop was reduced to ashes, and he was in the hospital, stricken with a heart condition. Faced with a world she no longer understood, Marlena's mother, Anna, had gone to pieces. All her deep-rooted precepts—speak the truth, owe nothing, keep your self-respect, never look down on another human being—seemed only words now.

Marlena learned to sneak forth to nearby farms and steal cabbages and turnips to keep them alive. "How can you bring yourself to do it?" Anna Eberhardt would lament, and Marlena could only reply, "*Mutti*, someone has to." In that week, when Germans and Russians battled for mastery of the street, Marlena learned other skills of survival. More than once she had to roll aside corpses to get to the street's one water source. And one day, when a horse fell dead, Marlena inched forward on her belly, a knife in her teeth, to rip steaks from the still warm rump.

Three months later Prenzlauer Berg had become part of the Soviet sector. Marlena found a job with the British Control Commission store and commuted daily to the West. Traveling by U-Bahn, the Berlin subway, she adopted the same smuggling technique as Ernst Reuter: some cutlery hidden in her shopping bag on Monday, a spare sheet wrapped around her body on Wednesday. The doctors said that her father was dying, and until that time her mother was staying put. But Marlena feared the Russian presence and sought a new life in the West.

By February 1946 she had made the break. Now a new problem arose: a permit to stay. The Western sectors were bursting with refugees, but through her work Marlena met a military policeman with the Green Howards Regiment. He fixed her up with a false permit. He also helped her find a room in Spandau, on Elisabethstrasse. Taking due note of her lithe young figure, her shoulder-length auburn hair, her full firm lips, he bided his time. Then one summer night, exacting a samaritan's price, he burst into her room and forced himself on her.

On April 27, 1947, Marlena gave birth to a premature five-pound baby. From birth the child, named Marta, was bitterly contested. For days after her delivery Marlena was barely conscious, with abscesses in her breast, scarcely able to feed her baby. One day when she awoke the child was gone. The landlady explained that during a bout of delirium her mother had come and taken Marta back to the Soviet sector.

Stormy scenes followed. Deeply shocked by what she saw as her daughter's moral lapse, Anna Eberhardt could pose only two alternatives. Either she marry the man responsible or give up Marta for adoption. Marlena saw no such choice. Marriage was impossible and adoption unthinkable. When she had told the man responsible about her pregnancy he had laughed in her face. Soon thereafter he was demobilized and returned to England. Now Marta was her sole reason for living, and Marlena could not give her up. As soon as she regained her strength, she snatched Marta from the clinic where her mother had put her and fled back to the West.

For eleven months she worked as a part-time nursemaid for a British military family, but the job ended when the sergeant was transferred out of Berlin. The law permitted no transit of illegitimate children from the city.

Now, with Marta to care for and currency inflation rampant, Marlena could find no work profitable enough to live on. She made a decision. The old strict training must go by the board. She would put herself beyond the law and become a black-market trader. Somehow, she and Marta would survive.

In the five days following the Control Council's break-up, General Lucius Clay was taking no chances. The tenor of his cables to Washington was becoming increasingly urgent. "The . . . conditions which exist in Central Europe today justify us in asking for special recruitment for this theatre," he urged General Omar Bradley, the Army's Chief of Staff in Washington. He stressed, too, that any evacuation of American dependents from the city, often mooted by the Pentagon, would be disastrous: "In Berlin, German people might become hysterical and rush to Communism for safety." Clay hoped to forestall potential trouble in the best way he knew, with what he termed his "Basic Assumption Plan"—on the assumption that the Russians would cut off supplies from the Western sectors and leave them destitute.

Incredibly, such a move was entirely feasible, for Berlin,

even in prewar years, had never been self-sustaining. Each week thousands of tons of freight had to travel over a single-track "international" railroad that ran 110 miles through the Soviet zone from Marienborn to Berlin. Virtually every item consumed by the Berliners—and by 6,500 Allied troops, their families, staff, and technicians—had to be imported along a lifeline that the Russians could cut at the border at any time.

Clay had no intention of being caught unprepared. Accordingly, he instructed Berlin's American commandant, Colonel Frank (Howlin' Mad) Howley, to reveal the plan to his Western colleagues. On March 25 Howley called a secret meeting with General Jean Ganeval, the French commandant, and Major General Otway Herbert, the British commandant. His colleagues listened attentively as Howley outlined General Clay's Basic Assumption Plan—or, as the fiery colonel had christened it, "Operation Counterpunch." Not only would it provide for food and coal stocks and the emergency use of what little power West Berlin possessed, he explained, but for the transfer of the City Assembly to the Western sectors and the use of the RIAS network, if necessary, for counterpropaganda against the Russians.

Ganeval was hesitant: Could the Russians really be planning a blockade of the city? "I can't believe that they would do such a cruel thing," he said dubiously, "but it is a possibility. I'm glad to know that the first steps to counteract it have been taken." Herbert's reaction, however, was withering. "It's preposterous," he pronounced. "They wouldn't dare, but if they did we could never hold out. The Russians could have us out in a month if they wanted to."

Hostility between the two-fisted Howley and the fastidious, patrician Herbert was never far from the surface, and the tension was now palpable. "Preposterous, my ass!" Howley shot back. "We'll starve, we'll eat rats, rather than quit Berlin."

Yet Herbert had logic on his side. In the winter of 1946, the coldest in a century, the temperature had dropped to minus four. The water supply had frozen, infant mortality had sky-rocketed, scores of Berliners were found frozen to death in the Grunewald. Hunger had driven wolves from the woods onto the *Berliner Ring*, the network of roads fringing the city.

14

Summarizing the plight of thousands was the bitter benediction chalked on the Reichskanzlei's famous balcony: "Blessed are the dead, for their hands do not freeze." In another such winter, if the Russians sealed off coal deliveries to the West, the Allies' position would be untenable.

Just how tenable or untenable the situation was Howley would not know until his departmental heads reported back to him. Earlier in the day he had called an emergency meeting of his twelve-man staff and presented them with a problem that seemed at best hypothetical, at worst insoluble. He had given each man exactly four hours to work out what his department needed to make Berlin self-sufficient for the next two months: food, fats, solid fuel for laundries and bakeries, medical supplies for hospitals, building material, clothing, every conceivable item from butcher's meat to laborer's overalls. Now all he could do was await their analysis and ponder the fate of Berlin.

A lean, rasp-voiced ex-cavalry officer, the forty-five-year-old Howley was already a legend in the city. The Berliners admired his gruff bravura, his tough no-nonsense approach, his custom of showing up unexpectedly in any location from a rubble-clearing site to a beer hall. Even the Russians, after many long, wearisome negotiations over everything from streetcars and sewers to riot control, had come to accord him a grudging respect. As Colonel Kalinin, Kotikov's chief of staff, put it, "We find him a hard opponent, but we like his frankness and his businesslike way of handling things."

It was not a tribute Howley reciprocated. Tough and uncompromising, he had arrived in Berlin believing, like most Americans, the Germans to be his enemies, the Russians to be his friends. Almost immediately he was disillusioned by the Soviets' cynical manipulation of their fellow man.

At one *Kommandatura* meeting, debating the inception of people's courts, Howley was appalled to learn from Kotikov that no man was brought before a Russian court for trial. "If he wasn't guilty he wouldn't be in court," Kotikov shrugged. "All the court has to do is sentence him." On another occasion, pressing for an increase in rations for the hungry Berliners, Howley argued, "We can't kick a lady when she's down."

15

Smiling coldly, the Russian Colonel Dalada replied, "My dear colonel, that is the best time."

At 12:00 noon Howley's departmental chiefs filed back to report. It was plain that no one had a true concept of what it would take to keep Berlin alive for the next two months. Every estimate was either grossly inflated or far short of the mark. Exasperated, Howley swung around to question the one man remaining obstinately silent on his list of needs, the Chief of the Public Health Division, Dr. Eugene Schwarz. But the doctor only shook his head. "I have no list."

"No list?" Howley could scarcely contain himself.

Schwarz stared back at him guilelessly. "May I remind you of a report I made two months ago of a conversation with my friend?"

Howley might not have believed the story, but Schwarz had, and accordingly he had ordered gauze, penicillin, vaccines, ether, and other medicaments by the ton. Every medical depot in the American sector was piled to the rafters.

"Two months," Schwarz told Howley evenly, "doesn't come into it. I can take care of this city's health for the next six months."

2

"If It's War They'll Get Hit Right Quick"

APRIL 1–APRIL 17, 1948

In the first week of April Sokolovsky followed up his Control Council boycott with a systematic campaign of harassment. Always stopping short of overt provocation, these incidents were nonetheless designed to make the Allied presence in Germany politically untenable.

At 2:00 A.M. on Thursday, April 1, the Frankfurt-am-Main–Berlin express, the crack "Berliner," was hammering through the night, nearing the frontier town of Marienborn. In the warm darkness of its passenger cars rode 300 American officers and enlisted men, some dozing uneasily, others unable to sleep. It had already been a nine-hour journey, and it would be another 110 miles through the Soviet zone to Berlin.

Captain Clarence Cummings, a young engineer who had recently completed an instruction course in Frankfurt, was particularly anxious to get back to his wife and two children in the Lichterfelde-West suburb of Berlin. A few days earlier he had received a tearful phone call from his wife, Vera, who reported that the city was alive with dire rumors. The Russians were "really acting up," she had told him, and unless he was "planning to visit us in Siberia," he had better hasten home.

17

Cummings wasn't really anticipating trouble, but he was anxious to be reunited with his family and calm Vera's fears. When the captain beside him noted uneasily that the train was coming to a halt, Cummings, who had made the trip before, reassured him that this was routine. At Marienborn, the door to the Soviet zone, the American zone engine would be detached and a Russian engine would transport them the rest of the way to their destination.

But in the chill small hours of this first day of April, Cummings and the others aboard soon realized that trouble was afoot. As always, Soviet zone police, armed with pistols and carbines, were lining the station platform, under the light of mercury vapor lamps. But this morning many of them were also armed with an unfamiliar item of equipment: short metal ladders. Stepping forward, a Soviet lieutenant with a loudspeaker issued an ultimatum to the train's commander: As of midnight on March 31, by order of Marshal Sokolovsky, the "Berliner" would not be allowed to proceed until every passenger's travel pass had been inspected. It was an arrogant demand, for while the Russians had on occasion checked the documents of German passengers traveling in Allied vehicles, they had no right whatsoever to inspect Allied military personnel.

From his carriage window Cummings followed the exchange with bated breath. The train's commander was adamant: Americans did not come under Soviet jurisdiction; if any Russian attempted to board, the MPs would open fire. The Soviet lieutenant was inflexible. No Soviet zone engine could be attached to the "Berliner" until all passes were checked.

Now enraged shouts and boos echoed from coach to coach. "If they want to shoot, we can shoot too," yelled a man close to Cummings. "Come on, Colonel, let's go through."

Hours of stalemate followed. At 9:00 A.M. a Soviet engine hitched onto the "Berliner's" rear and shunted it onto a siding. By now there were other trains similarly stalled—two more American trains, from Bremen, as well as westbound British and French military trains. The train commanders had gone to phone Berlin, seeking instructions, and the passengers descended, grumbling, to light fires and brew coffee beside the track. They all felt they knew what General Clay's orders would be: take over the controls, at gunpoint if need be, and bulldoze a way through.

But afternoon slipped into evening and no orders came. As dusk approached, the men clambered back aboard the trains. At 8:20 P.M. the men aboard the "Berliner" heard shouts. The train jerked abruptly, and everyone tensed. Now the crunch would come. Then, as the train jolted on the rails, picking up speed, the Americans exchanged glances of disbelief. The train was moving away from Marienborn—back toward Frankfurt-am-Main. For reasons incomprehensible to all, General Clay had backed down.

What the 300 men aboard the "Berliner" did not realize was that for almost twenty-four hours Clay, in the subterranean headquarters office known as "the telecon room," had been battling with Washington for a go-ahead to call the Soviets' bluff and had been rejected. It was an impasse that Clay had faced many times in the past—an impasse prompted, he felt, by a total incomprehension of Russia's brinkmanship strategy by the top brass in Washington. Both General Omar Bradley, the Army Chief of Staff, and his Director of Plans and Operations, Lieutenant General Albert Wedemeyer, were former infantrymen, as was the Secretary of the Army, Kenneth Royall. Thus, central to all their thinking was that Berlin, where only 6,500 troops existed to repel 18,000 crack Russian troops, could never be militarily defended in the conventional sense.

Even an influx of garrison troops from the United States would not be feasible, for in 1945 America had heeded the grass-roots plea to "bring the boys back home" by demobilizing her forces at alarming speed, often at the rate of 800,000 a month, until total U.S. Army strength stood at no more than 1,630,000 men. It was a situation Secretary of State George C. Marshall criticized as "the disintegration not only of armed forces but apparently of all conception of world responsibility."

Convinced that this latest Russian move was another case of saber-rattling, Clay again attempted to persuade the Pentagon that the only effective counter was a resolute show of strength.

No sooner had he received Sokolovsky's message of March 31 on mandatory train inspection than he cabled an urgent Eyes Only message to Bradley, advising, "Am instructing train commandants to resist by force Soviet entry into military trains if necessary." By late afternoon, having received only bare acknowledgment, Clay contacted Bradley anew. Again the reply was indecisive: The Joint Chiefs of Staff must consider the implications; meanwhile Clay must delay the trains.

As Clay had anticipated, Royall, Bradley, and Wedemeyer, a single-minded triumvirate, proved politely obstructive. If trains were halted, Royall stressed, "in no event shall there be shooting." Patiently Clay wired back: "Any weakness on our part will lose us prestige important now. If Soviets mean war, we will only defer the next provocation for a few days. I do not think suggestion realistic. . . .Any failure to meet this squarely will cause great trouble."

At 9:00 that night, with the "Berliner" already four hours out of Frankfurt, Clay was again closeted in an anxious long-distance debate with Bradley. By now the matter had been pondered at higher level, by Secretary of Defense James Forrestal and Under Secretary of State Robert Lovett, both of whom ranked among the doves of the U.S. Cabinet. Bradley's final instructions left Clay out on a limb. Though he could move trains as he saw fit, the train guards must not be increased. Nor could his men open fire unless fired upon.

Protesting that "I do not agree that this is a fair instruction to a man whose life may be in danger," Clay nonetheless assured his superiors that their instructions would be "followed to the letter."

Thus, when the "Berliner" and other military trains were stopped at the border of the Soviet zone, Clay had no choice but to direct the train commanders to back down.

The halting of the trains on the morning of April 1 had created another problem for Clay. It meant that 600 tons of vital freight had been lost to Berlin. The crisis he had envisaged through his Basic Assumption Plan loomed perceptibly nearer.

Clay summoned Colonel Henry Dorr, the commander of Tempelhof Air Base. How many C-47s, he asked, were available in Frankfurt? Dorr was explicit. Thirty-six planes of the

61st Troop Carrier Group were stationed at Frankfurt's Rhein-Main air base, although due to overhaul problems only twenty-five might be immediately available. Clay probed further. What cargo could a C-47 carry? "Two to three tons," Dorr told him. "No more."

Clay reached a decision. Before midnight on April 2, he instructed Dorr, thirty flights must somehow be made from Rhein-Main to Tempelhof. Then, as Dorr left hastily, Clay reached for his intercom and called his chief of staff, Brigadier General Gailey. Sixty tons of the most important supplies—just 10 percent of what the trains would have brought—must, Clay ordered, be loaded onto trucks to reach Rhein-Main by dawn. By midnight on April 2, at the latest, those sixty tons of supplies for Berlin's garrison must reach Tempelhof.

At Rhein-Main, some 275 miles from Berlin's Tempelhof base, the pilots of Major Albert Schneider's 53rd Troop Carrier Squadron were tense with expectation. For weeks their flights had been routine. Now, out of the blue, an intriguing announcement had appeared on the briefing room's bulletin board: Pilots were invited to volunteer for night flying missions to Berlin. In the excitement of the moment few even troubled to ask why. As one officer, Lieutenant Vernon Hamman, recalls, "We were so young and so dumb, all of us volunteered."

What baffled the pilots was the missions' seeming irrationality. No cargoes were to be carried; other squadrons were tackling that. Their sole instructions were to fly ahead of the cargo planes on a direct leg from Rhein-Main, circle Tempelhof, then return to Frankfurt.

No one had stopped to consider that at least two-thirds of the journey would be at 5,000 feet over Russian territory—a sure target for ack-ack or Yak 3 fighters if the Russians interpreted these night flights as an act of war. By the time the true nature of their mission finally sank in the crews of the 53rd had picked up a nickname wryly appropriate for the men chosen to test the Russians' will to oppose them: "Clay's Pigeons."

Fortunately the Soviets did not interfere with the cargo operation. The sixty tons of supplies were flown safely into Berlin as scheduled, and "Clay's Pigeons" went unmolested.

A few days later, however, the Russians were involved in an

air incident with tragic consequences. On April 5 a British Viking 1-B airliner GAIVP with ten passengers aboard was approaching Berlin in one of the three air corridors reserved for international use. Suddenly a Soviet Yak 3 fighter swooped down toward the British plane in a mock attack, narrowly missing the starboard wing. Zooming past the Viking, the Yak made a climbing turn and came back. At 1,000 feet the two collided head on and crashed in the fields below. There were no survivors.

For the most part, however, the British—like the Americans—felt the stepped-up Soviet activity as an exasperating, and sometimes saddening, experience.

At the Autobahn Aid Station, sixty miles from Berlin, the Union Jack fluttered to earth for the last time as the British prepared to pull out. It was a moment that called for ceremony, and Captain Desmond Haslehust stood rigidly at attention while the sad sweet notes of the Last Post echoed among the pine forests.

Even now Haslehust could scarcely credit what was happening. For as long as he had been in Germany there had been emergency aid stations, both American and British, sited at twenty-five-mile intervals along the *autobahnen*—precarious barbed-wire outposts inside Russian territory to aid Allied drivers facing breakdown problems or gasoline shortages. Commanding a staff of policemen and engineers, officers like Haslehust did one month's rotation duty. But on March 10, when he took up his post here, nobody had known it would be for the last time.

The trouble had started shortly after he arrived, when the artesian well supplying the station silted up. Haslehust had applied to Berlin for boring equipment, but within hours came bleak news: The Russians refused to allow it through. For two weeks the station had relied on water tankers from Helmstedt, in the British zone, filling every available receptacle from basins to jerricans. Then, on April 12, came more disquieting news from headquarters. The Russians had told the Allies that all aid stations must be closed down. To enforce the command they would allow no more tankers through.

22

"Leave nothing for the Russians, not even the barbed wire," Haslehust was instructed by phone. "Pack up everything and return to base."

Now these orders had been carried out. The dismantled barrack huts and workshops were piled aboard the trucks, along with the barbed wire. They were ready to go. The lingering notes of the Last Post died away, and Haslehust relaxed his salute.

Uncomfortably, he wondered where it would end. Were the Allies prepared to yield to the Russians every inch of the way?

This same thought was foremost in the mind of Colonel Frank Howley. Since the staff meeting of March 25 Howley had been studying the Russians in the weekly *Kommandatura* sessions with more than usual attention. Had the Control Council walk-out been a step toward the break-up of four-power control in Berlin as well? If so, how firm was the American resolve to stay?

As Howley and many Americans saw it, the Allied stake in Berlin was faith. Withdrawal would lead to despair—and to Soviet persecution—of the tens of thousands of anti-Communists who had been encouraged to speak their minds against the Reds. It would mean the retreat of forces which, however small, were the symbol of the Allies' commitment to halt the march of Communism across free Europe.

It was a concern that Clay had also voiced, in an impassioned plea to General Bradley. "[If] we retreat from Berlin," he had warned, "after Berlin will come Western Germany. If we mean that we are to hold Europe against Communism, we must not budge." But Bradley's response had mirrored the prevailing attitude of the Pentagon. Might not Russian restrictions be added one by one, he asked, "which eventually would make our position untenable unless we ourselves were prepared to threaten or actually start a war?" He saw the outcome as gloomy. "Here we doubt whether our people are prepared to start a war to maintain our position in Berlin."

Howley, who supported Clay's position to the hilt, had confided his own suspicions to the Chief of Intelligence, Major General Robert Walsh. At the *Kommandatura* meetings, he reported, General Kotikov was being reduced to a puppet, flanked always by his deputy, Colonel Yelizarov, and the political adviser Maximov, parroting speeches they had prepared. The Russians, Howley warned, were readying for a coup, designed to frustrate the Allies' plans for Germany.

Walsh brought in the State Department's Perry Laukhuff, who drew up a cautious report: "It would appear a possible responsible assumption, subject to later observation and study," that the Russians might at some stage kill the *Kommandatura.*

Midway through Saturday, April 17, Howley was more than ever certain he was right. Facing him across his office desk was his Chief Public Health Officer, Dr. Eugene Schwarz. "I'm sorry, Colonel," Schwarz was saying, "but the Russians have cut off the milk supply. Unless we get that fresh milk six thousand German babies in our sector will be dead by Monday." Even the farsighted Schwarz had not anticipated this eventuality.

Howley was appalled. Yet the logistics made sense: The Russians possessed the only dairy herds in Berlin. At the end of the war they had rounded up 7,000 cows and driven them into the Russian sector. Then, when the Allies arrived, the Russians had proposed a trade: a daily supply of American flour in return for over 18,000 quarts of fresh milk. For three years Russian and American trucks had carried on this exchange at the border.

Now, overnight, the Russians had clamped down a ban. Claiming that both labor and gasoline were short, they insisted that American trucks must collect the milk directly from dairy farms all over the Soviet sector. On a weekend, with many drivers on leave, it would involve a mammoth rescheduling operation.

"Can't you give these children anything else?" Howley pleaded.

Schwarz shook his head. "We've skimmed milk, but that's useless for their formula."

For a while Howley was silent. "All right," he conceded finally, "they've got us licked. I'll see about the trucks. Just for this once we'll have to eat crow." Privately, Howley was thinking, if the Russians would imperil the lives of 6,000

German babies, Clay's Basic Assumption Plan, or Operation Counterpunch, must sooner or later become reality.

Howley was not alone in his concern. At his headquarters in the old spa town of Wiesbaden, more than 250 miles southwest of Berlin, forty-year-old Lieutenant General Curtis LeMay, the taciturn commander-in-chief of the United States Air Forces in Europe, had, unknown to Howley—or even Clay—taken the final steps to ensure that if the Russians were bent on World War III, his crewmen would be ready.

Ever since taking command, in October 1947, the reduction in USAFE strengths had worried LeMay profoundly. His own available manpower had slumped from more than two and a half million men to 303,000. Worse, on the heady assumption that war was a thing of the past, vital defense equipment like bomb fuses and specific calibrated tools were being pulverized and consigned to the junk pile. In event of war, LeMay could muster against an estimated Russian fighter strength of 4,000 planes no more than thirty-eight combat groups of P-47s and B-29 bombers—of which only eleven were rated as operationally effective.

To LeMay the Pentagon's indecisive Soviet policy and belief in conciliation at all costs was cause for alarm. In the monthly commanders' conferences at U.S. Zonal Headquarters in Frankfurt, intelligence summaries and estimates of Russian intentions were almost never raised. Instead, LeMay, whose B-29s three years earlier had put a torch to fifteen square miles of Tokyo, listened impatiently to recitals of blanket returns and the incidence of venereal disease. This lack of finite policy had finally stirred LeMay to take the defense of free Europe into his own hands.

Chewing on an unlit cigar, scarcely seeming to move his lips, LeMay announced to his Chief of Staff, Brigadier General August Kissner: "We're not going to sit here fat, dumb, and happy—we're going to do something to get a little protection."

Both men saw the essential problem if war broke out. America's supply line from Bremerhaven in the northwest, at the mouth of the Weser River, was almost 250 miles from Frankfurt, where the bulk of U.S. troops were stationed—and

25

farther still from fighter fields like Fürstenfeldbruck, near Munich. If the Russians moved in to cut that supply line, only two American divisions and a handful of planes deep in southern Germany existed to oppose them.

What worried LeMay above all was the lack of American strategic bases situated well behind the Rhine. He and his staff officers had set their minds to the problem and come up with a bold and rather unorthodox solution. It was a plan that called for the formation of a small international defensive alliance with France and Belgium—an alliance that prefigured the North Atlantic Treaty Organization by a year and that LeMay was later to call his "own private NATO."

In meetings with General Charles Lecheres, Chief of Staff of the French Air Force, and his Belgian counterpart, Lieutenant General Lucien LeBoutte, LeMay had laid his proposition squarely on the line: "You know the situation as well as I do. If anything happens we're in a pretty bad position. I've got supplies. How about stocking up and getting ready to operate?"

Lecheres and LeBoutte did know the situation: Communism seemed to be spreading like a virus. Not only were Communists securing control of Eastern European states, but in Italy and France the Communist Party was powerful enough to make each successive government nervous about joining a Western bloc. And in Finland the Communists had recently forced through a new treaty of "Friendship." Thus, although it was illegal for American troops to set foot on French or Belgian soil in peacetime, both generals had assented to LeMay's proposals. How they squared it with their governments—or whether they even tried—LeMay never knew.

Now action was the keynote. Day after day one of LeMay's officers, Colonel Stanley Wray, flew from base to base, inspecting facilities. Week after week top-secret trainloads of materiel shuttled out of Wiesbaden, the boxcars laden with bombs, ammunition, aviation gas, field rations, and spare parts. In their wake went hundreds of USAFE ground crews, attired in civilian clothes, on temporary attachment to embassies and consulates—briefed to assemble the stockpiles at journey's end. "Zigzag those trains from hell to breakfast," LeMay ordered—for this masterpiece of deliberately snarled-up transportation was designed to deceive curious civilians as much as Russian agents. Bills of lading vanished without trace; whole boxcars of supplies sat on sidings for days before being attached to other trains and shuttled on.

Thus, by April 1948, LeMay's "private NATO" extended as far south as Istres, near Marseille, as far west as Bordeaux, and as far north as the Belgian bases of Liège and Charleroi: thousands of tons of materiel stored in warehouses, 200 technicians sited at each base. Only planes, deemed too conspicuous, were lacking, but if H-Hour came they could be flown in and armored for an anti-Russian strike.

Studying the charts his transportation experts had assembled, LeMay could now summon Kissner to announce with certainty: "If it's war they'll get hit right quick with all the air we have."

3

"You Have Done a Terrible Thing"

APRIL 17–JUNE 23, 1948

Lord Mayor-elect Ernst Reuter listened intently. The voices of the young men grouped around his desk in City Hall were restrained yet urgent. They were students of Humboldt University in Berlin's Soviet sector, and they were protesting Communist rule.

Reuter already knew part of their history. Most of them had seen war service in labor battalions or on the Western front; one, a former Allied POW, had been put to work transporting corpses in the Neuengamme concentration camp. All, without exception, had learned to loathe Nazism and propaganda. Theirs had been a shining goal: to build a new Germany, founded on truth.

Yet this had proved impossible at Humboldt University, the rambling old nineteenth-century building on Unter den Linden. In line with the Soviets' determination to instill Communism into every student, it had swiftly become, in one professor's words, "a charnel-house of academic thought." Lectures in Communist ideology became compulsory. In the canteen, propaganda broadcasts by the *Deutschlandsender* network were pitched at full blast to check "seditious" conversation.

28

History professors had to submit their texts in advance; instructions came from Moscow on the correct approach to Goethe; and Communist-sponsored students sat in on suspect classes, interrupting curtly, "No, no, Herr Professor, Lenin did not say that. . . ."

The backlash had been inevitable. In May 1947 Otto Hess, a lean, aquiline medical student, along with his friends Otto Stolz and Joachim Schwarz, had founded *Colloqium*, a campus monthly of criticism and comment. At first they trod warily, aware that more than 2,000 East German students had been arrested in this one year—more than 600 of them sent to Sachsenhausen, a former Nazi concentration camp twenty miles from Berlin. But in April 1948, following a student riot at Leipzig University, the three editors had courageously reprinted the Leipzigers' attack on their Soviet oppressors. In part it read:

> . . . Familiar visitors have reappeared in the universities of Germany's Soviet Zone. They are called Intolerance, Compulsion, Repression, Terror. . . . Whosoever does not preach that Marx, Engels, Lenin, and Stalin are the ancestors of all science is undesirable. Whosoever indulges in the concept that study is intellectual analysis, not taking orders from Moscow, is undesirable.
>
> Is This To Continue? No!

Within hours, students had thronged the corridors outside the rector's office, eager to learn the editors' fate. Soon Otto Hess emerged and announced the news: "We're finished—all three of us thrown out!"

The expulsion created a furor. At 6:00 P.M. on April 23, 2,000 students stormed off the Humboldt University campus and into the British sector to hold a protest meeting in the ruins of the Esplanade Hotel. They raised a defiant battle cry: "We demand a Free University in the West, one where we can pursue our studies in peace."

Now, one week later, a group of these students were in Reuter's office to plead their cause. "We are determined to fight the Soviet ideology right here in West Berlin," insisted

Otto Stolz, one of the expelled editors. "It's a question of either demanding truth in the lecture hall or emigrating," another student, Rolf Hildebrandt, summed up, "and we say emigrate."

Reuter was sympathetic. "Of course," he agreed, "you must have your Free University. But there are problems." Between puffs of his cigar he outlined them: no funds, no textbooks, no university building, and as yet no sector willing to take up their cause. In the City Council, Reuter might carry the motion, but this was only a beginning. Then it must go to the *Kommandatura*, without whom the Council could not even authorize funds for a tea party. And however the Western Allies voted, one Russian veto would still render the motion void.

Yet, as he looked at their despondent faces, Reuter sought some way to give them hope. Here was a group of Berliners who would somehow cling to their belief in the Allies. So the Allies must not relinquish them. At least, Reuter promised, he had power to do one thing: He would ask every department in City Hall, every suburban branch of the Social Democratic Party, to present the unborn Free University with one chair. It was not much, but it was a beginning.

For almost every Berliner, the black market had become a way of life. As prices soared ahead of wages, many found it impracticable to work for derisory take-home pay. An unskilled worker could command only 180 marks a month, yet the black-market price for a topcoat, if one could get it, was 600 marks. It was the same with other goods: butter was sixty dollars a pound, bread twelve dollars a loaf. For the cheapest of broken-down shoes a man paid upward of one hundred dollars. As one social-services worker described the situation in a report to General Clay: "Many people find it not worth while to work for a wage. It takes too much time away from earning a living on the black market."

Although barter was illegal, every neighborhood had its secret *Brotbaum* (bread tree), which each night sprouted small white leaves of paper: "Will sell linen curtains and tablecloths for potatoes." "Want bread, offer German cigarettes." But this was for the poorest and neediest. The nerve center of the biggest deals was the "Little Tiergarten," the parched expanse of grass that stretched away from the old Reichstag.

Marlena Eberhardt never forgot her first visit—or how the conductor actually called out "Black Market" as the streetcar approached the Tiergarten stop. Descending, she looked about, fascinated and repelled. At 10:00 on a May morning the place was alive with people, dragging suitcases, pushing handcarts. Children with pinched old men's faces offering cigarettes cadged from Allied soldiers. War veterans on crutches with medals to sell. Plump snide men with nylon stockings at 45 dollars a pair. Ragged men peddling yarn and soap powder.

The language of barter was surreptitious murmuring litany: "Gold, silber, dollaren, Ami zigaretten, schokolade . . ."

The three hardest currencies were cigarettes, coffee, and chocolate. One packet of cigarettes, worth at least 35 dollars, might change hands a hundred times. Sixteen cartons secured a Bechstein grand piano. One American technician at Tempelhof had acquired a $3,800 mink coat with 13,000 cigarettes.

Since her initial resolve, in March, to support herself and her illegitimate daughter, Marta, by black-market trading, Marlena had acquired a certain expertise. She had made a contact through a soldier working in the British NAAFI stores on Reichskanzler Platz. For a one-third cut he had offered to supply as much chocolate as Marlena could sell. There were forty-eight bars to a box—with each two-ounce bar worth 30 marks.

Only an overly suspicious policeman would have spotted her as a black-marketeer. On the surface she was a pretty young war widow who had chosen a sunny morning to air her daughter in her push chair. But in the base of the child's cart were four boxes of chocolate, 192 bars, almost 6,000 marks' worth. Between visits to the Tiergarten the stolen chocolate was hidden in the wardrobe of the flat she now shared with three other families.

One day the first week of June as she was making her rounds a whistle blast split the air. From a lookout atop a heap of rubble a cry went up: *"Razzia"* (raid). Blue-gray uniformed police from Berlin's black-market squad piled from a wagon and rushed toward them. The parched plain was suddenly a sea of shabby men and women, fighting to get away. The more agile sought refuge in the cavernous ruins of the Reichstag. Marlena

31

and her baby were among them. They were lucky this time, but would they be the next? Was this to be the price of survival?

That same week in June General Clay took a step to wipe out the black market and stabilize Germany's currency at one stroke. He acted with such lightning speed that many Berlin financial experts were convinced the Americans had gone mad.

On Wednesday, June 2, he summoned a group of Berlin's leading financiers to a top-secret conference that had all the elements of a cloak-and-dagger operation. Helmut-Otto Kruger, legal adviser to Berlin's Chief Postmaster, was told only: "Go straight home and pack—you'll be collected within the hour." Then Kruger was transported to the meeting in a blacked-out Horch limousine that veered all over the city in an attempt to throw him off the scent. But at journey's end he almost laughed outright. A native-born Berliner, Kruger knew the gray stone pile of York House, a British headquarters on Fehrbelliner Platz, as well as his own front door.

In the paneled first-floor conference room, clutching defensively to cheap cardboard attaché cases, were eleven other men whose names were bywords in Berlin financial circles. Each had been abducted in the same way.

The door to the conference room swung open and three men entered: Britain's Sir Eric Coates, France's Paul Leroy Beaulieu, and a man the financiers knew only by reputation, Jackson Bennett of the U.S. Treasury Department, General Clay's financial adviser.

"Gentlemen," Bennett greeted them, "we've invited you here to assist us in a crucial financial program."

All the German financiers were familiar with the problems of the country's faltering economy—and of the role of the United States in trying to solve them. As early as 1946 Clay, then Deputy Military Governor, and Robert Murphy, political adviser, had urged on Washington the issuance of a new German currency to replace the outmoded Reichsmark. For on the subject of inflation both men held strong views, repeatedly stressing that there could be no healthful German economy without a stabilized currency and a reformed decentralized banking system.

The Russians' plans to impoverish Germany as a first step

toward a Communist take-over had been laid long before VE day. Unwittingly, the Allies had played into their hands. To ensure that a single occupation currency was used by all four powers, they had supplied their own printing plates to the Russians. In a cynical attempt to bankrupt the nation, the Soviets had promptly printed occupation marks by the billion. Polish DPs with suitcases full of marks were shuttled into Germany on a nonstop spending spree. Every Red Army soldier in the Soviet zone was awarded up to six years' back pay—all of it in occupation Reichsmarks.

What followed was the economic nightmare that had spawned Germany's black market. Few farmers would invest in government bonds or carry out cash transactions; for a sack of potatoes they demanded a Persian carpet or Meissen china. No laborer worked more than the minimum hours necessary to earn the Reichsmarks to match his ration coupons. On every street the shopkeepers' shelves stood empty; their goods remained in the warehouses. Money became worthless. University lectures were paid not with money but with consumer goods: three pounds of flour per lecture, with a special monthly bonus of thirty herrings. The noted comedian Bruno Fritz rated eight ounces of bacon and eight of white beans for each performance. A hairdresser stayed in business with the aid of ham smuggled in from Poland; it was the sole currency that bought the needed dyes, pins, and hair conditioners.

For three years the Russians had worked diligently to ensure the continuation of this economic chaos. When currency reform was first discussed Sokolovsky insisted the new banknotes must be printed under the supervision of the individual zone commanders. But Clay and the Allies demurred. There was no guarantee that the Russians would not print more than the stipulated amount of notes—as they had the first time around.

Clay had suggested a compromise. The new currency should be printed by the State Printing House in the American sector, 100 yards from the Soviet border. During the printing the plant would be declared an international enclave, under four-power supervision. But the Soviets had resorted to delaying tactics, culminating in Sokolovsky's Control Council walk-out.

33

Now, Bennett told the assembled financiers, the Allies' patience was exhausted. In the three Western zones currency reform was going ahead. But Berlin presented a special problem. Since the city was under four-power occupation, no one nation could legislate on Berlin's currency—but of course on this matter there was no agreement between the Allies and the Russians. Suppose the Russians attempted to introduce a new currency of their own into Berlin? In that event the Allies must be prepared to defy them—and extend their new Western currency into Berlin itself.

It was to discuss these contingency plans that Berlin's financial experts had been called in. There were many hypothetical questions to consider. How much money should be put into circulation at one time? Should accounts be blocked, and, if so, to what extent? These were the problems to which they must quickly find answers. Until the eleventh hour they would be held incommunicado, working in York House, sleeping in a British barracks at Spandau. For at all costs the Russians must not suspect their mission.

As Bennett wound up, a low murmur arose in the conference room. Then Helmut-Otto Kruger spoke up. In the event that the Allies did find it necessary to introduce their new currency into Berlin, wasn't the State Printing House uncomfortably close to the Russian border?

Bennett's reply made them aware of how far things had gone. In a top-secret project, code-named "Operation Bird Dog," the money had already been printed in the United States in December 1947, and two tons of it was now stored in the vaults of the old Reichsbank Building in Frankfurt-am-Main. When and if the need arose, planes would be standing by at Rhein-Main Air Base to ferry 250 million crisp new blue-backed Deutschemarks into Berlin.

As the month of June wore on the Russians stepped up their slow tightening of the noose around Berlin. Shortly after 10:00 A.M. on Sunday, June 13, three khaki-colored Diesel buses, each bearing a forty-strong contingent of British soldiers and their families booked for leave in England, settled in for the two-hour journey to the Helmstedt checkpoint on the Berlin-Hanover *autobahn*. Toward noon the checkpoint came in sight: a huddle of drafty wooden huts, candy-striped poles supported by oil drums, Mongolian soldiers in smocklike uniforms with automatic weapons. Two hundred yards beyond a no man's land of sun-baked earth, the Union Jack fluttered above the British zone.

The coaches stopped, and there was a mood of silent tension. Finally a young Russian lieutenant boarded one of the coaches and demanded all passports. The officer moved slowly, scrutinizing each document minutely in a silent war of nerves.

Aboard the first coach, now checked out, Captain John Reynolds, who was in charge of the convoy, relaxed a little. Suddenly a harsh command brought him to his feet: "Everybody out of the buses and into the woods!"

Reynolds strode out to meet the Russian as the others were debussing. With the aid of a Russian-speaking passenger, Reynolds questioned this arbitrary action. A wordy argument ensued. Finally, Reynolds saw the light: A teenage girl aboard Coach No. 3 had covertly snapped a picture of a Russian guard. After an hour's wrangling, the Russian, angrily zipping the film from the camera, handed back the camera and released the coaches.

At 2:45 P.M., after almost three hours, the buses eased forward across no man's land and the British barriers rose to receive them. Looking back, Reynolds noted the convoy's good fortune. The Mongolian guards were now rerouting all vehicles—back toward Berlin. The road was closed.

The Helmstedt shutdown was one of a string of recent incidents. Two days earlier, on June 11, Britain's Major General Herbert, through whose sector all Berlin rail traffic was routed, was told by the Russians that no more freight trains could enter. Their excuse was "congestion in the Berlin yards." By 8:00 P.M. all trains on the decrepit *Reichsbahn*, spanning the Russian and British zones, had ground to a halt. Since eighteen trains a day were the city's lifeline from the West, more than two million Germans—and their Allied occupiers—faced potential starvation.

35

Twenty-four hours later the ban was called off, only to be followed by other bans. On June 14, following the Helmstedt shutdown, the Russians closed the temporary wooden bridge across the Elbe River near Magdeburg. The bridge, carrying *autobahn* traffic from Berlin to Helmstedt, was "in urgent need of repairs." All traffic must detour to Niegripp, fifteen miles downstream, to cross the river by hand ferry, two cars at a time.

On the same day the Russians turned back 100 out of 600 Berlin-bound freight trains, alleging "technical defects." Major Karl Mautner, Howley's liaison officer at City Hall, reported that 7,000 freight permits still awaited Soviet signature. And Mautner further spelled out Berlin's financial plight. Since April 1, the night the "Berliner" was halted, the city had accumulated a 400-million Reichsmark debt to Western suppliers of raw material. Worse, many plants vital to Berlin's economy were in danger of folding: the Blaupunkt radio works, the Osram light-bulb manufactory, the giant Telefunken works, which turned out radio tubes and equipment. At Marienborn the Russians had turned away 140 loaded coal cars bound for Berlin.

In a final act of insolence the Soviets had ordered that all Germans traveling to the Western zones could buy rail tickets only at Friedrichstrasse Station in the Soviet sector. Thus they assumed sole authority over which Germans could leave Berlin.

The situation became graver by the day. Under the pretext of clamping down on black-market deals, the Soviets had now put restrictions on the shipping of all goods. Every item transported must undergo their scrutiny. To what extent they would carry this harassment short of total war no one could be certain. But in an attempt to take soundings, Clay sent Howley to clarify the situation with General Alexander Kotikov.

"Find out if the Russians are just trying to annoy us," Clay instructed, "or if they really have a black-market problem. If Kotikov has anything reasonable to suggest we might be able to work out something."

But at his Karlshorst headquarters the pudgy silver-haired general smiled and avoided the issue. "I'll have to take this up with my superiors," he said. He would get back to Howley as soon as possible.

Forty-eight hours later Howley still had not heard from Kotikov. It was Wednesday, June 16, and a *Kommandatura* meeting was scheduled for that morning. Howley did not want to raise the issue in the overcharged atmosphere of the meeting itself, but before the day was through he resolved to sound out Kotikov in private. When he took his seat in the second-floor conference room of the *Kommandatura* building, however, Howley was taken aback. Colonel Alexei Yelizarov, the Deputy Military Commandant, was occupying Kotikov's seat. General Kotikov, Yelizarov was explaining to the chairman, France's General Ganeval, was "indisposed," and he was standing in.

Nodding his assent, Ganeval opened the meeting. As always, Howley noted, the agenda was uniformly tedious: the question of personnel employed at Spandau Prison, the reorganization of Berlin's administrative courts, the recognition of nonpolitical organizations. Each week *Kommandatura* meetings grew more protracted, so that fourteen-hour sessions were now commonplace, as the Russians attempted to wear down the Western Allies in trials of verbal strength. As he resigned himself to the long ordeal Howley looked out the window at a skylark, spiraling and swooping in Triest Park.

The meeting dragged on, interrupted at one point when a commissar Howley had never seen, wearing an exotic Ukrainian blouse, entered and whispered urgently in Yelizarov's ear.

At 10:45 P.M. Howley made an effort to end the meeting, proposing it should adjourn at 11:00 P.M. But Yelizarov refused, insisting they turn to a full-scale discussion of General Kotikov's "Fourteen Points for the Amelioration of Workers' Conditions in Berlin." It was a subject the administrators had debated for eight months now—always fruitlessly, since at city level, as Howley had stressed, they were powerless to act on many of the points. The nonexistent Control Council was the supreme arbiter on labor questions.

At 11:15 P.M. Howley came to his feet. His decisive rasp cut across Yelizarov's tirade: "Half an hour ago I suggested that we end our meeting. I'm tired. I am going home and I am going to bed. With your permission, General," he addressed the chairman, "I will leave my deputy, Colonel Babcock, to represent me."

General Ganeval graciously assented. As Howley strode across the room, there was a low buzz of comment from the Russian contingent. As he closed the door behind him a tumult of sound rose from the conference room. But he was past caring. The night air along the street was sweet and cool, and Howley felt cleaner now.

Using Howley's brusque exit as a pretext, Yelizarov seized his chance to sabotage the *Kommandatura*. Rising from his seat, the hulking Russian slammed his papers on the table. "It is impossible," he shouted, "to continue this meeting after an action that I can only claim as a hooligan action on the part of Colonel Howley. I consider we should finish."

"I will close the meeting if so requested" was Ganeval's tactful gambit, but Yelizarov would have none of it. "If Colonel Howley will not apologize, I will not remain here any more," he announced, moving fast for the door.

"It is the Russians who are acting improperly," Ganeval called out, but Yelizarov kept going. Amid the general hubbub, Ganeval made one last attempt to regain order. "We haven't settled the date of the next meeting," he reminded the Russian.

"As far as I am concerned, there won't be a next meeting," Yelizarov shot back.

The delegates stared at one another bleakly. With this one sentence four-power control in Berlin—and all hopes of averting a confrontation over the city—had come to an abrupt end.

In the shadowed anterooms of the U.S. Press Club in Zehlendorf, white-jacketed German stewards moved lethargically, emptying the last of the day's ashtrays, polishing tomorrow's glasses. At midnight only a handful of correspondents— among them *Newsweek's* John Thompson and the New York *Herald Tribune*'s Marguerite Higgins—still lingered over drinks.

As Howley strode into the main clubroom they exchanged puzzled glances. Though he habitually gave a half-hour press conference following each *Kommandatura* meeting, it had seemed too late to expect a newsbeat tonight.

Barely had Howley called for a martini on the rocks than a steward came hastening: The colonel was wanted on the phone. Repairing to the lobby, Howley heard Babcock's excited voice describing the upshot of his departure and Yelizarov's break-up of the meeting. The Russians had fulfilled his three-month-old prediction.

As Howley returned to the clubroom, he faced the correspondents, eager for a story. He briefed them on the situation, ending on a note of warning to the Russians: "All right, this may mean the end of the *Kommandatura*, but if any joker thinks the Americans, British, and French are going to be dealt out of Berlin he has another guess coming."

As the newsmen piled out, exulting over their scoop, Howley called Clay's Dahlem home to update him. To his astonishment, Clay, invariably courtly, was "hopping mad." "Get over here and fast," he said. "I want to see you right away."

At No. 43, Im Dol, Howley faced a commander angrier than he had known in three years. "You have done a terrible thing" were Clay's first words. Standing rigidly at attention, Howley remained discreetly silent. "And the worst of it is," Clay added, his voice made high by rage, "you're not even sorry about it." Now Howley could no longer contain his feelings. He snapped back, "You're damn right I'm not."

Coldly, Clay dismissed him with an injunction to return at 8:00 A.M.

The next morning the general was still agitated. The reasons were plain: Even at the eleventh hour Clay had hoped for a compromise over currency. Under quadripartite control the continuance of a common currency had been a possibility, however remote. Clay had even hoped that Ganeval, as that month's chairman, could call a meeting to discuss the mooted reform. Now, with the *Kommandatura* broken, the Russians could legitimately refuse to attend.

Chastened by Clay's contained anger, Howley sought to defend himself. The *Kommandatura's* status, he responded, was now the same as that of the Allied Control Council—

nobody knew whether it existed or not. "When it suits the Russians they'll say it does exist, and when it doesn't suit them they'll say it doesn't. And I have taken all I can stand from the Russians."

Clay was icy: "Your job is to sit there and take it."

In a flash of insubordination for which he "expected to be fired on the spot," Howley replied angrily, "I thought my job was to keep them from stealing the city of Berlin."

Clay was silent. A man who did not normally tolerate dissent, he was nonetheless a realist. He recognized that the damage was done and that, whatever followed in the days ahead, Berlin would need this volatile Irishman whose mental processes he could never plumb yet whose courage he could not impugn.

"All right, Frank," he said quietly, "I guess you've had your quota of conferences for one day. Go home and get some rest."

As late as June 17 the Russians were still in total ignorance that within twenty-four hours currency reform in the West would strike a lethal blow to the inflation they had created and nurtured. On June 16 Clay, in a top-secret Eyes Only teleconference with Under Secretary of the Army William Draper in Washington, announced: "Agreed to currency reform on tripartite basis as of June 18 . . . the money is en route to last stations, key officials are notified, all is in motion . . . the die is cast."

The night of June 18 was hot and airless. All over Germany families stayed tuned uneasily to their radios, alerted that an important announcement was to come. In a studio at Radio Frankfurt, almost 300 miles southwest of Berlin, the American Control Officer, Robert Lochner, whom Clay had briefed to inform the public, was still wrestling over last-minute translation details in a marathon telephone conference with one of Jackson Bennett's staff. It was a reform to tax the best financial brains—yet the basic provisions must be made clear. At one point Lochner complained, "This section just isn't clear to me." In a burst of frustration the expert shouted back, "But *I* don't understand that part myself."

Promptly at 8:00 P.M., however, Lochner's translation was ready to be transmitted to millions of Germans: "This is Radio

Frankfurt. You will now hear an important announcement by the three Western military governors."

As of midnight, Sunday, June 20, Lochner went on to explain, all old currency in the three Western zones outside Berlin would be invalid. Starting at 7:00 A.M. on Monday, June 21, Reichsmarks were to be turned in or registered at neighborhood food-ration offices in exchange for new Deutschemarks. For the first sixty old marks each citizen would get sixty new—forty on the spot, twenty within two months. Though the rate of exchange on the balance could not be revealed until registration was completed, it was, in fact, to be one new mark for ten old—a whopping 90 percent currency deflation.

As Lochner walked thoughtfully home he was intrigued to hear his own voice booming back from scores of apartment windows. To ensure that almost sixty-eight million Germans were made aware of the new reform, Radio Frankfurt was retransmitting every hour until midnight.

Still the diplomatic door was kept ajar. By 8:14 P.M. General Ganeval had called a Saturday morning *Kommandatura* meeting to discuss the reform, making it diamond-clear that these measures did not apply to Berlin. By midnight Yelizarov had replied by letter. "Owing to pressure of business" he was unable to attend.

The exclusion of Berlin from the monetary reform left one man—Lord Mayor-elect Ernst Reuter—sorely worried. Even before the reform was announced he had called on Howley's liaison officer, Major Karl Mautner, and urged him: "You can't leave Berlin out of the currency reform. We'll be absorbed into the Soviet zone."

His concern was well founded. On Sunday, June 21, Clay received a letter from Sokolovsky that left no doubt that a Russian power grab for Berlin was on. Protesting the currency reform, the marshal stated: "With respect to Greater Berlin, I consider it to be economically integrated with the Soviet zone."

Clay suggested a meeting of all four economic advisers to hammer out a solution. To his surprise the Russians agreed, and a meeting was arranged in the Control Council building for Tuesday, June 22. Even as the Control Council was meeting to discuss compromise, however, events were moving swiftly

41

beyond the point of negotiation. At 9:00 P.M. on June 22 Frau Louise Schröder, one of the three acting mayors, was summoned peremptorily to City Hall, accompanied by her deputy, Dr. Ferdinand Friedensburg. There the Soviet liaison officer, Major Otschkin, handed them some documents, along with a handwritten note from General Lukjantschenko, the Soviet Chief of Staff.

"These documents," ran Lukjantschenko's note, "provide for currency reform in Berlin. The Soviet Military Administration does not doubt that the Berlin City Council will carry out its instructions on the introduction of the currency reform. . . ."

Scanning the documents through gold-rimmed pince-nez, the prickly Friedensburg asked Otschkin if the reform applied equally to the non-Soviet sectors of Berlin. The Major said it did. "Then," Friedensburg challenged, "how can this point of view be reconciled with the provisional constitution of Berlin?" Otschkin was evasive: On this point he could make no statement. Friedensburg persisted: "What is the City Assembly to do if the other powers specifically make other arrangements for their sectors?"

"I don't think the Western powers will make any conflicting regulations" was Otschkin's complacent reply.

At this same moment, in the Control Council building on Elszholzstrasse, the four-power economic conference was nearing its inevitable conclusion. From the first Jackson Bennett had judged the presence of Russia's Professor Paul Maletin ominous. A prominent Communist, Maletin was brutally uncompromising: The Soviets had every intention of saving Berlin from the "economic collapse" that the new reform threatened. Thus the new Eastern zone currency, Maletin announced, would be Berlin's only valid money. From now on Russia would control the city's banking and finance.

Bennett resisted stubbornly. The Soviet writ did not apply in the city's Western sectors, he pointed out, nor had the Allies any intention of abdicating their sovereignty to Russia.

As the meeting broke up, Bennett's suspicions that the Russians had only been stalling for time were confirmed. A uniformed courier entered and approached Maletin. He kept

42

his voice low, but Bennett heard enough: "The proclamation is ready. Tomorrow we announce the new financial regime."

On the morning of June 23 Clay drafted a curt reply to Marshal Sokolovsky: "I reject *in toto* the Soviet claims to the city of Berlin." In the pre-dawn darkness of that same day, his contingency plans went swiftly into effect. At Kaufbeuren Air Base, near Munich, several pilots of the 39th Troop Carrier Squadron, among them Lieutenant Randolph Tully, received a cryptic order from the squadron's Operations Officer: Take off for Rhein-Main Air Base, pick up "a load of merchandise" for Berlin. At Rhein-Main the mystery deepened as crews began loading wooden boxes marked only "Clay" and "Bird Dog." In the Operations Office, the briefing officer pressed live grenades on Lieutenant Tully and his co-pilot. "If you have to crash-land in Russian territory," he ordered, "blow up the ship." Tully was mystified. Why the Russians would want the secrets of an antiquated C-47 was beyond him.

Once over Tempelhof, the whole operation assumed a nightmare unreality. Through his microphone, Tully, as instructed, intoned a code phrase with an Alice-in-Wonderland ring: "Tempelhof tower, Tempelhof tower, we have New York on board." The result was electrifying. As the C-47 slid down the runway, jeeploads of military police converged on all sides. As Tully cut engines, a harsh voice assailed them: "Get out of that plane, you two, and stand clear." Repairing to the snack bar for coffee and doughnuts, Tully and his co-pilot were still none the wiser as to their errand.

Then, soon after 3:00 P.M., in Western sector branch offices of the Stadtkontor Bank all over Berlin, the phones began to ring. Branch Manager Walter Karge, at Lichterfelde, in the American sector, received a cursory summons to report to the sector's head office in Steglitz.

There, along with other managers, Karge received instructions from the sector chief: The Western Allies were proceeding with Berlin's currency reform. As of June 25 Berliners, too, could convert Reichsmarks to the new Deutschemarks. They would be exchanged on a one-for-one basis up to sixty marks, the capital quota to be paid out in one installment. At 8:00 P.M. that night the listening public would learn full details.

In the hope of one day reaching agreement with the Russians, the Soviet Ostmark (East Mark) would also be legal tender—and thus, in the Western sectors of the city, either currency could be used to pay rent, taxes, gas and electricity bills.

To ensure top security, the managers were transported back to their branches by British Army trucks, wedged in among cartons of brand-new Deutschemarks—each note rubber-stamped "B" for Berlin. Ahead, they could only look forward to thirty-six hours camped out in their offices, along with their staffs, each group standing watch over some 20 million Deutschemarks, until borough officials arrived to collect them.

Karge's last instructions had been ominous: "And pick up some candles on the way out—the Russians may cut off the light."

Through the streets of the city the realization traveled like a shockwave: Money was for spending. As news of the reform passed from Frohnau in the north to Schönow in the south, Berliners had but one idea: The flimsy value of their Reichsmarks was numbered in hours. Clutching bankrolls, large or small, they formed long jostling queues at stores, railway stations, theaters, above all in the ubiquitous black markets. Rich and poor alike had just one purpose: to snap up some tangible item while the time remained.

In these last hours currency changed hands like paper money in a frenzied game of Monopoly. Everything from a race-track ticket to a cemetery plot was suddenly a desirable commodity. Along the line of the Iron Curtain, at Potsdam and Pankow and Lichtenberg, hundreds tried to slip through to dump their worthless notes in the Soviet zone. One man, arrested at the border, was weighed down by 400,000 Reichsmarks.

Never was there such a time for paying off old debts. Doctors' surgeries were inundated with conscience-stricken defaulters. Customers arriving at Madame Berthe's off the Kurfürstendamm, found the famous modiste in hysterics, scattering handfuls of Reichsmarks to the four winds: One and all, her debtors had discharged their obligations. Journalist Cornelia Herstatt returned to her Tiergarten apartment to find the letter box stuffed with 4,500 marks. Belatedly her publishers had settled the advance on her first book—and an estate agent, in the nick of time, had returned her 3,000 marks down payment on a new flat.

Some squandered every last cent, beset by a feeling that all money was now unreal. Paul Michael von Broecker, a student, made for the fairground by the Titania Palace. Between the rifle range and the test-your-strength machine, he rid himself of forty marks. Eva-Maria Niensdorff, General Ganeval's pretty interpreter, felt the same. Her last forty marks went on a bunch of wild roses, a wedding bouquet for a favorite aunt.

A few tried to strike last-minute bargains. As lawyer Horst Mühle queued in a Steglitz barbershop, a customer rushed in with a fistful of notes: "Take it—I'll pay for a year's haircut in advance." Some found loopholes the currency laws hadn't blocked. Bank clerk Johann Richter noted that small coins like pfennigs would be retained at a tenth of their old value—and set out to amass 5,000 marks worth of fifty-pfennig pieces.

Those who had come by their cash illegally found no redress. Aircraftman Danny Tremarco, from the Royal Air Force Station at Gatow, should never have had any Reichsmarks: British personnel were confined to occupation scrip called BAFs. Yet through black-market deals the young airman had salted away 10,000 marks—the price of the set of fine bone china he had earmarked for his mother in Liverpool. He arrived at the dealer's shop to find his money worthless.

There were special hardships for some. The old, living on savings, saw their money decimated overnight. So, too, did students living on Army gratuities and precarious budgets. Edith Alker, who ran the Protestant welfare agency, Innere Mission, returned from a trip to find the mission's funds frozen and her 3,000 D.P.s in dire want; it would be months before Internal Revenue vetted the funds of charitable institutions.

Yet for thousands, even as they formed into long lines at their local food offices, often for eight hours at a stretch, there was a resurgence of hope. In a corridor at City Hall, Otto Theuner, the Councilor for Personnel, jovially hailed Ernst Reuter: "These are very democratic times—all Berliners are equally rich and equally poor." Mayor Willy Kressman, in the

45

factory district of Kreuzberg, summed it up to his aides: "Out there they'll be queueing to start a new life. At last they've summoned up courage to think of the future, to hope."

To some that hope seemed dim. At 8:00 P.M. on Wednesday, June 23, eating her meager supper, Marlena Eberhardt heard the news. Through the living-room radio came the familiar tones of the announcer for RIAS (Radio in the American Sector): Berlin's currency reform, designed to destroy the black-market root and branch, was now an established fact. The measure that promised a new beginning for millions of Berliners put an end to Marlena's livelihood. She would once again have to find legal employment, and the wages, she knew, would be meager. But at least what money she did make would now have some value.

On June 23, at the seventy-fourth session of the City Assembly, 130 councilors were assembling to debate Marshal Sokolovsky's decree that only Soviet currency would be valid citywide. Through terror tactics reminiscent of Nazi days, a Communist rabble 3,000 strong sought to cow the city fathers into disavowing the Allies.

"Hands off Berlin!" "Down with the Split!" The raucous cries held an ugly edge of menace as the angry demonstrators gathered in the streets surrounding the red-brick structure of City Hall on Parochialstrasse in the Soviet sector.

From a loudspeaker truck the grating tones of Walter Ulbricht, the bearded fanatic whom the Kremlin had enjoined to communize German industry, kept the mob at fever-pitch. Parked in the side streets were ten Russian trucks crammed with Communists carrying red banners proclaiming "ONLY ONE CURRENCY WILL SAVE BERLIN." Others thronged the corridors that led to the third-floor Assembly chamber, a vicious gauntlet of jibing hoodlums.

Councilor Jeanette Wolff, a petite, sixty-year-old grandmother, stopped aghast at the sight. Suddenly a policeman blocked her path. "For God's sake don't go in, Frau Wolff. They're trying to stop the delegates—you'll get crushed."

She stiffened determinedly. "I spent six years in a concentration camp without being scared of the SS. I'm not going to run away from the SED." Then she passed resolutely through the mob, their spittle wet on her cheeks.

Inside, the long bare Assembly chamber with its rows of wooden benches more suggested a classroom besieged by unruly students than a parliament. Officers of the four powers, seated on high-raised benches, stared with growing alarm at the mob of SED demonstrators that packed the public gallery. As Jeanette Wolff entered, two councilors were battling for supremacy. The speaker, bald-domed Otto Suhr, was refusing to open the session until the demonstrators quit the chamber. SED councilor Karl Mewis, poised on a bench, his arms outstretched, was exhorting them to stay.

Sighting Jeanette Wolff, Mewis shouted, "You don't come in. Traitors are to stay outside." Frau Wolff's retort was brief and unparliamentary: He could shut his big mouth. Then, as he continued to hurl abuse, the five-foot-tall woman walked over and toppled him ignominiously from the bench.

It was symbolic of all that followed. In vain, Frau Louise Schröder, frail and neat in navy blue, pleaded for order. Hoots and catcalls greeted her appeal. Angered by this display of bully-boy power, Jeanette Wolff marched to the microphone and addressed a strident protest to the Soviets: "Gentlemen of the Soviet Military Administration—I may assume that you do not interrogate your prisoners under a thousand-watt lamp like the Gestapo did. . . . You are still supposed to be our liberators. . . ."

The Russians stared back impassively, one ostentatiously filing his nails, another flicking at the pages of a newspaper. From the gallery there now came a barrage of chilling vituperation: "Throw that bitch out!" "We'll shut your mouth for you."

Finally, after a warning that the meeting would transfer to the American sector if the mob did not disperse, the demonstrators trooped from the gallery, chanting the "Internationale."

There followed a meeting as turbulent as any in the Assembly's history. Shouts and threats from the Communist councilors greeted Frau Schröder's uncompromising stance as Acting Mayor: "I cannot take orders from one of the Allied occupation authorities conflicting with those of the others. We cannot obey Sokolovsky." A Communist delegate responded with a prophetic warning: "Two currencies will mean barbed wire on the Potsdamerplatz—the end of Berlin as a united city." Amid the uproar that followed, Gustav Klingelhöfer, City Hall's economic adviser, rose to propose a motion: Now that two currencies had been introduced, let them compete, for the canny Berliners would soon decide which one was the better.

This was a shrewd proposal, for Berliners in the Soviet sector were already discovering that the much-vaunted Russian currency reform was, in truth, no reform at all. To forestall the Allies, the Russians had hastily tricked out millions of old worn Reichsmarks with thumb-sized stamps held on with potato glue—money that the irreverent Berliners soon dubbed *tapetenmark*, wallpaper money.

By a vote of 106 to 24—with only the Communists dissenting—the Council overwhelmingly approved Klingelhöfer's motion. In staunch defiance of the Russian ukase, the city councilors had cast their lot with the Western Allies—at a meeting held fourteen blocks inside the Soviet sector.

At No. 4, Reichsstrasse, the clock in the newsroom of the British-licensed *Der Tag* showed 11:00 P.M. The morning edition of June 24 was almost ready, and political editor Margot Derigs, a comely war widow, was checking the last of the galley proofs. Just then, she remembers, the teletype machine of the Soviet-sponsored ADN news agency—often silent for hours at a time—began an ominous tac-tac.

Reporters called excitedly to one another, abandoning their typewriters to huddle around the machine. Margot Derigs joined them, watching the message as it stuttered out onto the teletype paper:

BERLIN, *June 23 (ADN). . . . Transport Division of the Soviet Military Administration is compelled to halt all passenger and freight traffic to and from Berlin tomorrow at 0600 hours because of technical difficulties. . . .*

Frau Derigs suddenly knew "that this was it, this was final." A blockade was no longer just in the making. It existed.

4

"There Was No Agreement. There Is No Agreement"

JUNE 23 – JUNE 25, 1948

*. . . It is impossible to reroute traffic in
the interests of maintaining rail service, since
such measures would unfavourably affect the
entire railroad traffic in the Soviet Occupation
Zone . . . water traffic will also be suspended. . . .*

The teletype clattered on. In newsrooms all over Berlin the
scene that Margot Derigs had witnessed was being enacted
time and again. More than any other body, it was the editors
and reporters who first became conscious that this late-night
flash marked the prelude to a lock-in bigger than anything
Berlin had known hitherto. For nine unenviable hours these
men and women were privy to this secret—until at 9:00 A.M.
the day's first newscast from the RIAS studio on Kufsteiner
Strasse brought the grim tidings to 2,500,000 Berliners.

*. . . Coal shipments to Berlin from the Soviet
Zone are halted. The Soviet authorities have also
ordered the central switching stations to stop the*

49

supply of electric power from the Soviet Zone and
Soviet Sector to the Western sectors. Shortage of
coal to operate the plants and technical
difficulties at the Czernowitz Power Station are the
reasons. . . .

All over the city, undeterred by a steady drizzle of rain, people gathered in uneasy knots on the sidewalks as the announcer's voice echoed from scores of windows. Because of "technical difficulties" the milk delivery from the Soviet zone to the Western sectors was once more halted. All deposits in the Stadtkontor bank were to be frozen. Food and drug stocks in the Russian zone were now reserved for the Soviet sector only.

The implications, shocking in their cynicism, could no longer be evaded: The city would acknowledge Russian dominion or be starved into submission. By rail, road, and water Berlin was cut off from the outside world.

In these first hours the Berliners reacted each in their own way. Some maintained that this was just one more Russian bluff. Some carried on determinedly. Others reacted with anger or fear—or became aware of a new sense of purpose, a solidarity engendered by a common plight.

In a Grunewald villa, Dr. Fritz Schieckel, a young pediatrician from the Children's Hospital, was talking over the situation with his wife, Vera. Often in the past the Schieckels had thought about emigration. Didn't both England and Canada offer a brighter future? Now, as the broadcast spelled out the shape of things to come, the Schieckels were one of many families to reach a crucial decision. "Let's stay," Fritz urged. "The West must help us if it wants to help itself."

Others reacted with resignation. For Marlena Eberhardt, after the fall of her black-market empire, it was one more tragic turn of the Russian screw. Hearing the news that morning, she said to her friend Hildegarde Lutz, "They've always had the door ajar—now they've locked it."

Thousands more wondered just what the future held. In Wilmersdorf, eighteen-year-old Kurt Arnold was just starting as a trainee at Berlin's last luxury hotel, the Park. Now the thought struck him: With Berlin cut off, would a hotel find trainees an economic imposition? Kurt's fears were well founded; the 200-room Park was soon reduced to five guests a day.

At Berlin's largest hospital, the 800-bed Rudolf Virchow, in Wedding, the Chief Medical Officer, Dr. Wilhelm Heim, called his doctors and interns to an emergency meeting. Owing to electricity cuts, surgery must be scheduled for one hour daily. Then Heim pointed out how the Allied bombings had, in one respect, proved a blessing in disguise. With the upper floors and elevator system destroyed, power cuts couldn't hamper the transfer of patients on the two floors remaining.

Others were appalled by the long-term implications. In her office in City Hall, Frau Louise Schröder was stricken by the news. She burst out to her Chief of Secretariat, Gerhard Lasson, "But it may go on for one year, two years, ten years—who can tell?" Erika Tausch, a senior secretary at the Texilwaren glove factory in Kreuzberg, remembers that the office staff of fifty spent that entire day in excited discussion. "The mood was 'Will the Allies stay? Why should they bother? Why start a war for our city?'"

One man determined to resist at all costs was Colonel Frank Howley. At 8:30 A.M., en route to his headquarters, the rock-jawed Irishman was angry beyond speech—conscious that June 24, 1948, was "one of the most infamous days in the history of civilization." The faces he saw in the streets as his open Horch sped by were more troubled than Howley had ever seen. Fear of the Russians lay over the city like a pall.

In his office, as Howley was briefed by Public Information Officer Fred Shaw, he understood all too well the fear in those faces. In an attempt to stampede the population, the Soviet radio was spreading awesome rumors. Berlin's streets were said to be torn by riots, its stores looted. Still other reports had it that Western troops had fired on German mobs; that hundreds lay dead where they had fallen; that the panic-stricken Allies, bent on evacuation, had begged the Russians to expedite their departure.

"The Americans will be the first to leave," ran one scurrilous newscast. "Mrs. Howley is packing her silver."

Would the normally skeptical Berliners take these Communist shadows for substance? Early reports suggested they might. At dawn, when the Soviets predicted the water supply would be cut off, nervous *hausfrauen* had reacted accordingly. Gauges at the sixteen water plants fell alarmingly as housewives scrambled to fill bathtubs, buckets, even chamber pots; in the French sector suburbs of Wedding and Reinickendorf, many taps had run dry.

Howley knew he must act fast. He phoned William Heimlich, head of RIAS, and within minutes they had hit upon a solution. By 10:00 A.M. a RIAS announcer was urging baffled housewives: "Forget about the water shortage—give your baby a bath. All of you take baths—use as much water as you want. There's plenty of it!"

The psychology worked triumphantly, for within hours the plants reported that water hoarding had ceased and the city's supply—1,200,000 cubic meters a day—was returning to normal.

Meanwhile, others were reacting to the rumors. Colonel Robert Willard, U.S. troop commander, called in alarm to say he had two battalions of fighting troops and was anxious to help. Howley assured him there were no riots and help was not needed. Next it was Major General Clarence R. Huebner, commander of U.S. forces in Germany, calling from zonal headquarters in Frankfurt: "What's the real situation?" he asked. "If you want any troops we'll rush them in right away."

With more confidence than he felt, Howley replied, "General, what you've heard is Russian bushwah. There's absolutely no rioting in our sectors. The situation is tense but I've got it in hand."

Actually, Howley was more disturbed than he could openly admit. All along the Russian border, at Potsdam and Pankow and Lichtenberg, worried observers reported Josef Stalin tanks maneuvering in strength, in plain sight of the Germans. Howley needed no military adviser to calculate the odds. In Berlin's East sector alone the Russians had 18,000 crack troops—as against 3,000 American fighting men, 2,000 British and 1,500 French. And those three-to-one odds could be further weighted by reinforcements from the 300,000 men encamped in the

Soviet zone, for the Red armies had never permitted large-scale demobilization as had the Americans.

In truth, all three Allied sectors were vulnerable to a surprise Russian attack. Across the 341 square miles of Greater Berlin, the subterranean U-Bahn and the rickety overhead S-Bahn crisscrossed from the Soviet to the Western sectors in a cat's cradle of steel. From any one of ninety-two U-Bahn stations— or sixty-six S-Bahn—Russian troops could pour into the West as effortlessly as Monday-morning commuters into Grand Central Station or Piccadilly Circus.

Of course no one could be sure of the Russians' intentions, but one factor was plain: The Berliners, who would bear the brunt of the blockade, must know that the Allies stood solidly behind them. Once again Howley called Heimlich, asking for a prime slot that afternoon.

As yet uncertain as to Clay's policy, let alone the State Department's, Howley was going out on a limb, but at 2:00 P.M. that day, as he sat beside the interpreter in a RIAS studio, he sought to reassure the Berliners.

The Americans, he promised, were not leaving; they were here to stay. He did not yet know the solution to the present problem, "but this much I do know," he said. "The American people will not stand by and allow the German people to starve."

Then, mindful of the tanks massing on the border, he wound up: "And now I will give the Russians something to chew on besides black bread. We have heard a lot about your military intentions. Well, this is all I have to say on the subject: If you do try to come into our sector you had better be well prepared. We are ready for you—and if that day comes, believe me, many a comrade will go across the golden Volga."

On the evening of June 24 General Lucius Clay's plane from Heidelberg touched down at Tempelhof Air Base. Addressing the newsmen massed to greet him, the general laid his position squarely on the line: "The Russians are trying to put on the final pressure—but they can't drive us out of Berlin by anything short of war."

Yet by midnight on this same day Clay would have cause to

wonder. Now that the chips were down, how much support could he finally command from those from whom he had most right to expect it?

At an early evening meeting with his staff to sound out opinion, Clay found them uncertain. Some, like political adviser Robert Murphy, believed passionately that the United States must stay. As Murphy had urged Secretary of State George C. Marshall that very morning: "Physically all that has happened is a pole across the road guarded by two Mongolian soldiers. *This* is the blockade, no more." Staunch support came, too, from Major General Robert Walsh, Clay's G-2. "The Russians are putting up a tremendous front" was his shrewd evaluation, "but they're weak, they're vulnerable—if we face them out they'll capitulate." Economics adviser Lawrence Wilkinson similarly assured Clay: "We're seeing eye to eye, Lucius—I'm as red-headed as you are."

Others felt that support from the Army and State departments, however, would be lukewarm for a variety of reasons: the lack of fighting men, the physical impossibility of defending Berlin, the conviction that in their drive to communize Europe the Soviets would resort to all-out war. As the meeting broke up there were no staff recommendations and no final consensus of opinion. The lonely decision was left with one man: Lucius D. Clay.

Around this time General Sir Brian Robertson arrived at Clay's headquarters deeply disturbed. Earlier that day Clay had come up with a plan to break the blockade: an armed convoy of 200 trucks, escorted by a constabulary regiment, a recoilless rifle troop, and an engineer battalion to proceed along the Helmstedt–Berlin *autobahn*. The battalion would be equipped with bridge, train, and road repair equipment to carry out all bridging and highway repairs necessary en route. His object was threefold: to call the Russians' bluff, to show the American intention to clear the road to Berlin, and to assert Allied rights to stay in the city.

It was a calculated gamble—yet all reports reaching Clay convinced him the Russians did not want war. For six months now Lieutenant General Reinhard Gehlen, former OKH Chief of Intelligence, and a staff 400 strong had been working under

American G-2 auspices to evaluate the "E" (for *ernst*, or serious) case that was Berlin. From his $3 million fortress at Pullach, near Munich, Gehlen kept daily contact not only with Frank G. Wisner, of the newly created Central Intelligence Agency in Washington, but with two vital Berlin "fronts," Major General Rudolf Kleinkamp's *Reklame und Werbe Zentrale* publicity firm and Erwin Bender's import and export agency.

Through agents in East Berlin these bureaus kept Gehlen, Wisner, and General Walsh in tune with Soviet thinking, and the tenor of all reports was that the Russians were saber-rattling—what the State Department's George Kennan, in an independent memorandum, termed "Moscow's attempt to play, before it is too late, the various political cards it still possesses on the European continent . . . in Trotsky's vivid phrase, 'to slam the door so that all Europe will shake.'"

Hence Clay's confidence that an armed convoy could still proceed unscathed along the *autobahn*.

Sir Brian Robertson was appalled by this concept. "If you do that, it'll be war—it's as simple as that." In the strained silence that followed, Robertson added uncomfortably, "In such an event I'm afraid my government could offer you no support—and I am sure Koenig will feel the same."

It was now that Robertson proposed an alternative plan: Supply Berlin by air. It was actually the brainchild of Air Commodore Reginald Waite, a wiry forty-seven-year-old flying-boat veteran, the Control Commission's Royal Air Force representative. Waite's complex logistics called for an all-out effort by British transport aircraft to supply Berlin's basic needs. Robertson had warmly approved the scheme.

Convinced that Clay would welcome the project, Robertson had already asked Air Marshal Sir Arthur Sanders to put the British side of the plan in motion. The first aircraft—a modest contingent of eight planes from Waterbeach, near Cambridge—would leave England after dawn on Friday, June 25.

But Clay was not as receptive as Robertson had anticipated. It was one thing to fly reinforcements into Berlin on a temporary basis, as Clay had done in early April from Rhein-Main to

55

Tempelhof. It was quite another to contemplate such a mission on an indefinite basis. When the New York *Herald Tribune*'s Marguerite Higgins had asked him at Tempelhof whether it was possible to supply Berlin by air power alone, he had replied flatly: "Absolutely impossible." At midnight on June 24 Clay saw no reason to reverse that view—nor the one he had expressed as recently as June 13 in a cable to Washington in which he said: "We can maintain our own people in Berlin indefinitely, but not the German people if rail transport is severed." This was the appraisal he now gave Robertson.

But something would have to be done, for Berlin was under siege without guns. In the darkness thousands lay awake, wondering and fearful, wooing a sleep that would prove elusive even in the small hours.

In Lichterfelde-West a telephone rang in a darkened two-room apartment, and Hans Hoehn, a nineteen-year-old clerk in the U.S. Military Government, groped to answer it. The voice on the other end said, "You are a traitor because you work for the Americans. All traitors will be shot when the Americans leave Berlin." His wife Astrid asked who was calling, and Hans told her it was a wrong number. He was too frightened to repeat what he had heard.

At about the same time Robertson's military assistant, Major Terry Coverdale, at home on Rheinbabenallee in Dahlem, came bolt upright in bed. Hastening to the window, he warned Nancy, his wife: "I think this is it—they're here." Then he returned, cursing, to bed: it was only a routine patrol of the 11th Hussars Daimler armored cars.

In a ditch flanking Montgomery Barracks, Kladow, Lieutenant John Horton, of the 1st Worcesters, on night patrol, froze into absolute stillness; ten feet away on the road he heard the stealthy sound of footsteps. A Russian sentry was heading directly for him. Quickly Horton ducked behind a bush. Too late, he realized the man sought the same bush—only for reasons of natural modesty. As the fine spray drifted down on him, Horton lay still, gritted his teeth, and thought of England.

Beneath the iron ribs of the Lehrter Railway Station, a confrontation of explosive dimensions was in the making. The incident had begun soon after midday as a petty wrangle. Around 12:30 P.M., in the mess of the block, which housed British detachments policing the Tiergarten, Sergeant Edmund Coslett of the 1st Worcesters was forking a mouthful of meat and vegetable stew when the alarm bell jangled into life. As he and his mates jumped into action, Coslett gleaned from a passing officer the only intelligence he was ever to receive on the situation: "There's skullduggery at the Lehrter Railway Station—the Russians are trying to pinch some scrap metal and you've got to stop it."

As the Worcesters' truck jounced toward the station, a mile away, the first intelligence reports were reaching Major General Otway Herbert in his Kaiserdamm headquarters. At first glance the situation looked like a genuine error over boundaries: Scrap-metal workers, under Russian orders, had begun loading scrap onto railway cars just inside the British sector. When police ordered them to stop, Russian officers arrived to countermand the order.

Nonetheless, Herbert ordered the Worcesters to move in, surround the Russians, and if need be dig in until they unloaded the scrap from the trains and withdrew.

It was a daunting task. Lacking entrenching tools, they could not dig in on the contested ground, a waste of weed-choked tracks lying between and below two bridges—the railway bridge that spanned the yard and the redstone Moltke Bridge crossing the Spree River to the south. As darkness fell, however, the Worcesters took up final positions, prone on their groundsheets among the sleeping cars, stationed behind empty freight cars, or crouched among wispy drifts of gray-white flowers along the rusty tracks. But the Russians, dimly seen figures in olive-green, showed no signs of withdrawal. Some dug in along the riverbank; others holed up in an abandoned ice factory 200 yards across the tracks.

At tenement windows overlooking the yard, Berliners clustered curiously on this chill June night, elbows propped on cushions for greater comfort.

Now, to Coslett's relief, Captain Albert De Quincey, an insouciant fair-haired youngster, arrived to take command. "We've got to stalemate them," he told Coslett. Already

57

reinforcements were arriving: thirty more Worcesters under Sergeant Jimmie Cushen, deployed in the attic of a ruined warehouse overlooking the Moltke Bridge; a company of the 1st Royal Norfolks; and three armored cars from the 11th Hussars, their two-pounder guns mounted, blocking the Moltke Bridge exit from the far side of the river.

At 9:00 P.M. a Russian limousine approached from the west. As Colonel Alexei Yelizarov descended, the light from his headlamps picked out a formidable barrier. The bridge was blocked by a bristling hedge of barbed wire. As De Quincey and his interpreter advanced to parley, Coslett heard Yelizarov's impatient command: "Remove these things immediately. Let the troops and the vehicles out."

De Quincey was courteous but firm. When the scrap metal was unloaded, the troops and freight cars would be free to depart.

Yelizarov peered into the darkness. "Have you troops?" he demanded harshly.

Hands in pockets, De Quincey lied coolly: "You're surrounded by them."

"Machine guns?"

"Hundreds of them."

"You may display machine guns and armored cars," Yelizarov threatened. "I can and will display tanks."

"Bring them" was De Quincey's nonchalant reply. "We'll blow them off the face of the earth."

When General Herbert heard the news he swore explosively. Though he had ordered a show of force, he had had no intention of holding a position from which one trigger-happy sentry could start a war. Immediately he wired a request for instructions at the highest level. After a hastily convened emergency Cabinet meeting at 10 Downing Street, he received his orders: For the next twenty-four hours, at least, the Worcesters were to hold fast.

It was a bold stand, for despite De Quincey's outrageous bluff, the yard was surrounded by barely a hundred men, armed with no more than rifles, two-inch mortars, Mark V Stens, and three light machine guns.

But the move paid off. After a night of electric tension, the

Russians finally capitulated. By eleven o'clock the next morning they had sulkily unloaded the scrap metal and were allowed to drive away.

As the air of crisis intensified, men sought desperately for a formula, some last-minute legal technicality that might yet avert the nightmare of war.

In his Dahlem villa RIAS Chief William Heimlich was retiring for the night when a four-alarm call from Brigadier General Charles Gailey, Clay's apopleptic Chief of Staff, startled him into wakefulness. Within the hour, Gailey shouted, Heimlich was to bring copies of all documents concerning road accessibility to Berlin to Clay's headquarters. The order made sense of a sort: Before taking over as civilian head of RIAS, Colonel Heimlich, as Assistant Chief of Staff, G-2, had sat in on the early Control Council meetings, parleying for countless hours with the Russians. But he told Gailey flatly: "I do not have any copies."

At the pitch of his lungs Gailey bawled, "You were there—you must have them. Now find those agreements and get over here."

Heimlich could offer nothing but the coldest of comfort. "I was there—and I know that there *was* no agreement, there *is* no agreement—on the roads or on anything else." As an afterthought he added, "It may just hold on the air—I wouldn't even know about that."

In the underground telecon office of his headquarters, Clay was alone. Now, early on the morning of June 25, the general was engaged in a battle of wills with two men located 4,000 miles away in Washington: Secretary of the Army Kenneth Royall and his Chief of Staff, General J. Lawton Collins.

The conference had no sooner opened than Royall, stressing that he did not want "any action taken in Berlin which might lead to possible armed conflict," suggested a concession that left Clay fuming. Might not "a few hours' delay" or a complete slowing up of the currency reform be advisable? If so, Royall insisted, "I would want it so delayed or slowed up."

Clay protested. The currency distribution had begun at 7:00

A.M.; already, outside food offices in the Western sectors, the lines were forming, thousands strong. Moreover, any such delay would be a betrayal of the City Council's courageous stand. The general emphasized: "There is no possible way now to suspend issue or to slow down."

Royall wavered. He felt that "the limited question of Berlin's currency" was not "a question to go to war on." Clay was withering. If the Soviets went to war, currency would play no part in it. It would be because they felt the time was ripe. Neither he nor Robertson had "any intent to start shooting"; both fully realized the desire of their governments to avoid armed conflict, but if the Allies were to hold their heads up in Europe, they had to stand firm. "We cannot be run over," he exhorted Royall, "and a firm position always involves some risk."

For the sixth time in as many weeks Royall reverted to his age-old obsession: the evacuation of U.S. dependents. Clay was intransigent. "Movement would be a mistake . . . our people are calm and quiet." Pointedly, he reminded Royall of the Berliners' courage to date. "We should not destroy their confidence by any show of departure," he affirmed. "Once again we have to sweat it out."

Toward noon Sir Brian Robertson once again called on Clay at his headquarters. "Our planes are coming in," he said. "Is it on as far as you're concerned?" Still Clay temporized. There was one man whose support would be crucial to his final decision, for to stand firm the West had to take into account the mood and the mettle of the Berliners.

As soon as Robertson was gone, the man in question, Lord Mayor-elect Ernst Reuter, was summoned to Clay's office. Accompanying him was his young aide, Willy Brandt. Political adviser Robert Murphy sat in, listening. This was a historic moment, for it was the first major test of the Allied will to check Russian expansion. "I may be the craziest man in the world," he told Reuter, "but I'm going to try the experiment of feeding this city by air."

Reuter smiled skeptically. For a moment the two faced each other uncertainly, both seeking the meeting of minds that might make this miracle possible. Then Reuter said gently, "We shall, in any case, continue on our way. Do what you are able to do—we shall do what we feel to be our duty. Berlin will make all necessary sacrifices and offer resistance—come what may."

He added but one rider: It was a mistake to believe that all would be well if the Berliners were fed and heated and clothed. Somehow Berlin's industries must still function as near normally as possible. "If the people have no work," Reuter said, "they will lose heart, whether they have enough to eat or not. Then they will surrender to Communism."

Outside the room Reuter turned to General Gailey. "Clay's determination is wonderful," he said, "but I don't believe it can be done." Gailey shook his head. He confided, "I don't believe it either."

Clay and Murphy were left alone. The general uncradled the phone. "Get me General LeMay in Frankfurt," he said. Murphy sat watching him.

Curt," Clay asked, "have you any planes there that can carry coal?"

"Carry what?" LeMay asked incredulously.

"Coal," Clay repeated.

"General," LeMay apologized, "we must have a bad phone connection. It sounds as if you are asking whether we have planes for carrying coal."

"Yes, that's what I said," Clay emphasized, his voice a shade higher. "Coal."

Another pause, then LeMay rallied. "The Air Force can deliver anything," he promised.

The Berlin Airlift—the first showdown in what the world would come to call the Cold War—was beginning.

5

"I Wouldn't Give That for Our Chances"

JUNE 25–JUNE 30, 1948

The decision to supply the entire city of Berlin by air was breathtaking, both in its simplicity and its temerity. Most of the men involved in the first freight hauls had little or no concept of the magnitude of the task ahead and reacted with consternation to the seemingly bizarre demands being made on them.

Around 4:00 P.M. on Friday, June 25, Captain Jack Olin Bennett, the senior pilot in the Flight Office of American Overseas Airlines at Rhein-Main AFB, Frankfurt, answered the phone. It was one of LeMay's staff officers asking to charter the fledgling airline's one DC-3, the civil version of the C-47. "You're going to be shocked at the cargo," the officer warned. "It's coal for Berlin." Bennett was incredulous. "Not *coal*."

"We'll put it in sacks," the staff officer assured him. But Bennett was unyielding. "Look, we're a passenger line. Getting dust over everything would kill our trade." But he sensed his caller was desperate. "Is it that serious?" The voice on the other end was sober: "It's that serious."

For some, the urgency took time to sink in. At Wiesbaden, Captain Francis Kennedy was straggling through the Operations Block's briefing room when he looked up in surprise.

Ahead of him was General LeMay himself, in overalls and peaked cap lugging his parachute and awaiting his flight clearance like any other pilot. If "Old Iron Pants" was in there pitching it must be a tough mission.

If the mission was indeed tough, no one alerted LeMay. While his immediate objective was clear enough, the long-term strategy was less certain. By nightfall on Saturday, June 26, having hauled 80 tons of flour and milk into Tempelhof, he telephoned Clay for further instructions. "Haul some more" had been Clay's curt and unrevealing directive. Thus LeMay still assumed Clay had embarked on an April-pattern mini-lift to supply the Berlin garrison.

As for Clay's own appraisal of the long-term strategy, he was contemptuous of the whole concept of a full-scale airlift. As he had told Enno Hobbing, editor of the U.S.-licensed daily *Neue Zeitung*, in a recent off-the-record comment, "I wouldn't give you that for our chances."

It was small wonder. On the face of it, Clay had just set in motion one of the most foolhardy rescue operations ever undertaken. In all, the British might muster a total of 150 planes, but even this was uncertain. The French, Koenig reported, could supply little more than personnel; their air fleet was busy in Indochina. Though the main burden of the lift would eventually be borne by the Americans, the only transport planes the U.S. Air Force had in Europe at the time were 102 twin-engined C-47s, nicknamed "Gooney Birds," with a capacity of less than three short tons—6,000 pounds—apiece. Unarmed, unarmored, cruising at a lumbering 180 miles per hour, these old workhorses of Arnhem and the Hump would be easy prey for prowling Russian fighters.

And though some pilots dubbed the C-47 "the most forgiving plane that ever was," all had seen better days. Lieutenant Joseph Kaeser, one of the first airborne from Rhein-Main, flew this and scores of other missions in planes whose gyroscopic instruments would sometimes fail—and since the instrument lights were often defunct, a flashlight was a must. Captain Francis Kennedy, hitting a storm en route, found his windshield leaking rain like a colander; at Tempelhof he had literally to empty the water from his shoes.

63

There were other crucial problems. Neither of Berlin's two airfields was remotely suited to a transport operation. The RAF Station at Gatow, ten miles from the city (and within perilous minutes of the Soviet fighter bases at Staaken and Schönewalde), lacked even elemental facilities. A former Luftwaffe training base, it was little more than a country strip, with a 1,500-yard pierced steel planking runway, likely to rip up the tires of heavy (31,000 pound) transports. A 2,000-yard concrete runway was under construction but barely three-quarters completed, and there was as yet no perimeter track.

And LeMay's pilots were quick to spot the hazards of Tempelhof, sited in the very heart of the city, for themselves. Sergeant Vernon Earley, a radioman, never forgot his first trip in. As his C-47 broke cloud cover the cockpit was all at once on a level with a seven-story building. As the plane let down to hit the runway, at a dizzying 750 feet a minute, the startled faces of apartment dwellers, gawking from their windows, were plainly visible. For Lieutenant Don Waters there was a greater terror still: the 400-foot brewery smokestack looming beside the perimeter. The dense yellow-white smoke, blotting out all vision, turned his stomach to ice.

One factor gave grounds for hope: Thanks to Colonel Frank Howley and his "Operation Counterpunch," Berlin's food situation was not yet desperate. On June 26, the first tenuous day of the airlift effort, the city's warehouses held seventeen days' supply of bread grains and flour, thirty-two days' supply of cereal, fats enough for forty-eight days, meat and fish for twenty-five days, potatoes for forty-two days, plus twenty-six days' supply of skimmed and dried milk—from which the health authorities had by now devised a special formula for Berlin's babies. Yet against Berlin's daily food need of 13,500 tons—ranging from 646 tons of wheat and flour to three tons of fresh yeast—LeMay's planes could haul in 700 tons at most.

But on Sunday, June 27, working serenely at his cluttered desk, Clay was not yet truly worried. The flurry of activity galvanizing Wiesbaden and Rhein-Main was in his timetable no more than a three-week operation—forty-five days at the most. By that time the Russians would surely lift their blockade.

Yet there was a nagging doubt. Suppose the Russians proved intransigent? How steadfastly would the United States government back him? How staunch would be the British reaction? Until he knew the answers to these questions, Clay could only take it a day at a time.

The impassive eyes of George II gazed down from the great oil painting at the six Americans, grouped in an expectant semicircle around His Majesty's Secretary of State for Foreign Affairs, sixty-seven-year-old Ernest Bevin. Bevin's first words were a body blow to all but one of his listeners.

"Gentlemen," his robust voice boomed out, "I have news I believe you will find extremely interesting. I have just come from a meeting of the full Cabinet at which it was agreed that under no circumstances will we leave Berlin."

A stunned silence followed, recalls Clay's economics adviser, Lawrence Wilkinson. For among the delegates present, almost all, aside from Wilkinson himself, favored the speedy and total abandonment of Berlin.

Lieutenant General Albert Wedemeyer, the Army General Staff's director of plans and operations, and Major General William Draper, Under Secretary of the Army, were particularly dubious. Along with a battery of staff officers Wedemeyer and Draper had flown to Europe on an urgent fact-finding mission for Omar Bradley, both to sound out British intentions and to advise on the feasibility of evacuating Berlin. Hence their embarrassment now, for if rationed, impoverished Britain, with two million unemployed, chose to make a bold stand in Berlin, it hardly behooved the powerful United States to pull out with ignominy.

As the silence grew more protracted, Wilkinson spoke up resolutely. "Well, Mr. Secretary," he replied, "on behalf of the Berliners may I for one say that this is the best news we've had in a long time." No one raised his voice to second this proposition.

Then Bevin, who was convinced that the blockade was no more than a nine-day wonder, told the Americans that six RAF C-47s, which the British called Dakotas, were already flying between Wunsdorf, near Hanover, and Berlin-Gatow, carrying a daily load of sixty tons. That service, he assured his visitors, could be continued for a few days, by which time, road and rail conditions would be normal. It was this belief alone that had prompted his government's resolution to stay put.

"It would never work long-term," he concluded, "you could never feed two and a half million people by air. But it's well worth trying. We must see this one through. Even if it fails entirely, you know, it will give us all time to negotiate."

Shortly after the meeting Wedemeyer was seated beneath the crystal chandeliers of the blue-and-silver restaurant in Claridge's Hotel. Worried by what he termed Clay's "cocky irresponsible attitude," he had called in his old friend, Lord Portal, former Marshal of the RAF, for advice. Although Portal had retired from the post three years back, the two men had been wartime comrades since the days of the Quebec and Casablanca conferences.

Wedemeyer launched into the subject of the airlift. It had been estimated that Berlin could exist on a survival level of 5,000 daily tons, but Wedemeyer thought a scarcity of transports would dictate a maximum ceiling of 3,000 tons—a quarter of Berlin's preblockade needs. What part, he asked Portal, could the RAF play?

Portal hazarded that in any such operation the RAF would have to call in the Dakotas of the British Overseas Airways Corporation. Between them they might muster a daily delivery of 750 tons. That left 2,250 tons to be made good by the Americans.

Wedemeyer still thought the answer was to withdraw American troops and their dependents from Berlin at an appreciably faster rate. This would cut down consumption of food. But Portal assured him that air access for three clearly defined air corridors to Berlin—from Hamburg, Frankfurt, and Bücke-burg, each twenty miles wide—not only existed but had been agreed to in writing by the Russians as far back as October 1946. The maximum permitted height in these corridors was 10,000 feet.

Somewhat more reassured, Wedemeyer sipped his coffee. Suddenly a chilling thought crossed his mind. "Supposing," he said, "when the Russians see this building up they won't let us use the airfields?" There was a dead silence. Portal could find no answer at all.

Even as Ernest Bevin was bidding farewell to his guests in London, the thirty-third President of the United States, at his desk in the Executive Office of the White House, was pondering the fate of 2,500,000 Berliners.

Grouped around him this morning were three of his top advisers: Secretary of Defense James Forrestal, Secretary of the Army Kenneth Royall, and Under Secretary of State Robert Lovett. Without comment, Harry Truman listened as Lovett recited the details of a meeting hastily convened in Royall's Pentagon office at 4:00 P.M. on the Sunday just past. There they had discussed three major alternatives to the problem of Berlin: to remain under the stress of weekly crises, to supply the city by air and risk war, or to quit Berlin.

Truman cut in abruptly: "There is no discussion on that point. We stay in Berlin—period."

At once the burly Royall expostulated: "Mr. President, have you thought this through?" He elaborated: It was unthinkable that the United States should be committed to a position under which "we might have to fight our way into Berlin," unless the possibility was clearly recognized and the consequences accepted.

Truman did not yield an inch. "We will have to deal with the situation as it develops, but the essential position is that we are in Berlin by terms of an agreement and that the Russians have no right to get us out by either direct or indirect pressures." The decision was now made irrevocably—a logical extension of the President's will to contain Communism in Europe.

Another radical decision followed. As from today the President wanted Clay's improvised airlift placed on a full-scale organized basis. Somehow Berlin would be fed until the diplomatic deadlock was broken—"even if it takes every Piper Cub in the United States."

Two points only remained to be settled: the feasibility of dispatching two B-29 squadrons from Goose Bay, Labrador, to Germany and of basing two B-29 squadrons in England (the latter having been agreed to by the British).

Truman approved both projects wholeheartedly. The position in Berlin was precarious, he knew, but "if we wish to remain there we will have to make a show of strength." If ever there was a show of strength that would convince the Kremlin the Allies were in earnest, it would be the dispatch of the B-29s—known throughout the world as the atomic bombers— to within striking distance of Moscow.

In Wiesbaden, these Cabinet-level decisions were so far unknown to LeMay. Yet on the morning of June 28 he too was driven by necessity to take positive steps. Already LeMay had called in planes from as far afield as Vienna and Bremen; every transport in the European theater was fully committed. Now, as Clay's command—"Haul some more"—sounded once again over the wire in his Wiesbaden office, LeMay was moved to protest: "Wait a minute, General! Are you trying to break a blockade? If you are, let's set about it in a businesslike manner. Send up a smoke signal back home."

Clay agreed to contact Secretary Royall, and LeMay and his chief of staff, Brigadier General Kissner, promptly settled to a teleconference with Washington. Many more planes were needed, LeMay stressed, especially Douglas C-54 Skymasters, with three times the C-47's capacity, and time was of the essence.

Next, the two men approached Brigadier General Joseph Smith, the gruff forty-seven-year-old Commander of Wiesbaden Military Post, to head up a newly created Airlift Task Force headquarters. But the Post Commander was oddly reluctant. Although his experience ranged from bombers to piloting an airmail plane, Smith could not picture what an airlift involved. Finally he promised, "I'll think about it and come back after lunch."

An hour later, Smith was still uncertain. He had no clear idea as to what steps to take. Kissner wheedled, "It's only a two-week job at most—how much staff do you need?" Smith, at last persuaded, replied, "I'm no empire-builder on a two-week job. Give me a couple of operations officers and a few maintenance people."

The màgnitude of the task ahead escaped him. When a Public Information Officer, anxious to dramatize the project, pressed for a catchy code name—Operation Lifeline, or, perhaps, Operation Airlane—Smith, more prosaic, growled, "Hell's fire, we're hauling grub, I understood. If you have to have a name, call it Vittles." So Operation Vittles, the greatest mercy mission in the history of aviation, it modestly became.

Up in the British zone it was called Operation Plainfare. But whether Vittles or Plainfare, both operations had one factor in common: a fire-alarm haste coupled with a total lack of long-range planning. At Wunsdorf, the RAF airport near Hanover, 150 miles west of Berlin, the chaplain, the Reverend Donald Cawthray, hastened with dismaying news to his wife, Dorothy: "There are a whole lot of transport planes coming in from England . . . the pilots will be sleeping in my church!"

It was true. A peacetime fighter field, Wunsdorf had barrack accommodations for 700, but within days the station was teeming with more than 1,600 men, forced to bed down as and where they could. Worse, though the field had a serviceable runway, loading areas for transport aircraft were nonexistent.

By dusk on June 28 Wunsdorf presented a picture of frenzied and uncoordinated activity. As the first planes, the Dakotas from Oakington and Waterbeach, near Cambridge, came coasting in over the pine forests, they made an oddly stirring sight, green and red wing lights glinting against the silver fuselage, the plumes of their exhausts blue and white in the night. But soon rain set in, driving from the North Sea, and as the planes touched down as haphazardly as crows on a plowed field, their heavy tires rapidly churned the grass to a gleaming expanse of mud.

Wild confusion reigned. Squadron Leader Andrew Johnstone, of No. 30 Squadron, bringing in seven Dakotas from Oakington, found no marshalers to guide him to dispersal and not a soul in station headquarters who could tell him what to do. Every corridor and stairway seemed alive with harassed blue-clad pilots vainly seeking instructions, "like Victoria Station in the rush hour." Squatting patiently on the Officers' Mess steps until the chaos had abated, Johnstone finally dumped his kit on a bed in an attic, along with seventy others. Squadron Leader Tom Churcher, bringing in No. 238 Squadron from Oakington later, wasn't so lucky. He had to make do with a mattress on the floor, with a journey down a ladder to the lavatory below.

In the Operations Room the situation was as bad. Anxious to be airborne to Berlin, Johnstone was told, "Lane A, Plane 7—it's loaded up with flour." But in the darkness he and his crew couldn't even locate the plane. For seventy-five wearisome minutes they picked their way through the aircraft parks, reading off the serial numbers by flashlight. Finally they tracked it down, stacked away behind some unserviceable Dakotas.

Pilot Officer Roy Jenkins, of No. 24 Squadron, landing from Bassingbourn, was told to make ready for a 4:00 A.M. take-off—but no one even gave his loft a wake-up call. As a result, many 24 Squadron pilots took off into the overcast sky that morning without navigators or even radiomen. Squadron Leader Churcher, visiting Ops for instructions, found no one to advise him on a route to Berlin or even to specify height limitations. As he watched, planes were rising from the runway at heart-stopping levels, barely clearing the tall trees that ringed the airfield.

Few pilots, in any case, had a clear idea as to what the operation involved. Squadron Leader Arthur "Pop" Salter, who led in No. 46, another Oakington-based squadron, didn't realize the Americans were even part of the show. His inner belief, which he kept to himself, was that "we should be stopped, seen off." To Salter, the whole mission had one likely end: a head-on encounter between Dakotas and Russian MIG fighters along the Bückeburg-Berlin corridor, in the style of a medieval joust.

Despite the confusion, enthusiasm was nowhere lacking. Fired by a belief that within days this glorious adventure would have ended, scores of RAF fitters and mechanics, armed with no more than a tool kit and a change of underwear, thumbed a ride out of England on the first Wunsdorf-bound plane— without checking out of their parent stations or even booking in on arrival. It took one officer, checking every station and every section, weeks to locate who had ended up where.

All over Germany, as the airlift gathered shaky momentum, this willingness to accept any challenge became the keynote. At a June 29 staff meeting, announcing that more planes were on the way, General Smith, at U.S. Task Force headquarters, called on his new Air Cargo Officer, Major Edward Willeford, for a forecast of future potential. "I estimate by July 20 we'll be flying in 1,500 tons every twenty-four hours," he announced confidently. On every face was consternation, for on this day, by straining to the utmost, the combined efforts of the 60th and 61st Troop Carrier Groups had hauled in 384 tons to Berlin. To predict that within three weeks that amount could be quadrupled seemed near insanity.

In fact, this target was achieved—yet at a superhuman cost. Forced to scrape the barrel, LeMay was now calling on every grounded flier in the command for part-time duty. Yet most pilots, even so, were lucky to snatch seven hours' sleep in thirty-six. Armed with the daunting knowledge that four hours in the cockpit was equivalent to eight hours' labor on the ground, the 60th's flight surgeon, Lieutenant Robert Miller, was treating men whose average flying time was 120 hours a month for everything from vitamin deficiencies to blocked sinuses—a medical-care program so intensive he scarcely once removed his clothes in five weeks.

One noncom, Sergeant Donald Fromme, was so disorientated as to time and place after two grueling missions that he inquired blearily of his roommate, "Hey, are we getting up or going to bed?" Lieutenant Vernon Hamman solved the problem by taking to his bed after twelve hours' flying and staying there until the phone awoke him. For Lieutenant Lewis Smith, the flying time was the least of his problems. At Wiesbaden AFB, with "planes nose to tail all over," it might take thirty hours to complete two missions; often a plane waited an hour at Tempelhof before an unloading crew even approached it.

In these first days the presence of men who worked strictly by the rule book made no one's task any easier. General Joseph Smith flew into Tempelhof to find not only a near-empty airfield but a wrathful LeMay demanding, "Why have you got all those planes stacked up down at base?" Hastily Smith made inquiries and unearthed the bottleneck. To his astonishment, Frankfurt Traffic Control was hewing to the old peacetime procedure of a twenty-five-minute separation between take-offs, regardless of altitude.

Promptly, LeMay placed the entire traffic control system

71

under Smith's aegis. From now on planes would take off at five-minute intervals or LeMay would know why.

Other customs died harder. At Tempelhof, the O.C., Colonel Henry Dorr, waged a losing fight against the old peacetime dispatching system. Before returning to base, each pilot must visit the Weather Office to sign a clearance form, and the Air Safety Center on Potsdamer Strasse must be briefed on every plane flying in and out. The advent of the Cold War seems to have passed some men by. Lieutenant George Kinser and his crew, forced to stay overnight in Berlin at a requisitioned hotel, were told: "You can wear flight suits in the dining room this once—but next time you'll observe dress rules or eat in the kitchen."

Already many pilots found their cargoes bewildering. Though signs loomed large in barrack rooms—"Conserve! Remember Everything You Eat Is Being Flown In"—it seemed, even to inexpert eyes, that a sense of priorities was lacking everywhere. Lieutenant James Wenk's first "priority" haul was 5,000 pounds of mimeograph forms. Lieutenant Lewis Smith was as baffled: His cargo was an entire planeload of shrubs "to help the city's afforestation program." And though Berlin was ringed by market gardens, Sergeant Edward Mantor was mystified to find himself unloading scores of bushel baskets of fresh spinach.

Some outgoing cargoes were so strange that many drew the line early at what they would or wouldn't carry. By order of the O.C. no man in the 12th Troop Carrier Squadron would haul a crate so heavy no loading crew could lift it. It contained a marble statue looted from the Tiergarten.

Day and night the planes kept flying, shuttling back and forth down the wide corridors, through the rain and murk that now blanketed more than three million square miles of Europe: 100 American planes and fifty British, their pilots loading up with any cargo that was ready, catnapping where they could, grabbing hasty snacks of coffee and doughnuts, their spirits lifted high by a new slogan out of Wiesbaden Headquarters, daubed everywhere from fuselages to flour sacks: "LeMay Coal and Feed Company—Round-the-Clock Service Guaranteed."

"It seems as if every plane in Europe is flying to Berlin," Lieutenant James Wenk wrote to his parents back in Vineland, New Jersey, but foremost in his and every pilot's mind was, when would the Russians come up off the ground and fight back? All of them felt it could not be long.

In the last week of June the politicians spoke. Their voices were defiant, even outraged, and as they echoed across the world the sentiments seemed pitched to the listening ear of history. In Washington, General George C. Marshall announced, "We intend to stay in Berlin." From Paris, Premier Robert Schuman warned the nation: "France would be a victim of any conflict even if she remained neutral." In London, Ernest Bevin told a packed and silent House of Commons: "None of us can accept surrender." The leader of His Majesty's Most Loyal Opposition, Winston Churchill, pledged his fullest support: "The issues are as grave as those . . . at stake in Munich ten years ago."

The issues were now broader than one city's food supplies, vital though these were. They embraced even more than Allied plans for a West German state with a stable currency, a thriving Ruhr on which the Marshall Plan depended. The siege of Berlin had become the siege of all Germany and of Europe as well.

What was now at stake was nothing less than confidence. In the teeth of Russian threats and intimidation, the Allies had invited the cooperation of the Berliners and encouraged them to speak their minds. The voluntary surrender of the Western-occupied sectors now would forfeit not only the trust of the Berliners but of all Germans and most Europeans. Each helpless surviving state would be left with one sole recourse: to make the best terms with Moscow that they could. Thus it was vital that the Allies should hold their heads high and stand firm.

Each day the headlines proclaimed a common resolution—

"WESTERN GERMANS BACK CLAY'S STAND"—
BRITISH ACCEPT RISK OF WAR"—STAND ON GERMANY BACKED
BY TRUMAN"—
"BRIDGE OF PLANES TO BERLIN IS SEEN."

But the problem remained: Which side would be first to yield?

What were the Russians seeking? Facing the increasingly hostile Germans, as they beat against the West's weakest salient, their position seemed unenviable, yet two possible prizes emerged: the surrender of Berlin, or the even bigger prize of a new conference, with Ruhr coal as a bargaining counter. If this was so, what options were open to the West? Certainly, any diplomatic counterattack—which must strive not merely for present withdrawal but future containment— must start with a formal protest to Moscow. Other possible countermeasures loomed large in Allied thinking: discussion before the United Nations, possible economic sanctions, such as closing the Panama and Suez canals to Soviet ships, a total diplomatic break.

But one secret fear obsessed the peoples of the West: that the Russians would be obdurate enough to resist all attempts at a compromise they did not seek, convinced that the Allies must ultimately surrender. As July dawned, all present hopes thus hinged on one imponderable: the fragile bridge of planes that the Allies were building across the sky.

6

"You Now Gave Your Lives for Us . . ."

JUNE 30–JULY 29, 1948

All day the thunder of the planes filled the city. The noise was deafening. It reverberated among the hollow buildings and the mountains of gray rubble; it throbbed above the graceful arches of the lime trees. Flight after flight of battle-worn C-47s and shining C-54 Skymasters swooped in over the tall apartment buildings. On the sidewalks Berliners stopped in their tracks, craning upward. Some were moved to tears by a display of Allied air power that only three years back would have spelled naked terror. In Tempelhof's orange-and-white control tower, where GIs worked around the clock to snatch order from chaos, the voices were a metallic nonstop hubbub: "Give me an ETA on EC 84 . . . wind is now north northwest . . . That's flour coming in on EC 72 . . . Roger . . . Ease her down."

To Colonel Frank Howley, waiting on Tempelhof's giant concrete apron for the Skymasters' nine-ton loads of flour, the snarl of their four Pratt & Whitney engines was like a defiant voice repeating over and over, "We're licking the blockade! We're licking the blockade!" Ever since the airlift gathered momentum, Howley had been in his element. Working with his

75

City Hall liaison officer Karl Mautner and councilor for food Paul Füllsack, he had spent long hours devising ways to cut payloads to the bone. Flying in bread from Army bakeries proved wasteful, for one-third of each loaf was water. The solution was simple: fly in only flour. It was discovered that dehydrating potatoes saved the lift 780 tons a day, while boning meat reduced its weight by a quarter. Within weeks, such meticulous slide-rule calculations had cut Berlin's minimum daily food requirements from 2,000 tons a day to half that amount.

As Clay's call for planes clattered by teletype across the world, thousands of airmen found their lives turned upside down. On Johnston Island, in the Pacific Ocean, Captain Clifford "Ted" Harris, returning from the operations office at midnight, was surprised to see a Jeep's headlights moving toward him. He heard brakes slam on, and from the darkness navigator John Campbell hailed him: "Ted, you've got to get yourself all together in thirty minutes. We're going to Berlin."

At Elmendorf Air Base, Anchorage, Alaska, the pilots of the 54th Troop Carrier Squadron, the "Eager Beavers," were rousted from the camp cinema at 6:00 P.M. to hear Lieutenant Colonel James Sammons announce tersely, "Gentlemen, this is what we've been waiting for." One lieutenant's muttered reaction—"Maybe *you* have but we haven't"—was typical: Fully a third of the pilots had wives and families there who would have to be left behind. Yet by 9:30 A.M. next day, the squadron—210 men in ten C-54s with scarlet tails and wingtips designed to be spotted in the arctic wastes—were airborne from Elmendorf. As a point of pride, every man took his snowshoes along to hang on the walls of their Rhein-Main operations room.

Many men got even briefer notice. In a bar in downtown Honolulu, Private William Glatiotis almost gagged on his beer when a sergeant hailed him casually, "Hey, Greek, you're shipping out in two hours' time." At Bolling AFB, Washington, D.C., Sergeant Albert Schmick's first intimation was a casual farewell from a colleague: "Good luck—and have a good trip." In these last frantic hours, men struggled irresolutely with the problem of what to take and what to leave behind. Lieutenant Edward Shack departed so fast from Westover that he left his

Buick in the parking lot without a thought of antifreeze—or of a Massachusetts winter that would drop to 40 below zero. In Mobile, Alabama, Lieutenant Gail Halvorsen, given less than an hour's notice, left his Chevrolet under a tree and hid the keys. A streaming head cold determined his main priority: a barracks bag stuffed to the brim with handkerchiefs. Philosophically, Halvorsen reassured himself that it would be a two-week trip at most, "because no foreign power would ever be allowed to starve a city to death."

Many men didn't even have the necessary five minutes to make out pay-allotment forms, and hundreds of Air Force wives were left penniless for weeks, forced to ask for yet more credit from the milkman and the butcher. Typical was the plight of the 19th Troop Carrier Squadron. Airborne from Hickam Field, Honolulu, their 11 C-54s skimmed over the very troopship that was bringing their wives and families from San Francisco to Hawaii. Three days later, when the distraught dependents reached Hickam, no one could tell them how long their men would be in Germany—or whether they would ever return to Hawaii.

Most men expected crew rest on a journey totaling twenty-four hours' flying time, but not all were so fortunate. Lieutenant Joe Tytus, one of four C-54 pilots to leave Fairfield Suisun AFB, California, arrived at Westover to endure a four-hour briefing on the next leg of the trip; neither he nor his fellow pilots had ever flown outside the Pacific. Once in Newfoundland, a further five-hour briefing ensued on weather conditions as far as the Azores. It was small wonder that many men no sooner hit Germany than they dropped in their tracks.

The British, too, were throwing in everything they had. By July 3, forty Avro Yorks, from the RAF stations at Abingdon and Lyneham, had swung into the battle. As Transport Command versions of the old Lancaster bomber, each plane, based on Wunsdorf, could carry up to nine tons of cargo.

And one day earlier Premier Clement Attlee's decision to "put everything into the sky that we've got" led to one of the most astonishing spectacles Berliners had ever witnessed. On that Friday night, July 2, the pulsing beat of "In the Mood" drifted through the shrubberies and across the moonlit water at Castle Archdale, on Lough Erne, Northern Ireland. It was 8:00

P.M., and the airmen of 201 and 230 squadrons, RAF, were enjoying an other-ranks dance with the local colleens. Suddenly Squadron Leader Tony Payn, 230's commander, shouldered his way to the bandstand and seized the drummer's wire brushes to beat an urgent tattoo for silence. "Sorry, chaps," Payn apologized, "but we've got to get loading the planes. We're recalled to base."

It was no easy instruction to follow. The ten Sunderland flying boats that made up the Coastal Command squadrons were secured to mooring buoys in the middle of the lough, approachable only by marine tender. Moreover, each plane was loaded with 2,500 gallons of fuel in readiness for a combined operation with the Royal Navy. Before take-off they would have to be defueled or the combined weight of the 120 airmen and their kit would render them top-heavy.

Now all was action. A fueler went to work on each Sunderland. Then, for eight hours, a long chain of airmen and colleens worked side by side manhandling kit bags and spare parts down to the tenders. By 4:00 A.M. they were ready. At 9:00 A.M. on Saturday, July 3, Payn's Sunderland, trailing a giant plume of spray, was already touching down at the base on Calshot Pier, 360 miles distant, on Southampton Water.

As yet, no reasons for the recall had been given, and Payn was convinced that 230 were destined for the Thames to break a current London docks strike. Squadron Leader Denys Horner, commanding 201, had direr forebodings. Unlike Transport Command's planes, Sunderlands were equipped with gun turret and depth-charge racks. His private bet was on war.

In the officer's mess, the Station Commander now broke the astonishing news: The planes were to join the Berlin Airlift. Operating from the old Blohm and Voss basin, at Finkenwerder on the Elbe River near Hamburg, they would ferry their nine-ton cargoes to the Havel See, two miles south of Gatow.

But at Finkenwerder there were problems. They found not the familiar scarlet rubber mooring buoys but cast-iron battleship buoys—a perilous proposition given a lively tide and the Sunderland's fragile outer skin, barely a tenth of an inch thick. Fueling, too, was difficult, for as yet no fuelers had arrived and each Sunderland, its mainplane twelve feet above the water, had to be hand-pumped from forty-gallon drums loaded aboard a DUKW—which took up to an hour per plane.

It was soon clear that the Sunderlands were being accorded VIP status. On Monday, when rain set in, Payn's emergency call brought two truckloads of gumboots within the hour—and all his adjutant's offers of a signature were brushed aside. Scrawling "Operation Plainfare" across the invoice, an equipment officer assured him, "That gets you anything you want around here, old boy."

And as Payn's Sunderland bored down upon the Hamburg corridor, skimming 100 feet above the pine forests and the silver vein of the Elbe, the sense of status was heightened. From Russian fields all along the route planes of every shape and description from MIGs to R-1 spotter planes, their observers armed with cameras, rose up to focus on them. Then, as the flying boat, carrying its first token load of three and a half tons of Spam, hit the Havel "like a pelican landing on a puddle," Payn and his crew were astonished by the city's reaction: Paddling toward them like a Hawaiian war party came scores of canoes steered by lustily singing Berliners, bearing garlands of summer flowers.

The Sunderlands were not the only ones to receive a warm welcome. All over the city the grudges and the alienation of the past were forgotten. On a balcony in Zehlendorf, Frau Schulz, a tenant in the house she had once owned, flung her arms around Dorothy Madison, a noncom's wife, as the first Skymasters thundered overhead, weeping unashamedly, exclaiming over and over, "*Der wunderbar Amerikaner.*" On a street corner in Lankwitz, Sergeant-Major Jim Madison of the 18th Constabulary Squadron was as moved as his wife—"standing there with forty Berliners I didn't know, but we were just one person as the planes went over." Secretary of the Air Force Stuart Symington, at Tempelhof on an inspection trip, felt a lump rise in his throat as he watched little girls with pigtails, wearing white puff-sleeved blouses and velvet bodices, pressing nosegays of flowers on the pilots as they piled from their planes. The wife of Berlin's American Overseas Airlines chief, Barbara Parsons, summed up the mood that the armada evoked: "It was no longer 'them' and 'us'—it was '*us.*' "

What stirred the Berliners above all was the realization that the Allies were staying to share their plight—and many of the Allies took pains to make this resolution plain. At 10 Höhmanstrasse, Sir Brian Robertson's wife, Edith, gave instructions to butler Carl Kunse: From now on the family silver must be displayed daily on the sideboard. It was one more earnest that the Robertsons were staying. When some senior American officers sought permission to transfer their families to the safety of the zone they were told: "That's fine, they can go—but you'll go with them." Scarcely a man took advantage of the offer.

The sense of solidarity was evident everywhere. At Gatow, Berliners pressed against the fences surrounding the old Luftwaffe barracks, clapping and cheering like spectators at a circus as the four-engine Yorks taxied in. On the streets around Tempelhof, pedestrians acquired the "Berliner Look"—left shoulder hunched, right ear perpetually cocked to the sky. Often up to 10,000 men, women and children lined Berlinerstrasse, bordering the field, perched in the forks of trees and on the walls of ruined houses, waving from the roofs of parked cars and trucks. Many of them brought gifts for the fliers—treasured family Meissenware, lucky charms, even dachshund puppies.

Ernst Reuter spoke for the majority of citizens when he pledged: "Berlin will be the German 'Stalingrad' that will turn back the tide of Communist pressure." When someone voiced doubts, worried that "the Russians will force us all to our knees," Reuter's faith remained unshaken. "No," he averred, "this will shake the conscience of the world."

On the face of it, this steadfast confidence was puzzling, for Berlin, as visiting author Rebecca West put it, was now "the largest prison ever known, with walls that rose to the sky, as thick as the whole Soviet Zone." And despite the steady roar of the planes and the warm comradeship, which springs up among those living under threat, there were manifold problems to be solved.

The first—and the worst—was coal. At first LeMay's staff envisaged a nonstop daily drop from the bomb bays of B-29s, followed by an all-night floodlight operation in which gangs of workmen would load up the coal. But the first trial drop proved a dismal failure; the fuel inside the sacks was reduced to useless dust. Thus, not until the night of July 7 did Berlin's first coal consignment arrive: a meager 160 tons packed in American Army duffel bags, ferried in by Skymasters.

Watching the teams of sweating German workers grapple the 100-pound bags toward the tailgates of parked trucks, Frank Howley knew the implications were grave. To be sure, Berlin now had six weeks' provisions in store—but the incoming shipments were meager indeed against a basic daily need of 3,000 tons. "The shortage of fuel can be tolerated now," gibed the Communist daily *Vorwaerts*, "but how will it be in the autumn and the winter?"

The Allied newspapers' official pronouncements gave scant cause for comfort. From July 8, Howley and his fellow commandants were forced to decree sweeping 75 percent power cuts. All streetcars and subways were halted by 6:00 P.M. Domestic electricity was limited to four hours a day. Occupation troops had electricity for two daily periods, totaling less than eight hours a day, but many small industries were denied any power at all. Ahead loomed the specter of 300,000 unemployed, for within eight days 1,000 Berlin firms would have only two alternatives: restricted short-time working or total shutdown. Too late, Ernst Reuter's prophetic warnings to rebuild the Kraftwerk West Power Station were recognized as all too accurate.

Anxious to prove their mettle, the City Hall officials did their best. On Dr. Ferdinand Friedensburg's orders, drill tests for soft brown coal were undertaken on the city boundary at Reinickendorf, in the French sector. Rickety derricks sprang up above three trial pits christened "Ferdinand," "Louise," and "Ernst," after the three mayors. But though "Ferdinand" uncovered a five-yard seam forty-two feet down, "Louise" and "Ernst" yielded only crumbling brown peat.

By July 9 the gasworks' daily coal consumption was cut by 500 tons, reducing the gas supply within the Western sectors by 50 percent. It was becoming clear that in the foreseeable future the planes could haul in little more than a drop in the scuttle.

Despite these setbacks, ground workers and pilots alike were fired by a fierce resolution. At Gatow, a station with 580 British on its rolls when the lift began, the staff was doubled within weeks, and the June strength of 1,400 German casual workers was trebled. By July 17, with the aid of borrowed American equipment, they had completed the new 2,000-yard concrete runway. As planes touched down every eight minutes, ten large hangars were now in use by the Army Service Corps experts— among them No. 10 Hangar, nicknamed "Newcastle," whose coal cargoes were sped along a spur railroad to Kladow Wharf and loaded onto barges.

Resources were sucked up as if a giant siphon had passed over airfields and depots. At Erding Depot in Bavaria six months' supply of aircraft windshield wipers was consumed in 12 days, and the mechanics were reconditioning more than 60,000 spark plugs each month. It was touch and go with the gasoline, which had to travel 250 miles by railroad tank car from Bremerhaven. Only the emergency turnaround of three tankers in mid-Atlantic kept the airlift going through July. Rhein-Main alone swallowed up almost three million gallons.

At Wiesbaden, faced with Berlin's insatiable demands, Brigadier General Smith battled to streamline both turnarounds and payloads. Time was saved by chalking a plane's maximum load on the aircraft door, along with a colored flat code: Red (I Need Gas), White (Coming in for a Load), Blue (Prepare to Unload Me), and Yellow (I Need Oil). By reducing gas loads to a perilous minimum, C-47 pilots of the 60th Transport Group could sometimes up their payloads to four and a half tons.

But already high-speed emergency servicing was taking its toll: One C-54 touched down at Wiesbaden with no less than sixteen faults listed on its "squawk sheet." And throughout July British planes were involved in more than a score of accidents, many caused by slapdash servicing—from failed pistons to broken pressure filter gaskets.

The most disquieting news came on July 8, in a meeting between General Smith and Tempelhof's commander, Colonel Henry Dorr. Tempelhof's one runway, a pierced steel strip resting on a shallow foundation of crushed rubble, was fast going to pieces. Under the constant pressure of full-load landings, deep and dangerous depressions were already beginning to form. The Air Force engineers predicted that within two months at most it would collapse.

Smith faced a painful dilemma. As a temporary reinforcement, the engineers urged that 150 tons of steel planking be flown in each day—yet that would mean reducing the food loads, which would soon bring the Berliners to near starvation level. Just fifteen days after its inauguration, the Berlin Airlift showed every sign of grinding to a halt.

Twenty-two miles from the Soviet zone's border, in the old walled town of Melsungen, in Hesse, the stentorian voices of the town criers volleyed through the narrow streets: "Come to the Schlosshof! Come to the Schlosshof and give aid to our beleaguered countrymen!" Within the hour, the crowds jammed the main square to hear Social Democratic Leader Ernst Spars, pointing upward to the cloudy skies, declare: "Up there the American people are showing their faith in the cause of our Berlin brothers every hour of every day. Yet we, their fellow countrymen, have done nothing! Now we must act . . . let us share with those brave Berliners what little we have!" A mighty roar of *"Ja!"* greeted the appeal. Then and there the townsmen agreed to a contribution of four freight cars of grain, dried fish and fresh vegetables to be flown into Berlin.

In cities and towns all over Western Germany there were similar scenes. Local governments in Hamburg, Bremen, and Lower Saxony passed resolutions donating one full day's rations to Berlin from every citizen. In the Ruhr, where the slogan "Coal for Berlin" was blazoned on the miners' barracks, 100,000 tons of coal slated for local homes was diverted instead to the city. The Berlin Airlift—or Die Luftbrücke or Le Pont Aérien or Vozdukny Most—was capturing the imagination of the world.

It was none too soon. All over Berlin, as the electricity cuts bit deep, the lights were going out. In the brief summer darkness, Berlin became again a city of night, devoid of traffic and streetcars, recalling the city's first terrible postwar summer. And there loomed a more immediate problem: how to win the battle for the minds and hearts of the citizens when power cuts were robbing millions of the broadcasts that linked them with the free world.

Midway through July, Rudolf-Gunter Wagner, RIAS's chief newscaster, hit on a solution: a car equipped with a loudspeaker from which he could read news bulletins at random points throughout the city.

The success of the operation astonished even Wagner. At 8:00 A.M. the next day, along with a police driver and a jeep with a loudspeaker on its fender, he halted in Wittenbergplatz, off Kurfürstendamm. Minutes after the first news items crackled through the speaker, a crowd was pressing around the jeep avid for every scrap of news Wagner could offer. When the car reached the next point, the reaction was the same. For twelve long hours, until dusk was falling, Wagner met with grateful crowds every mile of the way.

Within days a fleet of twelve newscasters was cruising the streets—hailed, like the airlifters themselves, as public idols. Many were hard put to reject the pathetic gifts pressed on them—a carrot, a potato, two teaspoons of coffee wrapped in paper. At one point Wagner had to use all his wiles to dissuade a small boy from parting with his pet canary. In their eagerness for news Berliners showed the same cavalier disregard for weather as the newscasters. Approaching one predetermined news point in torrential rain, Wagner, seeing no one about, told the driver to move on. But suddenly the jeep was besieged by Berliners with dripping umbrellas. All had been sheltering in doorways, hanging on for his arrival.

The venture's success proved an inspiration to William Heimlich, the RIAS chief who went to new lengths to spread the work beyond Berlin as well. Heimlich assembled a team of radio personalities who, even though encircled by the Russians, could fight back at them with the two weapons they feared most—truth and ridicule. Armed with a 100,000-watt transmitter, the most modern in Europe, reaching a listening public of forty million, Heimlich stepped up the transmissions to an unprecedented twenty-four hour operation: a nonstop barrage of newscasts, current-affairs talks, satirical playlets, even broadcasts giving the names of undercover Soviet agents.

Although sixty Russian jamming stations sought to silence these transmissions, 6,000 fan letters a week, most of them from behind the Iron Curtain, testified to their failure. As Lucius Clay later put it: "Next to the airlift, RIAS was the strongest American weapon in the Cold War."

Every facet of the Soviet tyranny was fair game to RIAS, from Stalin's baggy pants to the poker-faced East Berlin automatons who had embraced the dictator's cause. On the last Saturday of each month, thousands tuned in at 5:00 P.M. to hear the Insulaner (Islanders) Kabarett, in which comedian Walter Gross impersonated a pompous Communist stooge. Others opted for the savage gibes of the Hungarian political commentator, S. S. von Varady, whose broadcasts were heralded by a Berlin Philharmonic rendering of "Who's Afraid of the Big Bad Wolf?" When rumors abounded that the Americans were pulling out, Varady riposted through RIAS: "Rumors have it that the Russians are leaving Berlin. No! After a great deal of effort, I have established that the report does not conform to the facts . . . no power can force the Russians to deliver the toiling masses to American oppression and capitalist-monopoly terror."

Often the satire was gentler; one of RIAS's main aims was to help the Berliners shrug off hardship, to make fun of their own plight. A cheeky young librettist, Curth Flatow, was a byword for wry conceits that became part of blockade legend: To ensure that every Berliner had a warm room at Christmas, the date was being shifted to July 24. Nor would decorations present a problem. The Allies were flying in powdered Christmas trees, easily reconstituted with water.

By degrees the old irreverent Berlin humor was daily more in evidence. Jokes on the monotonous diet abounded. The slices of warmed-over toast that were many a family's dinner became "Stalin cutlets." Of the dehydrated potato known as "Pom," those who remembered the rapes of the "Russian time" joked: "Better 'Pom' than *Frau komm.*" In the cafés, where regulations decreed one pound of coffee must be stretched to fifty cups, the customers quickly thought up a name for a brew so watery you could see the floral pattern at the bottom: *Blumen* (flower) *kaffee.* "We're really in luck" was one favorite sally.

85

"Just imagine if the Americans were blockading us and the Russians trying to airlift us."

Heimlich and his team saw reason to rejoice: Laughter was returning to Berlin.

One man in these weeks unwittingly won the hearts of more Berliners than any other. He was Lieutenant Gail Halvorsen, the shy young Mormon from Garland, Utah, who had left for Berlin beset by a streaming cold and the conviction that it would be a two-week trip at most. Halvorsen's first days at Rhein-Main were like any other pilot's: fly, sleep, fly again. Convinced the Russians would soon yield to world pressures, he was afraid he would go home without ever setting foot in Berlin.

At 8:00 A.M. on July 17, Halvorsen took steps to rectify this, catching a ride to Tempelhof on a friend's plane. Intrigued by the dizzying angle of descent of the incoming flights, Halvorsen hoped to capture this maneuver on film. He trudged across the airfield's two-and-a-half-mile diameter, camera shooting upward as the planes swooped in.

He had reached the high perimeter fencing before he even saw the children—about a dozen—watching him carefully, not speaking. Their patched clothes, the pinched cellar-bred faces were almost the badges of postwar Europe. The older ones were learning English in school, and a tentative conversation sprang up. Did they get a kick out of watching planes? Halvorsen asked. They smiled uncertainly. "We watch planes all day." As they chatted on Halvorsen thought there was something strange about these kids. What was it?

Abruptly it struck him. All through his war service—on Ascension Island, in Latin America, ferrying planes to England and North Africa—there was always a string of street urchins cheerfully demanding gum and candy. Yet this group had never even raised the subject. Knowing nothing better, they expected nothing. It was that simple.

Halvorsen was in a dilemma. He was pressed for time, and he had only two sticks of gum in his pocket. He took them out, dividing them into four. As the children craned closer their expressions were full of awe—as if they were entering wonderland. Halvorsen felt a sudden rush of emotion: pain for youth beyond recall, compassion for kids who missed out, whose sole consolation was a wrapper to lick or to sniff. For thirty cents, he thought, I could put these guys on Easy Street.

On an impulse, Halvorsen reached a decision. "Now all you guys come back here tomorrow," he instructed, "and when I fly my plane over I'll drop you gum and candy if you promise to share it equally." Hasty translations and consultations, then wide smiles on every face. "But how will we know you?" one boy asked. "Planes fly over all day." "Watch the wings," Halvorsen told them. "Mine will be the plane that wiggles its wings."

Back at Rhein-Main, he almost regretted the promise. To acquire candy was easy, but how to drop it? On a C-54, the one viable exit was the ten-inch flare chute behind the pilot's seat, but what to use for parachutes? Moreover, any such maneuver was counter to USAFE regulations, and despite his easygoing manner, Halvorsen was a stickler for flight rules. Now he faced a bleak alternative: to break the rules or to break a promise.

Halvorsen swore his co-pilot John Pickering and his flight engineer Sergeant Elkins to secrecy, then retired to his billet, in the loft of a brick barn near Rhein-Main. The realization had struck him that he had all the "parachutes" he needed: almost a barracks bag full of handkerchiefs brought to combat that cold. Filling the handkerchiefs with small stones that would equal the weight of the candy, he began to practice drops down the grain chute at the far end of the loft.

Suddenly he looked down. Two pilots from the 17th Troop Carrier Squadron were watching him in incredulous silence. One of them tapped his head significantly. "Better watch it, Halvorsen," he called up, "or they'll be shipping you back to the States." Halvorsen smiled back nervously. "Well," he joked, "you know how easily a guy can get lift-happy."

All that night he worried that they would spread the word, and in the early-morning light, as the Skymaster jounced up Rhein-Main's runway, Pickering was in no reassuring mood. "Man," he prophesied, "you'll get in real trouble." Halvorsen only growled back, "I might—but I'm going to try it."

On the floor beside him were three handkerchiefs, knotted parachute-fashion. As the plane broke through the ragged deck of stratus over Tempelhof he saw that the children had remembered his promise. There they were, in a tight knot beside the fencing. Halvorsen moved the control column from left to right to oscillate the wings, and the children broke ranks, scattering in a wide circle. "Get ready," he yelled to Elkins, then the handkerchiefs were gone and he saw nothing.

As the Skymaster sank gracefully to the runway, and all through the turnaround, he fretted. If that candy had landed on the airfield, Colonel Dorr would be "real mad." With relief he taxied out.

Then, as the ship climbed for cruising altitude, he saw alongside the perimeter the kids bouncing up and down, joyously fluttering his handkerchiefs. "I wish they wouldn't do that," Halvorsen muttered, but he felt better. The promise had been kept, and that ended it.

But to Halvorsen's dismay it had only begun. As the days passed, the boys didn't go away. The numbers grew until more than 100 of them were pressed against the wire, watching in vain for the telltale wiggle of wings. In the 17th's Operations Office, the pilots grew curious. "How come those kids are always there waving?" one asked. Halvorsen now made a fateful error of judgment. "If I make just one more drop," he told himself, "they'll be satisfied and go away."

But they didn't, and in a desperate attempt to appease their hunger and get rid of them, Halvorsen did two more six-handkerchief drops. At last, one afternoon coming in to land, fog was stealing over Tempelhof. Halvorsen felt relieved. Unable to see the perimeter, he deluded himself the kids were no longer there.

Preoccupied with the weather, he hastened to the Base Operations Office, in case an alternate field was needed to Rhein-Main. As other pilots moved ahead of him in the line, Halvorsen glanced down at what looked like fan mail piled on the counter awaiting a claimant: stacks of big brown economy envelopes bound with twine.

Halvorsen went numb with panic. They were all for him.

Some were addressed in bright red or green crayon, with childish sketches of Skymasters dropping parachutes, and bore the legend "Onkel Wackelflügel" (Uncle Wiggly Wings) and others were addressed to *Der Schokoladen-flieger* (The Chocolate Flier). Holy smoke, he thought distractedly, if they're writing me letters, this is the end. It would mean a summons to LeMay himself and a court-martial for sure.

Not that he had any intention of claiming his fan mail, for mercifully none of them knew his name, but sooner or later Halvorsen knew he faced the worst kind of trouble. For now he stole discreetly away.

In the ordered chaos of his office, with only George, his Scottie, for company, Clay, as usual, was working late. He scribbled minutes, kept his telephone humming with constant calls to LeMay and Howley, briefing himself on every facet of the airlift's progress. A picture was emerging that disquieted him. More planes were desperately needed to haul in the city's coal, yet despite Truman's ukase to step up the airlift, the Pentagon, fearing that any greater aerial commitment would increase the risk of war, seemed reluctant to grasp the urgency.

On July 10, Clay had impressed on Bradley the need for fifty additional C-54s, requested by LeMay. Shrewdly he had pointed out that "if the Allied [formal] notes to the Soviet Government are to be taken seriously, it is extremely important that the airlift be successful." Yet, to date, the Pentagon had not acted on the request.

Clay had also urged again the one countermove that he believed would reveal the hollowness of the Russians' bluff: the dispatch of an armored column from Wiesbaden to Helmstedt and thence down the *autobahn* to clear all obstacles between Helmstedt and Berlin. "The intransigent Soviet position," he counseled, "should be tested, and I see no way in which it can be tested except by proceeding promptly with the movement of the armed convoy. . . ." But again the reply was ambivalent: "We are not yet prepared to reach a firm decision."

Then, on the evening of July 17, twelve hours after the first sixty B-29 bombers touched down at their British bases, Clay's secretary, Captain Margaret Allen, handed him an urgent cable from Secretary Royall: "Essential that you should return to Washington to discuss with General Bradley, the State Department and myself the entire Berlin situation. . . ."

89

The chance to put the case for Berlin that Clay had so long awaited was now at hand.

But by midafternoon on July 22, Clay, in Washington, was close to despair. In the Cabinet Room of the White House, at an emergency meeting of the National Security Council, he saw all his hopes evaporating. From the first he sensed that most of the fourteen men assembled at the long table saw Berlin as no more than a liability.

To make matters worse, ever since arriving in the capital he had endured the agony of a pinched nerve in his neck. The pain was so acute he could scarcely turn his head.

The one consolation was that President Harry Truman, listening alertly to the arguments, was showing more resolution than many of his advisers. All three Joint Chiefs of Staff— Bradley, the Air Force's General Hoyt Vandenberg, Vice Admiral A. W. Radford for the Navy—had estimated gloomily that following her headlong demobilization and destruction of war materiel America would need eighteen months to prepare for war if the Russians were challenged over Berlin.

As verdict followed verdict, Clay and his political adviser, Robert Murphy, heard the experts writing off their city. Berlin was "indefensible." Berlin needed "not only to import food but raw materials too." Berlin's supply line was costing $1,500,000 a week. Berlin was "vulnerable." So withdraw the B-Mark from Berlin and accept a Russian-controlled currency as a fact of political life.

All eyes now focused on Clay as Truman called for his summary. He knew that today he must fight as never before, not only for a city and its people, to whom he had pledged his word, but for the freedom of Europe as well. "Mr. President and gentlemen," he began unequivocally, "the abandonment of Berlin would have a disastrous effect upon our plans for Western Germany. . . . We should be prepared to go to any lengths to find a peaceful solution . . . but we have to remain in Berlin."

His voice resolute, he went on. To date, he reported, the airlift was averaging 2,500 tons of food a day. Thus, food requirements were adequately cared for; the problem was coal. As winter drew on, the city's minimum fuel needs, if extreme hardship was to be avoided, would be in excess of 4,500 tons a day. Given the present allotment of planes—fifty-two C-54s and eighty C-47s—Berlin would not survive. To ensure that it did, Clay needed nothing less than a fleet of 160 C-54s.

An audible gasp echoed around the table. Then General Vandenberg voiced his protest: More planes for the airlift would gravely disrupt the global role of the Military Air Transport Service. Secretary of State George Marshall cut in: What problems would the maximum use of planes on the lift involve? Vandenberg saw all too many. In the event of hostilities, many of the planes might be destroyed. That would seriously impair America's ability to wage strategic warfare, making it nearly impossible to supply troops and hold outlying bases. Moreover, Vandenberg pointed out, the air lanes to Berlin were as much Russian as American. If America increased traffic to the point where the Russians were forced out, that could give rise to international incidents culminating in world war.

Truman took up the question of an armed convoy. What risk of war did Clay think this entailed? Clay guessed the Russians would first set up road blocks, which his engineers would remove. Royall intervened: He would favor the convoy proceeding only if the trooops were unarmed. Clay was withering: "But that's ridiculous. If they stop us we shall have to move backward. And I'll never order troops of mine to run from the Reds without a fight." It was now that Murphy sensed Truman's sympathies moving toward Clay.

The subject moved back to the airlift. Under Secretary of State Robert Lovett asked about the risk of Russian fighter attacks on airlift bases. Clay thought there was none, unless the Russians wanted war—but he believed no Pearl Harbor strike was involved. Their aim was to force the Allies out by every aggravation short of war.

Truman interceded. "If we move out of Berlin," he said thoughtfully, "we shall lose everything we are fighting for. The question is: How to stay in Berlin without risking all-out-war?" Sensing he was losing ground, Vandenberg again interposed. To concentrate more aircraft in Berlin meant reducing air strength elsewhere, both in planes and personnel. An emergen-

91

cy elsewhere would find America more exposed than she could afford.

For the first time Truman showed a flash of impatience. Would the air chief prefer to see Berlin supplied by convoys? And if Russian resistance to them led to war, wouldn't the Air Force have to play its part in defending Berlin? Before Vandenberg could reply, Truman answered his own question: Since the airlift was less risky than an armed convoy, the Air Force must accord the lift the fullest support.

Truman rose decisively, announcing that he had another appointment. The meeting would continue with Marshall in the chair. But nothing had been formally agreed upon, and Clay was afraid that despite the President's sympathy, the Joint Chiefs would find sound reasons, both strategic and logistic, to change his mind. His mission would be a failure.

Then, by way of farewell, Truman turned to him, "Drop in by my office before you leave, General," he said cheerily, and he was out the door.

His features showing the effect of stress and the increasing pain from his pinched nerve, Clay once more faced the President. Chipper as always after his breakfast and his walk, Truman's demeanor seemed to match the morning—the bright sun sparkling on the buoyant Potomac.

"You look like you feel badly, General," Truman chaffed him.

Despite the stolid presence of Kenneth Royall, Clay could not hold back. "Mr. President," he spoke out, "I'm very disappointed. Without those planes I just don't think we're going to make it in Berlin." Suddenly the President's smile seemed the most dazzling thing he had ever seen. "Oh, you're going to get them," Harry Truman assured him, adding with an almost boyish air of conspiracy. "I've just overruled the Joint Chiefs."

Even in his astonishment Clay's shrewdness did not desert him. Inevitably, he told the President, the White House press corps would be waiting at the entrance in the west wing. Could he safely confide this decision to them? Just as he hoped, Truman waved a casual hand. "Yes, you tell them."

Clay left the Executive Office with lifted heart. In the

corridor, his aide was astonished to see his chief, so recently downcast, "beaming like a little kid." "We're getting the planes," Clay told him excitedly as they hurried to meet the press. With so many powerful men opposing his plans, the general wanted the news out immediately. Once those headlines hit the newsstands, Berlin would survive, for no one in Washington had the power to reverse a Presidential edict.

Later that day the Joint Chiefs held a meeting at the Pentagon. With the air of a man putting a brave face on things, Vandenberg announced that since the President had given the airlift his blessing, no effort must be spared "to make it an operation worthy of the name."

Wedemeyer, sitting in on the conference, thought it was vital to put the one airlift expert in the world in charge. With memories of his command in wartime China, he urged, "Why don't you send over Bill Tunner? He ran the airlift over the Hump."

Vandenberg's reply suggested he was a long way from grasping the magnitude of the Berlin airlift. "Any of my senior officers can handle a thing like that," he announced. "If I just tell LeMay to step up the organization, it'll be done."

In the week that saw Clay's departure for Washington, four students gathered for a jubilant meeting on the empty ground-floor room of the former Kaiser-Wilhelm Institute, a three-story, red-brick building in the suburb of Dahlem.

On the face of it, there was little cause for exultation. There was but one chair and as yet no table on which to stack their papers. But in the course of the day the telephone on the dusty windowsill would ring eighty times—and more than 120 callers would knock diffidently at the green-painted front door seeking guidance on enrollment. One extra-welcome visitor was a volunteer secretary who had thoughtfully brought a typewriter in her rucksack.

To the four students—Otto Hess, Helmut Coper, Horst Hartwich, and Otto Stolz—it was an historic event: the founding of a new Free University in the West.

Just as Lord Mayor-elect Ernst Reuter had predicted, the way had been long and arduous. On May 11, the City Assembly had approved the foundation of a Free University by 105 votes, with only the Communists dissenting, but as the rift with the Soviets widened, it seemed pointless even to raise the issue in a *Kommandatura* meeting.

But luck was on the students' side. From June 16, the Russians' boycott of the *Kommandatura* ruled out all need to consult with them further—and within days an enthusiastic newsman, Kendall Foss, had sold Clay on the idea that a Free University in the American sector would strike another blow in the battle to win the Berliners' trust and confidence. Then, a week later, the city's currency reform had netted the students an astonishing windfall. Appeals for funds in American clubs and canteens, plus the profits from U.S.-licensed newspapers, had brought in a titanic twenty million Reichsmarks, which even at the one-for-ten exchange rate totaled two million new Deutschemarks. Promptly the canny secretary of the University Founding Committee, Dr. Fritz von Bergmann, slipped into East Berlin to convert Clay's highly prized currency into five million Ostmarks.

At last the students had funds to buy chairs, desks, and microscopes in the East—besides the gift of buildings like the Kaiser-Wilhelm Institute from which to operate.

As the four-man committee talked things over there was still much to achieve. Professors must be found, as well as such major teaching facilities as auditoria, up-to-date projectors, and laboratory equipment.

For the newly enrolled students there would be many personal hardships. Some could cross freely from East to West, but others, such as Otto Stolz, could no longer cross with safety. The NKVD had a dossier on all leading dissidents. These, and others forced to flee homes in the East, would need financial assistance.

But all these problems would be worked out. They had funds and promises of aid from the Western Allies. A start was being made.

On July 24 banner headlines proclaimed: "AIRLIFT TO BERLIN REACHES NEW HIGH." Until this moment, Sokolovsky and his advisers had viewed the lift as a nine days' wonder, doomed to failure, for the countless concessions of the past had left the

Soviets skeptical of the Allies' strength of purpose. Now their resolve was plain for all to see.

At Tempelhof, General Smith, faced with the runway's imminent collapse, had begun a new runway 3,000 feet long and 140 feet wide, an avenue of broken bricks clawed by steam shovels from the ruins of the city and topped with asphalt from abandoned streets.

In the four-power Air Safety Center, when America's Captain V. I. Gookin spoke worriedly of reaching "saturation point," his Russian colleague, Captain Zorchenko, asked hopefully when that might be. Defiantly, Gookin snapped back: "When we're landing five hundred planes a day!"

Determined that this should not come to pass, the Russians built up their harassment by the hour. As Yak fighters thronged the corridors, swooping in dizzying 370 mph power dives, urgent instructions went up in American and British crew rooms: Fly above 5,000 feet. For the first time Russian barrage balloons swam perilously in the sky west and southwest of Berlin, above the fighter fields at Köthen, Dalgow, and Brandenburg. At Wunsdorf, in the British zone, RAF pilots reported 100 Yaks in readiness at every airfield along the Bückeburg corridor. Sokolovsky announced that night flights would take place at 2,500 feet somewhere between Frankfurt and Berlin—with Soviet pilots relieved of all obligation to give the Air Safety Center any details.

For the pilots, there were many near catastrophic incidents. Leading in No. 46 Squadron from Wunsdorf, Squadron Leader "Pop" Salter was faced with MIG fighters that spun and snarled around his formation every mile of the way, bulking 200 yards distant in his windshield. Conscious that one Dakota was close behind him, another in front, Salter held his breath and told himself, "No Charlie operation, this." Squadron Leader Denys Horner, bringing his Sunderland in for a Havel See landing, found himself above a Soviet practice range, the bombs from a squadron of Ilyushins hurtling past as he jinked and dived.

Not only the pilots faced Russian molestation. Berliners who had lent them support were now at risk as well. Comedian Walter Gross, famed for his broadcast lampoons, got a tip-off from Dahlem police precinct: A plan was afoot to abduct him to the East. Each night thereafter police mounted a guard on his Bitterstrasse home. Schoolteacher Kurt Foljanty, living in Grünau, in the Eastern sector, found himself in peril for another reason. An ex-POW from Poznan, he spoke fluent Polish and could stand in as an interpreter. When an officer arrived at his door unannounced, Foljanty sensed he was in danger and stalled for time. Lunch was just then on the table; could he finish? "You eat," the officer told him. "We can wait." Peering through the window, Foljanty spotted several cars drawn up along the street and a troop of soldiers. Hastily he laid plans with his wife, Maria, and thirteen-year-old Klaus, his son. The meal over, Kurt and Klaus strolled casually into the back garden and vaulted over the wall. Zigzagging, panting for breath, they scaled wall after wall, reaching the next garden, then the next, and finally Grünau S-Bahn. Twelve stations ahead lay Wedding, in the French sector, where Kurt had a cousin. Half an hour later they reached the freedom of the West.

Some 150 East Berliners a day would follow their example. Everywhere fear was in the air. On July 28, following his return from Washington, Clay agreed that up to 20,000 Berliners who might expect Soviet reprisals would rate priority evacuation. At RIAS headquarters, William Heimlich's desk was piled with U.S. passports hastily granted to his German writers and artists. Many who rated no preferential treatment, such as twenty-year-old housemaid Anna Suess, clung to a cyanide capsule; it was a last gift from her officer father, who had died in the battle for Berlin.

In Wiesbaden, 275 miles southwest of Berlin, the Americans and their dependents were on tenterhooks. How soon would the Russians break through? Every family had one suitcase packed with three days' supply of food and clothing. Every transport driver knew the escape route for dependents if the sirens wailed—to the French zone by Kreuznach, thence into France via the border at Metz. Brigadier General Arthur Trudeau's Task Force had a new mission: the mining of twenty-five locks on the seventy-mile stretch of the Main River between Wiesbaden and Wurzburg, as well as the giant Eder-see Dam. If the Russians did come, millions of tons of water would surge eastward to stall their advance.

Berlin's first airlift tragedy came on the night of Sunday, July 25, as a C-47, heavily loaded with flour, bored blindly through the foggy sky above the city. As the pilots, Lieutenants Charles King and Robert Stuber, sought Tempelhof in vain, their plane lost height alarmingly before plunging with appalling violence into a chestnut tree and through the side of an apartment house. Fire chief Rudolf Harder and his crew found the crewmen dead, the building on fire—and, incredibly, in the untouched basement, an entire family at work in their night clothes sawing up chestnut branches for winter fuel.

Yet the Berliners cared. Next day, at the base of the shattered tree, there appeared a wood-and-glass frame flanked by a small bunch of asters in a cracked drinking glass and forget-me-nots in an empty grapefruit tin. In the frame was a note, touching in its simplicity, a humble In Memoriam for those who died so that Berlin should survive: "Two American fliers here become sacrifices of the blockade of Berlin. . . . Berliners of the western occupation sectors will never forget you. We stand deeply moved at this spot which has been dedicated through your deaths. Once we were enemies, yet you now gave your lives for us."

At dusk on July 29, Wiesbaden Air Force Base was a scene of frenzied activity. A score of cargo carriers, dusty with flour, were moving out nose to tail from the ramp; in the thick haze gathering over the field, the orange runway lights glowed a muddy ocher. Polish and German DPs, in fatigue caps and grease-stained overalls, swarmed everywhere, but few had time to notice the battered old C-54, bearing the serial number 5549, as it swooped in to land. None gave more than a passing glance to the twenty men, many of them wearing the bright distinctive patch of the China Theater, now deplaning, along with two secretaries purposefully armed with their own type-writers.

At their head strode a tall, fair-haired, two-star general, aged forty-two, whose steely blue eyes were already taking in every facet of the activity about him and filing it for reference in his card-index brain. Major General William Tunner, known to his faithful entourage as "Willie-the-Whip," the one man ever to have masterminded an airlift, had arrived in Germany.

7

"It's Got to Be Regimented as Hell"

JULY 29–SEPTEMBER 8, 1948

The day was overcast. North and east of Wiesbaden, thick yellow-white clouds blanketed the Harz Mountains. In Berlin the ceiling dropped to 100 feet, the height of the apartment buildings rimming Tempelhof Field. Shortly after 9:00 A.M. a white hissing curtain of rain scythed the runways. In the control tower the five noncoms on duty could see nothing at all. It was Friday, August 13, 1948.

Ten thousand feet above the city, in the jump seat of his C-54 5549, Major General William Tunner swore explosively. Barely fifteen days had elapsed since Tunner and his team of experts had arrived to streamline the airlift into a miracle of aerial precision, yet now, in his earphones, Tunner could hear the operation disintegrating into panic-stricken chaos. Ahead of him, flying the same route through the murk, were twenty C-54s stretched out like machines on a conveyor belt—each plane three minutes apart, each boring at a steady 180 mph. Yet no radar, Tunner knew, could penetrate that driving rain—and the tower's talk-down procedure was falling pitiably apart.

Already one C-54, overshooting the runway, had crashed into a ditch, exploding into fire as the crew scrambled clear. To

98

avoid piling into the flames the next pilot braked with everything he had, blowing both tires. A third, swooping in over the apartment buildings, let down on the first solid ground he saw—an auxiliary runway still under construction. For seconds the plane yawed and side-slipped in the sticky rubber base, then ground-looped ignominiously.

Faced with a traffic jam of epic proportions—with planes leaving the unloading line for take-off, as well as planes coming in—the frightened controllers took the only course left to them and began to stack those planes still aloft at heights ranging from 3,000 to 12,000 feet.

Tunner was furious. Stacking planes was accepted emergency procedure—but it required an allotted area fifty to one hundred miles from the field. The island of Berlin allowed barely twenty miles of latitude; beyond that the cargo-laden planes were at the mercy of any Russian fighter bent on harassment. There was only one solution. Tunner grabbed the mike, and his voice was harsh in the controller's earphones: "This is 5549—Tunner talking, and you listen. Send every plane in the stack back to its home base."

A moment of incredulous silence, then a chastened voice queried, "Please repeat."

Tunner was curt. "Send everybody in the stack below and above me home. Then tell me when it's O.K. to come down."

Within the hour, Tunner, Lieutenant Colonel Robert "Red" Forman, his chief of operations, and Lieutenant Colonel Sterling Bettinger, his air traffic expert, were standing on the tarmac. Angrily, Tunner issued an ultimatum: "I want you two to stay in Berlin until you've figured out a way to eliminate any possibility of this mess ever happening again—ever! I don't care if it takes you two hours or two weeks—that's your job."

But the chaos of "Black Friday" did not entirely surprise him. From the moment of arrival it was clear that only a radical rethinking of the airlift could enable Berlin to survive. Tunner's first words had set the keynote for all that was to follow: "I'm not asking you to put in twenty-four hours a day, but, dammit, if I can do eighteen hours you can do fifteen."

No one in his twenty-strong team caviled at that injunction. The problem was plain for all to see—and not only in the skies

99

above. On this first day, Airlift Task Force Headquarters was a warren of empty rooms silted with debris, lit only by naked bulbs, innocent of desks and chairs. It was the only building LeMay had been able to find on short notice. To shield her desk from the noonday sun, Tunner's secretary of eight years, Catherine Gibson, had to improvise window blinds from wrapping paper. Toilet rolls were pressed into service as adding-machine tape, maps secured to the walls with mail censor stickers. While Air Installations expert Kenneth Swallwell set to work repairing the elevator, Lieutenant Colonel Manuel Fernandez, Tunner's communications chief, went in search of the team's first telephones.

Thus to Tunner's crisp instructions—"Get off your tails and get out on the road"—his team responded with enthusiasm. By 9:00 A.M. on July 30, after whirlwind surveys of Wiesbaden, Rhein-Main, and Tempelhof, his men were back with their reports, squatting on orange boxes in a semicircle around their chief, spotlighting the flaws that years of training had enabled them to detect at a glance.

Captain Jules Prevost reported that production-line maintenance was close to breakdown. Groups and squadrons were rushed off to duty, hampered by shortages of tools and spare parts, striving to carry out both daily routine checks and the major inspections planes needed after 200 hours of flight. Lieutenant Colonel Kenneth Swallwell was appalled by Tempelhof's runway system. A force of 200 men, equipped with landing mats, sand, and asphalt, made what emergency repairs they could; then scattered widely each time a plane zoomed in. Three runways, Swallwell predicted, would be minimal for the task that lay ahead. Major Edward Guilbert commented on the lack of loading expertise. Few cargo officers had the know-how to marry light-density loads like dried vegetables with high-density items like steel. Captain Harold Sims saw the old Transport Command System as the true bottleneck: Planes took off as a group and landed as a group, then often waited an hour for an unloading crew to reach them.

No man had run across a situation more bizarre than Chief of Staff Colonel Theodore Ross Milton. So scarce were briefing kits that one pilot, with the navigational frequencies of radio stations scrawled on the leg of his coveralls, had been unable to change his flying suit for two weeks.

It was plain that if Berlin was to survive the winter ahead, the airlift must be transformed from the gay derring-do affair of the first fifty-one days into an operation as inflexibly systematic as a metronome.

No team was better fitted for the task. In 1944, Brigadier General Tunner—along with many now picked to work alongside him in Berlin—had been assigned to India to take charge of the Air Transport Command airlift flying "the Hump" between Assam and Kunming, China, an airlift that was transporting 69,300 tons a month in its first year of operation. It was this feat which had led Lieutenant General Albert Wedemeyer to suggest him to Hoyt Vandenberg as the one man to see this job through.

Sounded out by Vandenberg, LeMay had agreed. "I don't think I can afford to turn down any offer of help" was his first reaction, adding with terse finality, "Let's use him."

By August 15, Red Forman and Sterling Bettinger, aided by Major Harold Sims as draftsman and navigational expert, had come up with a revolutionary solution to the Black Friday chaos at Tempelhof Field. In a room hazy with tobacco smoke, overlooking the field, they had devoted forty-eight hours to reshaping the airlift Tunner-style.

The room had taken on a surreal aspect: a cat's cradle of string looped from the window to door and back, supporting a baffling array of GI coat hangers tagged with model airplanes. But from the elaborate maneuvers the planes had performed and from Sims's drawings had emerged the flight patterns that were to govern the airlift for the foreseeable future.

Essential to this new operational plan was one-way traffic. Planes would fly up the southern corridor to Berlin, unload, and exit via a central corridor. The indiscriminate traffic flow of the past, with its constant risk of midair collisions, was out. Now each pilot must pass the checkpoints—the Fulda beacon near Frankfurt, the Frohnau beacon on the outskirts of Berlin— dead on time, using each beacon like a signpost in the sky, keeping an exact distance behind the preceding plane, maintaining precise altitude and speed.

101

Moreover, planes would now fly in alternate blocks to avoid confusion between the slower-paced C-47s, cruising at 165 miles per hour, and the C-54s, capable of 245 miles per hour.

Stacking over Berlin was also ruled out. As Forman and Bettinger twirled the coat hangers, it became apparent that in this intricate operation, with a safety margin of barely two and a half minutes, no plane could be given a second chance to land. Any plane that missed the first time must return to base with its full load, rather than disrupt the traffic flow.

Once a plane rolled to a halt, it was to be met immediately by an unloading crew and a refueling truck. From now on, no pilot would be allowed to leave the orbit of his plane. A mobile briefing truck would bring him the weather and a mobile snack bar coffee and hot dogs. In the spirit of Tunner's credo "When a plane's sitting on the ground it's going to waste" the plan was as near metronomic as could be. "We've just got to eliminate all individualism in the cockpit," Bettinger summed up. "It's got to be regimented as hell from now on."

For the British this was Dunkirk all over again—and they responded with the same fighting fervor. On August 7, Foreign Secretary Ernest Bevin, determined that England should play her part to the full in the battle for Europe's freedom, urged his Secretary of State for Air, Arthur Henderson, "We must fill the sky with our planes." Yet so hard pressed was the RAF that Henderson's one solution was to call in "the sky tramps," a score of air charter directors whose shaky old crates earned a precarious living hauling cargoes all over the globe.

With an offer of £45 per flying hour—almost £8 above the commercial rate—there were few who didn't jump at the chance.

In Berlin, the man slated to coordinate the civil lift, Edwin Whitfield of British European Airways, had a formidable task. Between them the firms could throw in 104 planes, but they were all geared to different speeds, altitudes, and load factors—from Aquila Airways' twelve Hythe flying boats, the civil version of the Sunderland, to the lumbering Bristol Freighter used on the Lympne–Le Touquet car ferry. Nor were their radios tuned to airlift frequencies. Among the twenty

Dakotas pressed into service none was sufficiently airworthy to carry more than 6,000 pounds—1,480 pounds less than the standard RAF load. Few were equipped for a speedy turnaround.

Many were in sorry shape—subject to maverick engine spasms, constant oil leaks, frayed brake cables, and cracked exhaust stubs. Their servicing was often slipshod. At Bovingdon, Hertfordshire, where his Halton's floorboards were raised to increase loading capacity, Chief Pilot Edward Hood, of British American Air Services, found three inches of wellmatured cheese—the fruits of an earlier Belfast milk run. Most had flown any cargoes they could get—racing pigeons to Turin, prize bulls to Argentina. Tunner-style regimentation was alien to them.

Typical of the crews signing on was First Officer Dennis Ormerod. Tramping London in search of work, Ormerod dropped in at Ciro's night club, whose two Dakotas, which ferried wealthy patrons to the French Riviera, had signed on for the lift. In answer to Ormerod's query—"Want a keen young pilot?"—the manager handed him the uniform of a man who had just quit. "Try that for size."

That first flight to Germany was one Ormerod never forgot. Only three times in a C-47, his memory for details was hazy. When the captain, on take-off from England, ordered "Wheels up," Ormerod asked shamefacedly, "Which lever do I pull?" Worse, the flight included a landfall at Geneva to deposit some of Ciro's revelers—with only a Mercator's plotting chart aboard to point the way. At 5,000 feet over Lake Geneva, Ormerod sought out a knowledgeable passenger. "Which end of the Lake is the airport?" Hastily the man instructed him: "Turn south."

Once at Wunsdorf, most charter crews found only confusion. Though Gatow's Wing Commander Flying, Tim Piper, had decreed they must fly in a separate block, no one knew which cargoes they would carry—or when. Eagle's chief pilot, Jim Hepburn, returned from Operations to find a bowser had backed into his Halton's aircrew, bending it to a misshapen "J." Undeterred, engineer Ray Lamb took an eight-pound hammer and banged it into shape. When Hepburn inquired dubiously,

"Will it be all right?" Lamb was philosophic. "We'll know as soon as we're airborne."

In a trailer at Tarrant Ruston, Dorset, Hugh Johnson, Operations Chief for Sir Alan Cobham's Flight Refueling, was stark naked in his shower when a phone call from the Foreign Office sent him groping for the receiver. Were the company's four Lancastrian tankers, which could hold 1,500 gallons of fuel, available to handle a "wet lift" of Diesel oil into Gatow? Offered £98 an hour, Johnson agreed on the spot—though how the fuel would be unloaded at Gatow no one knew. After frantic phone calls all over Germany, Johnson, briefed on the measurements of threads and unloading pits, handed his chief engineer a daunting weekend assignment: Design special tubing to connect the aircraft's belly tanks with Gatow's ground installation.

One man was determined to join the lift from the first—and for reasons far removed from hard cash. Pacing the grass airstrip at Blackbushe Airport, Camberley, Surrey, Air Vice Marshal Donald Bennett, chief of the brand-new charter firm Air Flight, was out to vindicate a belief in an ill-fated plane that had recently cost him a lucrative job.

At thirty-seven, Bennett was already a legend, with a brilliant succession of flying "firsts": the still-unchallenged world's long-distance seaplane record, from Dundee, Scotland, to Alexandra Bay, South Africa, in the autumn of 1938; the first direct-flight mail from England to Egypt two months later; the first commercial load flight across the North Atlantic. Even his textbook, *The Complete Air Navigator*, was still, after twelve years, the standard work.

During the war Bennett headed the world-famous Path Finder Force of Lancaster and Mosquito bombers that bombed a score of German industrial targets, and at war's end, appointed managing director and chief executive of the nationalized British South American Airways, his peacetime course had seemed secure.

Then, on January 29, 1948, disaster struck. One of B.S.A.A.'s crack airliners, the Avro Tudor IV, four-engine passenger plane, carrying a crew of six and twenty-five passengers, took off from the Azores for Kindley Field, Bermuda, and vanished forever into the night. Bennett, who had piloted the Tudor on its 16,500-mile proving flight from London to Chile and back and had never ceased to laud its airworthiness, was sacked with redress.

It was Bennett's first defeat, and it stung. With the Tudor near grounded as unreliable, he used his £4,500 severance pay to snap up two from the government and formed Air Flight. As he told his technicians: "We must prove that this is a good aircraft—the best."

Now that chance had come. The Foreign Office had made their bid and Bennett had clinched the deal. Within days, Tudor II G-AGRY, stripped of all save essentials, would take off for Wunsdorf with Bennett at the controls. The second Tudor would remain behind for conversion into a tanker: five large tanks, to hold a total of nine tons of Diesel oil for every trip he flew.

It was a characteristic Bennett venture. He was going to match aviation's most jinxed plane with a high-risk load against some of the world's most hazardous flying conditions.

For one airlift pilot there would be no regimentation. With the full backing of Generals Clay, LeMay, and Tunner, Lieutenant Gail Halvorsen would continue his candy drop. For in this improvised operation Halvorsen had done more, perhaps, than any other flier to capture the Berliners' hearts and minds.

The showdown Halvorsen had dreaded had been swift to come. One morning he was called before the 17th's commander, Colonel Haun. "What in the world," Haun led off, "have you been doing?" Halvorsen was guileless: "Flying like mad, Colonel." Haun exploded. "Look, I am not *stupid*—it's all over the front pages of the Berlin papers. You nearly hit a journalist on the head with that candy." Then, in a mellower tone, he added: "A good thing for you General Tunner says to go ahead."

From that moment, the candy lift—soon christened "Little Vittles"—snowballed to amazing proportions. When Halvorsen ran out of handkerchiefs, every man in the 17th chipped in

105

with their own handkerchiefs, shirttails, even sleeves. Each night when he returned to his billet, his bed was piled high with boxes of gum and Hershey bars.

From the salvage yard, a supply captain donated twelve surplus parachutes, and the base wives took over and organized "Little Vittles" sewing bees. To each miniature chute they made they attached a note reading, "Please return this chute for reuse to the first M.P. you see." The cynics laughed scornfully. "The *frauleins* will have that silk for blouses and panties," scoffed one. But of the first twelve chutes dropped on the next morning's flight, nine had been returned to Tempelhof by 4:00 P.M.

Others were drawn into the scheme willy-nilly. Sergeant Vernon Earley, parking his car in a restricted zone in Rhein-Main, was waylaid by a passing M.P. who gave him two choices: a parking ticket or 70 cents worth of candy for "Little Vittles." Delighted, Earley paid up.

Overnight, Halvorsen found himself a celebrity—not only in Germany but across the entire United States. Radio stations from Los Angeles to Boston took up his cause—"Send in a handkerchief and we'll play your request tune." Soon Halvorsen was receiving five sacks of mail a day. Every envelope contained handkerchiefs—some drenched in seductive perfume with lace edging.

By now Tempelhof's perimeter was wall-to-wall children. The pilots needed safer dropping zones. Thus the men in the 17th were assigned special dropping areas at 2,000 feet—over the Tiergarten, over schoolyards and recreation areas. As the cardboard boxes hurtled into space they burst open, and a thistledown cluster of tiny chutes floated down over the parks and gardens.

With Tunner's permission, Halvorsen was given clearance to range at 1,500 feet all over Berlin, following specific instructions: "Fly along the canal and turn right. We live in the bombed-out building and I'll be waiting in the backyard at 2:00 P.M." One small girl was reproving: "You fly so low our hens have stopped laying—so please drop some candy."

For Halvorsen, childhood was something outside politics.

When East Berlin children complained they lacked candy he widened his orbit, dropping parachutes over Weissensee and Pankow. Within days he was stopped. A Soviet protest note to the State Department had condemned the flight as "an outrageous capitalist trick."

Only one problem remained: the language barrier, for many of the children knew no English and Halvorsen no German. The problem was solved when Rhein-Main's base commander assigned Halvorsen a full-time German social secretary to answer his fan mail. It was a rare accolade for a humble first lieutenant—and a measure of the success of his own personal airlift.

Daily, the tempo of the lift was increasing. To some the day-long roar of the planes was already the sound of victory, but neither Clay nor Tunner was taking chances. Tunner continued his frantic pace. "He wanted everything done as of yesterday," secretary Cathy Gibson recalled.

Despite the airlift's undoubted triumph, the West still seemed prone to seek appeasement. On August 2, the three Western envoys in Moscow—America's Walter Bedell Smith, Britain's Frank Roberts, and France's Yves Chataigneau—met for two hours with an impassive Josef Stalin in his third-floor office at the Kremlin. Puffing blandly at an English Dunhill pipe, doodling red wolves' heads on his blotter, Stalin seemed genuinely anxious to settle the blockade. "After all," he told his visitors, "we are still Allies."

As it turned out, however, Stalin's proposals had changed little since Sokolovsky's obdurate stand in June. He still insisted on the replacement of Berlin's Western B-Mark with the Soviet zone Deutschemark as a condition to ending transport restrictions. The dictator's sole concession was that he no longer made it a "condition" that the Allies abandon the formation of a West German government; it was merely "an insistent Soviet wish." The stalemate continued.

Despite the all-out efforts of Clay and Tunner the airlift was running into some snags. On August 14, in the worst summer since 1919, with drenching, near-tropical rains, Berlin had just

107

twenty-seven days' food supply. Thus they saw but one solution: The lift must be stepped up—on the ground as well as in the air.

For thousands of Berliners, this decision proved to be a double blessing. Not only did it mean more food, but those whose jobs had folded now found work alongside the Allies, striving to make the airlift a success.

It was work that often taxed their bodies to the breaking point. Insurance clerk Heinz Pischke, joining an unloading crew at Gatow, found that all the other men in the twelve-strong team were professional coal heavers. But the job entitled him to a No. 1 heavy workers' ration card and a hot midday meal, so he struggled on, though the wire fastening the coal sacks scraped his hands red-raw. Bank cashier Erich Ungnad thought he would never make it. Staggering three yards with his first 200-weight side of bacon, he collapsed like a rag doll. Slowly he learned the secret of balance, stooping to take the weight on his haunches. A fierce pride was reborn in him; he could once more support Vera, his wife.

Not all were so conscientious. Stonemason Karl-Heinz Meissner, working on Tempelhof's runway, found some of his workmates surreptitiously drilling a neat hole in the center of each twenty-inch-square stone slab. When he asked why, he received withering looks. This ensured that all kept eating, for the slabs would crack when a C-54 hit them and need replacing. But the American engineers soon spotted the ruse, and Meissner was put in charge of another team of workers checking every slab for holes.

For thousands of men and women their guaranteed meal ticket for much of that autumn was a new airfield at Tegel, in the French sector. Without it Berlin could not last the winter, for the two existing fields could no longer handle the rising demand for coal shipments.

Yet before the Berliners could set to work, Tunner needed heavy machinery—and every available item was in use at Tempelhof. The solution marked the genius for improvization that was rapidly stamping every facet of the lift. Airfield engineer H. P. Lacomb, who had learned his skills in the Amazon jungle, was dispatched by the Pentagon to set up shop at Rhein-Main. Working with an oxyacetylene torch on bull-dozers, graders, and crushers shipped in from Bremerhaven, Lacomb sliced them up as easily as segments of pie, to be flown into Tempelhof in a Globemaster C-74 with a twenty-five-ton capacity. At Tempelhof Lacomb took over again, welding together what he had divided.

By September 1, with the heavy machinery assured, 19,000 Berliners had gone to work to build their own airfield. As they streamed across the rolling land, once a practice ground for Goering's flak divisions, their shovels shouldered like muskets, it was an unforgettable spectacle. Almost half were women—some wearing slacks and kerchiefs, some silk dresses, others in beach costumes and high-heeled shoes—yet they toiled as gamely as any man hauling pulverized bricks for the runways and carrying rocks to the crusher. Onetime professors in old frock coats labored along with war cripples and peasants in wooden clogs. By night, under the glare of arc lights, they worked on, eight-hour shift following eight-hour shift, to make Tegel a reality.

Though the pay was only one mark 20 per hour, the midday meal of vegetable stew and black bread was for many their only meal of the day. Many found the going tough and inevitably there were hazards. There were even some casualties. Sports-writer Kurt Felgentreff was on a gantry feeding granite into the fifteen-foot maw of the rock crusher when the man behind him slipped, tugged forward by the three-hundredweight slab. It was so sudden that Felgentreff stood mesmerized, noting dully that the man didn't even shout or cry out. Afterward he thought the first impact must have severed the nerves before the machine chopped limbs and torso into bloody chunks.

Ferdinand Schreck, one of a long line working on the runway close to the asphalt plant, looked up and saw thirty feet above, another man lose his footing and plunge headlong into the boiling bitumen. The scream resembled nothing he had ever heard. The line paused. On the faces of those around him Schreck saw conflicting emotions. A life had been lost, but winter was coming and the runway had to be finished. "There was just a silence, like you get on Armistice Day, then the line moved on."

By August, following the collapse of the black market, Marlena Eberhardt's fortunes had reached an all-time low. Marta had developed rickets. A pediatrician had counseled irons, but Marlena, recalling an old recipe of her grandmother's had resisted. Instead she bound Marta's legs in poultices of horse bone marrow, all the time kneading with her hands to force the bowed legs inward. Though the child moaned and writhed with pain, the symptoms diminished daily.

Ironically, the blockade saw the black market flourishing again, even with a pound of potatoes priced at a dollar—but Marlena's role as nurse allowed no time for that. But as a part-time checker in a British Control Commission store she could supplement her pay by stealing items the British didn't even miss.

Touched by the story of her little girl, the storekeeper turned a blind eye to Marlena making off with dozens of empty whisky miniatures, which she said were for Marta to play "Chemist's Shop." Instead, she and Hildegard Lutz used them to bottle their own "whisky," a concoction of tap water convincingly darkened with vanilla essence. Then, her auburn hair covered with a scarf, her face innocent of make-up, Marlena set out by night to sell her ersatz wares at the sleazy bars along Kaiser-damm. It wasn't a fraud that would bear repetition—but at five marks a bottle it was worth the risk. Leaving the bar, Marlena took care to walk confidently as far as the first street corner, then "ran with sparks coming out of my heels."

Absorbed in her lonely battle for survival, she gave little thought to the blockade. Theft had become the motive force in her existence. When Hildegard reminded her that in just over three months it would be Christmas and wondered if the Russians would relent before then, an appraising look came into Marlena's eyes. "I wonder," she pondered, "just where we can steal a tree."

Tunner's quest for perfection continued unabated. No source of information went untapped. One overcast August morning a group of thirty pilots were gathered in the ground-floor meeting room of Wiesbaden's four-star Schwarzer Bock Hotel. They had been summoned by Tunner, but no one knew why. Few were accustomed to rub shoulders with two-star generals. The only reassuring signs were a keg of German beer and a table piled with assorted cold cuts.

Promptly at 10:00 A.M. Tunner strode in, followed by his staff. "I called you men here today," he began, "to ask you some questions—and I want to hear some biased answers."

Then, for nine hours, the pilots held the stage. Beer steins in hand, platters of *wurst* parked comfortably on their knees, man after man aired his grievances without restraint, emboldened by the fact that Tunner had refrained from inviting group or squadron commanders. "There was an awful lot of frank talk," recalls a secretary who took the notes, "but they'd already seen Tunner out on the flight line—they knew he was no cardboard general."

Encouraged to "take it from warm-up to take-off," several pilots had a common gripe: When passing over a beacon in the climb-out and making the sharp 180-degree turn required, there was a general fear that another plane might climb up their backs or turn into them on a bend in the course. Clearly more beacons were needed. They also requested that climbing speeds for all pilots should be rigidly enforced by Operations and that there be constant flight checks for crews to ensure standardization.

Tunner listened intently, muttering curt asides to his aides, who scribbled notes and reached quick decisions. Normally beacons took up to a month to install, but by rushing forty-foot beacons on trucks to the required sites, Communications Chief Manuel Fernandez found he could meet the pilots' needs within the day.

Other pilots complained about the overly stringent supervision of the GCA (Ground Controlled Approach) controller. Recently, a Tunner staffer had laid down that in the air pilots should report their positions to the hour, the minute, even the second. Tunner passed the problem to Harold Sims, his navigational expert. "I agree with the pilots," said Sims. "It's valueless and restrictive. It's just stretching the transmission procedure that much longer." Promptly Tunner countermanded the order. The pilots exchanged glances.

111

There were other complaints—about food, mess halls, crowded barracks, taps that ran only cold water. Given the airlift's awesome daily growth, few of these problems would be solved overnight—yet the fact that Tunner had cared enough to sound out their opinions was to be a powerful boost to morale in the grueling weeks ahead. As Tunner later put it: "It wasn't a meeting following any known military procedure but it *was* democratic."

At 7:00 P.M. one young pilot, emptying his stein for the last time, felt emboldened to ask a final question. Granted that the pilots must function almost as auxiliaries to their planes, he sought Tunner's considered view: "General, do you think the C-54 can ever replace sex?"

For once in his career, his staff noted gleefully, Tunner could find no answer.

That same evening Tunner was in an analytic mood. Already more American planes than British were landing at Gatow Airfield. The first seeds of Anglo-American cooperation had been sown. Further, from August 21, Tunner had gained reluctant British assent to his basing three squadrons of C-54s at RAF Station, Fassberg, near Hanover, 140 miles northwest of Berlin in the British zone.

The advantages were manifold. The American corridor into Tempelhof was half again as long as the British corridor. To haul tonnage from Rhein-Main meant a round trip of over five hours as against two and a half hours from Fassberg. Thus Fassberg planes could achieve five round trips a day, compared with three and a half from Rhein-Main, with a saving of 100 gallons of gas per plane. And while Fassberg planes operated over terrain as flat as a football field, pilots from Rhein-Main and Wiesbaden faced the hazards of the deadly Taunus Mountains.

Yet one thing was certain: With the Americans and the RAF using the same corridors—along with the as yet untried charter pilots—a higher degree of coordination would be needed than ever before.

In Tunner's view that coordination could be achieved in only one way: by placing every plane flying the Berlin Airlift under his personal command. There was some resistance, he knew, within the RAF, but he could count on the wholehearted support of Curtis LeMay.

On August 21, goaded beyond endurance, the Allies paid the Russians back in kind. Across the Potsdamer Platz, in the heart of Berlin, the barricades went up for the first time. Provoked by four unauthorized Russian sorties into the Western sectors—ostensibly in pursuit of black marketeers—the Allies now blocked all access to the West, with stockades of steel rods and wire manned by 600 armed military policemen.

The Soviet reaction was to intensify their campaign of oppression, notably abductions. Day by day the Berliners' anger mounted as the seizure of both soldiers and civilians grew more cruelly haphazard.

One of their victims was Boy George Lea, a seventeen-year-old trombonist with the Worcestershire Regiment. Early one morning, following a twenty-four-hour ceremonial guard, he did what he had done scores of times: Ignoring standing orders, he slipped under the barbed wire dividing Montgomery Barracks, Kladow, from the Russian zone and set off through the pine woods toward the village of Gross Glienicke. For months Lea had been visiting a girl friend, Inga Braun, who lived in the British sector of the divided village—but to reach her involved crossing Russian territory.

He had just broken from the woods onto the sandy track leading to the village when he saw a five-man Russian patrol, headed by a sergeant with a pistol and a corporal with a Tommy gun. Lea froze. If he ran they would shoot, and he knew it.

The sergeant seized him, and the patrol frog-marched him to a wooden command post. From here he was taken by car on a three-mile journey to a white-painted mansion with barred windows.

In a ground-floor office, faced by a woman in a tailored black suit and an elderly lieutenant, Lea had his first interrogation. Who was he? Why had he been visting Gross Glienicke? They seemed irritated that he had been walking in and out of the Soviet zone for months without their knowledge.

The questions took a sinister turn. Who was his commanding officer, his adjutant, his company commander? Lea gave the classic response: "I am required to give you only my number, rank, and name." Then a slow chill invaded him as the woman triumphantly rebuked him: "You would be wiser to cooperate. We already know your commanding officer is Lieutenant Colonel Tuckey, your adjutant is Captain Durrant, and your company commander Captain Brown."

It was curiously humiliating, as if someone had been rifling through the pages of his private diary.

Finally, after two hours of questioning, Lea was taken to the cellar, which he was always to think of as "The Pit," and there they left him for seven days.

Long afterward the memory of those days swept back over him so that he sweated and shivered and paced the floor of his room, sleepless for nights on end. He knew his cell's dimensions by heart—ten feet by six feet—and he remembered too the low-watt bulb that burned in the ceiling day and night. High up in the rear wall was the sole ventilation, an air vent eighteen inches wide, so that the air was always humid and sticky, tainted by the stench from the brimming bucket toilet. Once a day a warder brought him a bowl of gray greasy soup and a chunk of sour-tasting bread. He was hungry all the time, dreaming of fruitcake.

On the seventh day he was awakened by the warder and led down the corridor. To his surprise, he was allowed his first bath, in a battered zinc tub, and given a razor and a rough corn cigarette rolled from a strip of *Pravda*. Then the warder gestured. "Follow me."

Upstairs he was ushered into another ground-floor room. It was simply furnished—a single bed, a chair, a small desk, an enameled coal-burning stove—but after the squalor of The Pit it was luxury that made Lea blink. The warder left, locking the door behind him.

Through the two barred windows Lea could see a green lawn sloping to a high fence and a lake fringed by reeds. The lake was perhaps 400 yards wide, and beyond it he could see a hill, crowned with trees. Suddenly it occurred to him. I've seen that hill before. Then, borne faintly on the morning air, he heard a ragged volley of rifle fire. The sense of familiarity quickened. All at once he knew where he was. The lake was the Havel See. Beyond that hill, tantalizingly out of his view, was Montgomery Barracks and the Worcestershire's rifle range.

General Lucius D. Clay (left) and Britain's General Sir Brian Robertson, chief architects of the Berlin Airlift. *(Keystone)*

Major General William Tunner, commander in chief of the Combined Airlift Task Force, who streamlined the lift into a miracle of aerial precision. *(U.S. Air Force)*

Colonel Frank Howley, hard-hitting American sector commandant. *(Keystone)*

Lord Mayor Ernst Reuter of Berlin, whose election was vetoed by the Russians. *(Ullstein—Stark Otto)*

A line-up of C-47s, with a capacity of less than three tons apiece, unloading at Tempelhof. Nicknamed Gooney Birds, these antiquated twin-engine planes were nonetheless dubbed by the pilots "the most forgiving plane that ever was." *(U.S. Air Force)*

Lieutenant Gail S. Halvorsen, originator of a candy drop dubbed "Operation Little Vittles," surrounded by a group of appreciative Berlin children. *(National Archives)*

Crews at Rhein-Main air base undergo briefing on approaches, return routes, beacons, and altitudes. *(U.S. Air Force)*

The C-54, with a capacity three times that of the C-47 soon became the mainstay of "Operation Vittles

Every available British plane was pressed into service. An R.A.F. C-47, called a Dakota, is loaded with spare wheels, ready for takeoff to Germany. *(Syndication International)*

Here the large planes prepare for takeoff from Fassberg as the airlift becomes an around-the-clock operation.

An R.A.F. crew lands a Sunderland hydroplane on Berlin's Havel See. *(British Crown Copyright Reserved)*

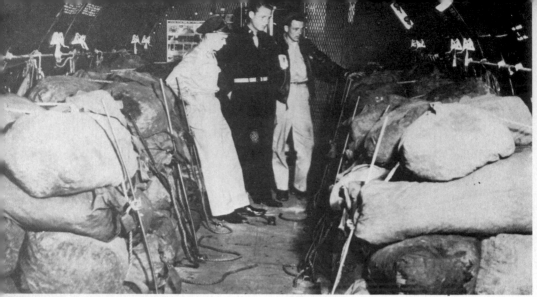

Crewmen check lashings on a 10-ton load of coal enroute from Fassberg to Berlin. *(U.S. Air Force)*

Construction of an unloading ramp continues at Tegel airfield in the French Sector of Berlin, as C-54s maintain a steady stream of traffic on the runway behind. *(U.S. Air Force)*

Flying conditions into West Berlin were hazardous. Here, a steeply descending transport plane flies into Tempelhof air base in the heart of Berlin, situated perilously close to a row of seven-story apartment buildings. *(U.S. Air Force)*

As the blockade continued, Berliners used every available spot of land to grow food. Here, a woman tends a vegetable garden on a boulevard in Berlin. *(Keystone)*

Young Berliners watch a C-54, loaded with much-needed supplies, nearing Tempelhof. *(U.S. Air Force)*

Jubilant Berlin residents mass in front of City Hall on May 12, 1949, to celebrate the lifting of the Berlin blockade. *(Wide World)*

He was within sight of home, yet powerless to get word to them or even to call for help. He began to cry.

Toward the end of August, all evidence suggested that a solution for the blockade was in sight. Following two meetings of the Western envoys with Stalin in Moscow, the four military governors of Germany were instructed to convene again on August 31 to work out an agreement in practice. It seemed likely that a compromise was in the offing. If the Allies would accept Stalin's condition that the Russian mark was to be Berlin's currency, Stalin would lift his objections to Allied plans for a West German government.

Indeed, the Allies' plans were already moving ahead. In a few days' time, with Christian Democrat Konrad Adenauer in the chair, West Germany's leaders were to meet beside the Rhine in the shiny modern auditorium of Bonn's Pedagogical Institute to thrash out details of the republic's constitution. The goal for which Clay, Robertson, and Koenig had so long fought was at last in sight.

Scarcely had this new meeting of the governors been announced, however, than Ernst Reuter called on Frank Howley to seek his advice. Reuter was in a quandary. The City Assembly was soon to be convened, and the SED (the Communist-dominated Socialist Unity Party) had announced their determination to disrupt it.

Howley thought hard. Why, if the blockade had almost run its course, should the Communists be readying for another power play? His inner belief was that the Russians, as always, were resorting to their old tactics of using the mob as an accessory to conference-table negotiations. But it would not be good for the city government to capitulate without taking a stand. "By all means hold the meeting," he advised Reuter. "If you have to leave, then leave under pressure from the Communist stooges." If the Assembly asked for sanctuary in the West, he added, it must be clear to the free world that the Russians had forced them out.

Afterward he wondered if his advice had been sound. The way Howley saw it, he may have just invited 100 Social Democrats, Catholics and Liberals, to lay their heads on a Communist block.

The honeymoon was over almost before it began. Within days the Berliners heard with stoic resignation that the four-power talks had come to nothing. The Allies were willing to accept the Soviet zone Deutschemark as Berlin's currency provided they could share in its control. But this proviso was rejected out of hand. The Communists were still obdurately bent on the seizure of all Berlin.

Consequently, the Russians once more unsheathed the one weapon of which neither diplomacy nor the airlift could deprive them: the mob. As Reuter had warned and Howley had feared, their target was the City Assembly, for their closing-down would be the first stage toward bringing one sector of the city under total Communist dominion. Just as in June, the Communists whipped up a frenzied mob of demonstrators. This time they stormed the gates of City Hall, scattering the police and breaking up the Assembly with brutal force. In effect, the total split of the city was now complete. Reuter and his co-workers were forced to move into new offices in Schöneberg borough, and Speaker Suhr would soon convene the Assembly's first Western sector meeting in an abandoned academy in Charlottenburg.

On September 8, word reached Major General Otway Herbert that Reuter, Franz Neumann, and their fellows planned a mass counterdemonstration of Berliners before the six-columned entrance of the ruined Reichstag to protest the routing of the elected government from City Hall. Once the seat of Parliament, which the Nazis had deliberately set ablaze in 1933, the gutted building remained a symbol for every free Berliner.

But its ruins, sited in the British sector, lay barely 200 yards from the Brandenburger Tor that marked the Soviet-British boundary. In the belief that the demonstration would be "as provocative as you can get," Herbert had banned the meeting.

The result had been a firm rebuke from Sir Brian Robertson and political adviser Christopher Steel. Despite Clay's avowed opinion that the demonstrators were "playing with dynamite," Robertson and Steel deemed the meeting "psychologically right." It must go ahead as planned; to retire from the Reichstag would be interpreted by Moscow as a major Western retreat.

Reluctantly, Herbert countermanded his order. But on the eve of the demonstration, timed for 5:00 P.M. on Thursday, September 9, the British commandant, unknown to Robertson and Steel, had taken precautions of his own. When darkness fell, 500 men of the Royal Norfolk Regiment, under Lieutenant Colonel George Turner-Cain, would deploy secretly, at night, through the Reichstag's bat-haunted ruins to stand fast for twenty-four hours until the meeting had ended.

Would Britons be forced to open fire on Russians—or on hostile Berliners intent on storming the Soviet sector? At 5:00 P.M. on September 8, Herbert didn't know.

8

"You Cannot, You Must Not, Forsake Us"

SEPTEMBER 9–DECEMBER 5, 1948

All through the warm overcast Thursday, with the thermometer hovering in the high seventies, the tension mounted by the hour. From early dawn the RIAS newscasters, led by Rudolf-Günter Wagner, had been cruising the streets, exhorting the crowds to make their feelings known: "Berliners from East and West, from Schöneberg, Wedding, Weissensee—to the Reichstag! Today at 5:00 P.M., Berlin calling the world! Against the blockade, against the Markgraf police, against Communist terror! The decision lies in your hands."

Now, toward 5:00 P.M. on September 9, an army was coming. They came on foot and by bicycle; they thumbed rides from cars and trucks along the street. They poured from the old Hansa quarter, across the Potsdamer Platz and from the bowels of the Lehrter Railway Station, like a football crowd heading for a stadium.

At his microphone beside the speaker's platform at the base of the Reichstag's stone steps, RIAS reporter Franz Zimmermann was reminded of Goethe's *Egmont*: "Behold they stire in thousands! They come! . . . The gates give way, the bolts are crushed, under their hand crumbles the wall." For *Time* correspondent Emmet Hughes, the throng was charged with "enough mass power to change the face of Europe." Susanne Suhr, wife of the City Assembly's Speaker, still recalls the poignancy of that moment. "I never cried during all the war—but I cried then."

The sun beat down on them, and the air was heavy with sweat and swirling dust and the odor of Linden blossom. Still they came, watched curiously through binoculars by Soviet officers standing in their staff cars beyond the Brandenburger Tor. Almost 300,000 of them, blanketing the parched grass of the Tiergarten and the rubble-strewn acres of the Platz der Republik, conscious that in this historic hour they would see freedom reborn or reburied.

As speaker after speaker took the podium, the crowd's emotions were stirred to fever pitch. They heard Ferdinand Friedensburg pledge "We shall not cringe. We shall go on defending the rights of decent, brave and loyal people." They heard Dr. Otto Suhr: "Today the Russian general gets the answer to his behavior from the mass of assembled Berliners." They heard railroad labor leader Gustav Pietch bellow hoarsely: "The blockade has failed, and now the Communists can only wait for the help of General Hunger and Generalissimo Winter. Again they will fail!"

But it was Ernst Reuter who captured the day. As he rose to speak, his fine tired eyes swept the crowd, and in the shadows cast by the tall pillars his features took on the roughness of a medieval woodcut. This was not, he told them gently, a day for generals or diplomats to speak or negotiate. This instead was the day on which the people of Berlin raised their voice. And that voice was calling out to the whole free world.

Then, in the soaring tones of an Old Testament prophet, Reuter spoke for Berlin: "We cannot be bartered, we cannot be negotiated, we cannot be sold . . . Whoever would surrender this city, whoever would surrender the people of Berlin, would surrender a world . . . more, he would surrender himself. . . . On this day, if only they could, the people of Leipzig, of Chemniez, of Dresden, of all the cities in the East Zone, would stand like us in their public squares and listen to our voice." And with passionate sincerity he concluded: "People of the world, look upon this city! You cannot, you must not, forsake us! There is only one possibility for all of us: to stand jointly together until this fight has been won."

A tidal wave of applause followed, for Reuter's words had truly embodied the Berliners' resolution to face the rigors that lay ahead.

Nobody had planned trouble, but as Herbert had feared, trouble was swift to come. As the meeting broke up, thousands, pouring through the massive Doric columns of the Brandenburger Tor on their way to homes in the Russian sector, met up with an open truck carrying Soviet sector police. And though the encounter began with jeers—"*Ivan, 'raus!*" "*Raus mit Kotikov*"—all at once the jeers were followed by rocks and the stage was set for tragedy.

The Royal Norfolks could hear the ruckus as they crouched in the darkness of the Reichstag, but Herbert had given them no orders to go troubleshooting in the Soviet sector. Perturbed, Colonel Turner-Cain muttered: "If we have to get out of here in a hurry the whole place will fall down."

From the shell of the old U.S. Embassy, a hail of bricks sent the first Soviet policemen scattering. Then, as reinforcements arrived, the crowd fell back. Pistol shots announced the first casualty: fifteen-year-old Wolfgang Scheunemann, who had stepped forward to shield a nurse, fell, mortally wounded in the groin. Chaos erupted. Screaming execrations at their Russian oppressors, the crowd surged back and forth through the columns of the Tor. One Soviet policeman, his face a mask of blood, fell at his post, to be dragged to safety by British MPs. Vainly Russians tussled with Britons, trying to drag him back.

Suddenly a gasp went through the crowd. Scaling the spiral staircase inside the Tor, a youth had reached the roof and was tearing at the Red flag. Soon three comrades joined him. To cries of "*Anbrennen*" (Burn it) they wrestled with it and sent it fluttering to the street. With matches and cigarette lighters, the crowd moved in. Through the struggling throng came a twelve-year-old boy toting a ten-foot section of the flagpole behind him. To those impeding him he explained: "I'm taking it to my uncle. We need fuel for the stove."

Suddenly the whine of a racing motor sent the crowd

scattering. A jeepload of armed Russians had driven headlong through the Tor into the British sector. Actually, they were merely part of a time-honored daily ritual—the changing of the guard at the Russian War Memorial just inside the British sector. But today the crowd was in no mood to honor the Russian dead. A volley of rocks found their mark, and the Russians recoiled, firing wildly into the air. Then, in a spaced, dangerous line, guns at the ready, they began a slow purposeful march toward the Memorial, driving the crowds before them.

Only the courage of a lone Briton, Major Frank Stokes of the military police, averted a mass slaughter. Advancing coolly to meet the Russians, his swagger stick swinging loosely in his hand, the major beat a gentle tattoo on their gun barrels, like a schoolmaster admonishing refractory pupils. It was the shrugged-off gesture to effectively defuse the tension. Sullenly, their guns lowered, the Russians beat a slow retreat back toward the Tor.

Slowly, in ones and twos, the crowd began drifting away, with only a litter of broken brick, the smoldering embers of the flag, to mark that on this ground the Berliners had shown decisively that they would resist. Overhead the thunder of the planes never ceased. It was almost like an affirmation that their faith was not in vain.

On the flight line the pressures mounted intolerably as more and more men were absorbed into the lift, living and working under conditions that were to worsen with every week that passed.

At RAF Wunsdorf, David Whalin, part of the Avro-York servicing flight, fought a daily battle against grinding fatigue. "Those going to work showed no concern for those trying to sleep, and on night shifts, sleeping by day, you always missed pay parade." For those billeted under canvas the consequences were often dire. Flight Sergeant George Leigh, on Operations Control at Wunsdorf, was confronted at 2:00 A.M. by an irate sergeant-major clad only in pajamas and a battle-dress top. For the third successive night, he screamed, his troops' bell tents had collapsed on them—sucked into the air by the Yorks' prop wash as the planes taxied out. So what was Leigh going to do?

121

All Leigh could do was tack one more notice on the bulletin board: "Air crews are requested to exercise moderation in flying over Army tents."

Conditions were as bad for the Americans. At Rhein-Main the mechanics of the motor servicing pool, stationed twenty miles from the base, bedded down each night in their trucks rather than endure the journey back. At RAF Fassberg, near Hanover, the first C-54 pilots to move in reacted bitterly to a British diet composed mainly of kippers, fried tomatoes, and overcooked Brussels sprouts. To Lieutenant Colonel Harry Mosely, USAFE's Deputy Air Surgeon, Fassberg's cramped, chilly dormitories, the almost total lack of hot water and latrine facilities, resembled "conditions . . . similar to those found in Nazi concentration camps."

It wasn't surprising that some men went spectacularly to pieces. "I saw much tension," Private Earl Vallier recalls of Wiesbaden. "Some of the crypto boys would go around talking to themselves in Morse Code." The fatigue there was so great, Private John Dubiel remembers, that three men in succession jumped from windows and broke their legs. And at Tempelhof, where Sergeant Reginald Clark and his military police literally prayed for bad weather to give them respite, Captain Michael Metz observed one of the strangest crack-ups of all. A C-54 overshot the field and crashed, and Metz and a noncom, racing to the spot, pulled the crew chief clear. Incredibly, both pilot and co-pilot were missing—and Metz learned that the men, escaping through a broken window, had at once gone AWOL in Berlin.

Yet every man, however grudgingly, acknowledged one truth: None worked harder than Tunner. Night and day, wearing an old olive-green flight jacket stripped of rank badges, a baseball cap crammed on his head, he shuttled from Wiesbaden to Tempelhof to Fassberg and back, grabbing coffee and doughnuts where he could. Often he shared a joke with his men—like the pilot who told him, "There's one thing we can be thankful for, General, hauling all this coal—we don't have to haul out the ashes." At day's end he slumped on a makeshift bunk in his office, too weary to cover the extra yards to his room. Noncoms working the "In Commission" board recalled

122

how time and again they looked up around 3:00 A.M. and there was Tunner, alert blue eyes scanning the charts: What planes were out of commission, how many, for how long?

Yet each day at seven in the morning Tunner and his experts were again in session: How could the lift be perfected further still? Base commanders were swift to learn what made Tunner angry—to see more than five planes on the ground at one time—and group commanders kept a wary watch on their hardstandings. If a plane lingered more than twenty minutes, it meant waste motion. In the airlift book there was no room for waste motion.

But to Tunner this was no mere exercise in logistics. Many times, striding Wiesbaden's streets at night, hashing over problems with an aide, Tunner would stress what the airlift meant to him: "The chips are down and the Berliners have chosen freedom. This is the first conflict between the free world and the slave world. We can't afford to lose it."

This shared ideology gave impetus to many changes. Under Cargo Chief Ed Guilbert's guidance, standard loads—coal, flour, powdered milk—became the sought-after norm, each load secured by web straps unfastening as easily as a passenger seat belt. Soon unloading periods had been cut from a time-consuming thirty minutes to the record Captain Michael Metz's team notched up at Tempelhof: twelve men hauling 172 sacks of coal in five minutes forty-five seconds.

Out to bolster sagging morale, Tunner pioneered other innovations: the "Howgozit" board, which set a daily quota for each unit, then reported how they shaped up. Thus a healthy rivalry grew up between the bases, fanned by Lieutenant Bill Thompson's *Task Force Times,* an irreverent daily news sheet enlivened by the salty cartoons of Technical Sergeant John "Jake" Schuffert. Not even top brass were immune from Schuffert's pen. One pompous base commander, who rode everywhere on a bicycle, was immortalized by a Schuffert strip of a crew chief beckoning in an invisible plane, at last signaling "Cut engines and park"—with a final shot of the O.C. dismounting from his bicycle.

One restriction Tunner balked at was the regulation that no German could be employed in any save a menial capacity. It

123

was an edict only Clay could rescind, and one day, as Clay passed through Tempelhof, Tunner saw his chance. His problem, he told Clay, was a shortage of skilled maintenance men—"but I think I can whip it if you'll allow me to hire some skilled German mechanics." Clay nodded incisively. "Go ahead and do it."

Almost overnight crack mechanics flowed in, their efforts coordinated by Major General Hans Detlev von Rohden, a onetime Luftwaffe maintenance chief. Von Rohden at once set a section to work translating the C-54 training manual into German—a first step toward the day when eighty-five German mechanics would be assigned to every airlift squadron.

Even so, Tunner lacked facilities to carry out the 200-hour major inspections that kept the battered planes flying. Inspections to date had been carried out at Oberpfaffenhofen (to the GIs, Oberhuffin' puffin') near Munich, where planes were washed down with kerosene and water on open-air ramps. As winter drew on, inspections would have to be made undercover, or the water would freeze as applied. But the problem was soon solved. The shell of a major wartime repair center still existed at Burtonwood, near Liverpool, England, and experts from Tinker Air Force Base, Oklahoma, with experience of a similar facility, began reactivating it. By degrees they evolved a three-quarter-mile assembly line where eight planes daily were sucked free of dust and grime by commercial-type vacuum cleaners, then cleansed of their patina of oil and grease with scalding sprays of detergent.

In mid-October Tunner was at last given the authority he needed to run a coordinated lift. After some pressure from LeMay, the British agreed to his appointment as Commander-in-Chief of a Combined Airlift Task Force, with the RAF's Air Commodore John Merer as his deputy. Now Tunner could coordinate the British, as well as the American lift, into a unified operation.

At last, Tunner seemed close to achieving his goal: a smoothly running mechanism capable of launching an airborne cargo every three minutes day and night. To be sure, the British, with their ragtag of planes, were still flying the block system—with groups of aircraft picked out for identical cruising speeds taking off for Gatow hourly. But after a bold decision to eliminate the C-47 from the American lift, Tunner could fly a nonstop conveyor belt of C-54s, with skilled Ground Controlled Approach operators picking up the planes forty miles out and taking them down like traffic cops, three to four planes at a time.

Meanwhile, more bases were opening in the British zone to capitalize on the shorter corridor—one outside the ancient Baltic city of Lübeck, 160 miles northwest of Berlin, a second to be constructed by the RAF for American use at Celle, 160 miles west.

Tunner's driving presence inspired infinite ingenuity. Suddenly the unwritten watchword was "Don't do it by the book—improvise!" That was the spirit that inspired Gatow's C.O., Group Captain Brian Yarde, alarmed by flocks of birds imperiling landing operations, to send for a squadron of falcons from Malta, 1,200 miles away. Within days the field was clear. Equally ingenious, a Wiesbaden sergeant, troubled by a freak fall of early snow, mounted jet-fighter engines on special trucks, melting tons of ice from frost-coated planes with the exhausts' searing heat.

At Tempelhof, upended steel landing mats seventy-five feet high stood in successfully as approach-light towers to guide the pilots on murky nights. At Erding depot, Bavaria, a shortage of emergency repair stands was quickly solved by welding together hundreds of steel-frame bed bunks.

Pilots thought long and hard about their planes and came up with novel ideas. DaVania's group increased tonnage by 500 pounds per plane by stripping the oxygen tanks—unnecessary at their allotted height of 7,000 feet. And when Berlin's thirty daily tons of salt proved a problem, Air Commodore Reginald Waite, the city's senior RAF officer, hit on the answer: ferry it in by flying boat. Normally, seepage from the salt packages penetrated the floorboards, corroding a plane's control wires—but a Sunderland's control wires were in the roof.

Captain Jules Prevost, Tunner's Chief of Production-Line Maintenance, was deeply disturbed. By the third week in October the airlift's demands were becoming inexorable. Foremost in Prevost's mind loomed two questions: How long could men and machines endure such strain? And if either were to crack, how long could Berlin endure the Russian pressure?

The statistics on Prevost's desk bore out his concern. Each four-engined C-54 was now taxed to its limits, with 60,000 hours of air time per month—as against the normal USAFE usage of 400 hours. Scores of planes that would once have rated a "Red X" (unsafe to fly) on their servicing sheets now received no more than a "Red Diagonal," signifying the faults as acceptable.

Pilot after pilot experienced the sweating fear of engines that balked and fell away, of planes that rode inexplicably heavy, of landing gear that malfunctioned. But the ruthless priorities of the lift decreed that many men lay their lives on the line. At Rhein-Main, Sergeant Emery Hedges, red-lining a plane for cracked landing gear, was shocked when the Operations Officer erased it from the sheet. "We want this plane to fly," he told Hedges coldly. Lieutenant Edward Weber, heading for Berlin, found his plane with a cracked high-pressure hydraulic line and a defective compass. Over Tempelhof everything jammed; Weber couldn't even slam down the landing gear. Minutes of terror followed as the plane swooped in over Gatow, missing a construction crew by inches, to belly-flop like a beached whale in a sea of mud.

The British planes were as bad. Leading Aircraftman Charles Armstrong recalls Wunsdorf's Yorks as a nightmare of ailing engines, their propellers and windscreens chipped by stones. Often the servicing was so hasty that the tires, ripped by pierced-steel planking, were patched by flashlight at night with a tube of Bostik. One charter pilot, Eagle's Captain Alan Duckworth, airborne from Wunsdorf, found his Halton almost falling apart; the spars running through the plane's center section shook as if alive. He landed just in time. In the upper-air turbulence, the rivets between the tank bays had worked loose. The entire plane had to be reriveted.

The British Dakotas were being withdrawn for use in a training program for new pilots—and two squadrons of Handley Page Hastings, based on Schleswigland, flew in to fill the breach.

The need for trained replacements was growing urgent, for

pilots even more than planes were under severe pressure. Despite the stresses, however, most early blockade runners, both American and British, shared Tunner's indomitable spirit. RAF Station, Lübeck, had a target of 102 daily return flights—then ran short of crews. Promptly every man available, from off-duty controllers to Ops Room clerks, formed into scratch crews and took off in any plane available—upping the total to 125.

One American crew, plagued by a hydraulic leak, declared an emergency and climbed to 9,000 feet—to find a tailwind that wafted them to Berlin in record time. Until Tunner clamped down on it, every plane in the squadron, declaring an emergency, shuttled to and from Berlin like a jet storm.

Few pilots evinced more determination than Air Vice Marshal Donald Bennett. Ever since his arrival at Wunsdorf, Bennett and his Tudors had caused comment: No ordinary man daily risked his life to justify a faith in a jinxed aircraft. Some looked askance at his inflexible rules. His pilots were forbidden to drink twelve hours before a sortie, and no man overslept twice. Yet Bennett quickly won a grudging respect. His pilots had to double as mechanics or navigators, but he was not a man of double standards; on engine changes, Bennett worked in oily dungarees alongside them. He once entered the officers' mess so daubed with grease that an unwary steward tried to eject him. When a distraught soldier, whose son had been injured, sought a mercy flight to Leeds, England, Bennett flew the man to Air Flight's home base, where his own private plane took over to continue the journey north. After that, Wunsdorf's fuelers saw to it that Bennett's Tudors were always first in line for take-off.

On Sunday, October 31, Bennett undertook a grueling flight that tested the endurance of man and machine. At 8:00 A.M., huddled with the forecasters in Wunsdorf's tower, Bennett heard their decision. The first wave must be airborne in minutes, before the drizzling overcast deteriorated. Bennett reacted promptly. Co-pilot Ken Hagyard and Radio Officer Vic Brennan were already aboard Tudor V G-AKBY, parked on the tarmac beside the tower, loaded with nine tons of Diesel fuel. As Bennett doubled for the plane he noted that the three elevator locks on the portside had already been removed for take-off. Clambering aboard, he called to Hagyard, who was doubling as both navigator and engineer, "We're off. Start engines."

Hagyard, shuttling from the navigator's table to the engineer's table, set the engines to idle, then hurried back to his flight plan. Taxiing out toward the runway, Bennett, as always, checked dials and controls—all were impeccable.

"Off we go," Bennett called, and Hagyard, after checking the magnetos at the engineer's table, strapped himself into the co-pilot's seat as the plane rolled into the take-off down the rain-slicked runway. Six hundred yards ahead they glimpsed the runway's end—and beyond it, looming in the murk, the high dunes of shingle and sand, where German construction crews were working on the new extension. At a speed of 110 knots Bennett began to exert the small, familiar backward pressure on the control column. He was barely off the ground when he felt the controls stiffen, then lock solid. The elevators had jammed.

Bennett did not know that due to the hasty take-off the starboard elevator lock, an external device fitted out to prevent damage to controls during the high winds on the ground, had not been removed, nor had it been correctly applied. Only now, at flying speed, had it snapped home to jam the elevators. He knew only that the Tudor was fixed irrevocably on the horizontal plane. It could not climb, nor yet descend. Nor could he halt its juggernaut collision course toward the construction site.

Bennett said nothing. Though his face was gray, beaded with sweat, his mouth had set in a tight line. Somehow he had to nurse the plane aloft to a height of 100 feet to clear the construction dunes ahead.

Now came the first test of his stubborn faith in the plane. His fingers probed for the small wheel below the throttle levers that operated the elevator trimming tabs. Normally, these tiny control surfaces, built into the much larger elevators, were used to adjust minor changes of the center of gravity—as when passengers moved about the aircraft. But by operating them gingerly in reverse Bennett knew that the plane's tail would drop—and the nose would then come up. As ungainly as an albatross, the huge plane fought upward as it neared the extension site.

From the co-pilot's seat Hagyard could see the construction crews, flinging picks and shovels aside, hit the dirt face down as the Tudor thundered over them. Now they were headed for the thicket of approach lights half a mile beyond. But again Bennett applied reverse trim. The plane cleared the lights with feet to spare.

Now, desperately using both knees, Bennett jammed the control column forward in an effort to shear and buckle the elevators' external locks. The starboard lock, though, held fast. To Hagyard it seemed Bennett had done no more than delay disaster. At any moment the Tudor must either stall-spin or plunge downward like a meteor. At this moment they were flying with the undercarriage down, with 60 degrees of flap, and engines at full power. But to retract the undercarriage or reduce the flap extension called for elevator control. Bennett's one hope was to stay within the Wunsdorf circuit and try to line up on the runway.

His voice calm, Bennett called Wunsdorf control: "The elevators have seized solid. Will endeavor to get back onto the ground. Please clear the runway."

Now, on the airfield's north side, he began his slow timed circuit. Constantly juggling the two center throttles operating the inboard engines, Bennett kept the plane to level flight, 300 feet over the circuit.

The secret had to be faith. The Tudor was flying level and true.

Fire engines and crash tenders stood by as pilots and flight crews held their breath. Three times they saw the Tudor try to line up on the runway—but always at too oblique an angle. Checking his compass reading, Bennett swung into another timed circuit. Each turn demanded a more intense concentration to avoid a fatal loss of height.

At last, with the voice of the GCA controller in his headphones, Bennett lined up on the runway. Now, in the most dangerous maneuver of all—the gentle loss of height—he knew it was too risky to use reverse trim. He would have to coax the

Tudor down on throttle alone, easing back on all four throttles at the same moment.

The air speed was falling now, the nose dipped forward, the Tudor went into a dive—steeper by the second. The speed soared to 130 knots, and Bennett, fighting the urge to tug again on the jammed elevators, momentarily opened up all four engines before throttling back. The Tudor's nose lifted only marginally; the dive went on.

Another burst of throttle, but the nose stayed down. The speed increased, fearsomely, to 150 knots. Yet that fractional lifting of the nose had arrested the angle of the dive, miraculously carrying the Tudor over the last 100 yards of the approach. It would just—though only just—reach the runway.

To scores gathered on the tarmac, it didn't seem that any crew could survive that horrifying angle of descent. In the last seconds, while Hagyard, rigid in his seat, anticipated the tanks in the fuselage behind must break loose to crush them, Bennett was still manipulating the throttle levers—though what alteration in the angle of dive he achieved he never knew. As the Tudor hit the tarmac, undercarriage first, thin black smoke streamed from the tires, which flattened to the wheel rims. At that moment the head of Radio Officer Vic Brennan was visible above the fuselage, making ready to jump as he hurled loose the Plexiglas astrodome.

Only now, with the undercarriage down, could Bennett apply the brakes, and abruptly Brennan vanished from sight as if plucked by a giant hand. Jarred and buffeted, Bennett fought the plane with all his strength, bringing it to a screaming, slewing halt as the runway petered out. It was then that he and Hagyard, climbing through the cockpit to inspect the tail, found the starboard control bent and buckled—but still intact.

It had been a human error. His Tudor had stood the test—but at what cost.

The dead leaves shivered from the trees in the Grunewald, and the frosty air along the shores of the Havel was pungent with the smoke from autumn bonfires. By day, a pumpkin sun glowed wanly in a leaden sky. In the huge chilly sheds where the loaders congregated at Gatow and Tempelhof, men stamped their feet and fretted gloved hands striving to keep warm.

"Generalissimo Winter," the Communists' long-awaited ally, had come to Berlin.

As Berlin winters went, it was a mild one—by day the temperature in mid-November rarely dropped below 50 degrees. But with the night came razor-edged winds from the lake, and the thermometer dropped to 20 below. In windowless apartments, plugged with ill-fitting rags and cardboards, it was minimally warmer—given luck, only 10 below freezing.

The Allies calculated that at most they could allot every household twenty pounds of coal for the entire winter—hardly more than a teaspoon a day.

No Berliner would ever forget those bitter months. Frau Helene Guhse, of Ernst Reuter's staff, was trying one night to open a jar of autumn-bottled blackberries when the black juice suddenly sprayed out. It froze on the wall of her apartment and stayed frozen until the spring. Comedian Walter Gross, playing a theater on the Kurfürstendamm, arrived to find the stage like a skating rink, following a burst pipe. Undaunted, the company bound rags around their shoes and carried on—before an audience shrouded in topcoats and rugs. "They applauded like crazy," Gross reported dryly. "They wanted to keep warm."

Always resourceful, the Berliners devised their own remedies. Waitress Elisabeth Hiller found the warmest place off duty was the cinema—cuddling beneath her topcoat a brick preheated in the oven. Others tore up once cherished parquet flooring to fuel their stoves, or broke up their scanty stock of furniture piece by piece. Journalist Cornelia Herstatt, in Tiergarten, burned bundles of old love letters—"but all their passion wasn't enough for real warmth."

Some children, like thirteen-year-old Klaus Hartwich and his sister Nora, spent all that winter as if bedridden. For lack of heating, school attendance was now optional, and Klaus and his sister passed almost five months under the bedclothes fully clothed, absorbed in quiz games. For many, hospitalization, with its priority coal allotment and 1,800 daily calories guaran-

131

teed, was a blessing. At Rudolf-Virchow Hospital, many patients, in the hope of staying on, secretly aggravated sores and rashes.

It was almost as bad for the Allies. The officers ate dinner by candlelight, incongruously clad in mittens and balaclavas, with pajamas under their uniforms.

Some Berliners found ingenious if illegal ways to "beat the meter," exceeding their electricity quota of eighteen kilowatt hours per month. Some were fortunate enough to lay hands on a magnetic device called "Little Gustav" that tugged the meter hands backward. Others drilled tiny holes in the meter covers and inserted thin wires to drag on the hands. Hotelier Heinz Zellermayer bribed electricians to link up his apartment with a British Army hotel nearby, but he soon found unbidden guests capitalizing on his hot-water bonanza. Once, entertaining friends at tea, Zellermayer found a total stranger who had slipped in behind them enjoying a shower in his bathroom.

Soon the felling of the trees began. Teams of Berliners went to work thinning the woods and the parks, digging up half-buried roots for fuel—but it was a halfhearted effort. For to Frank Howley's astonishment, the *Kommandatura*'s orders to the city fathers—to cut 350,000 cubic meters of winter wood—met with bitter opposition. To cut down trees wholesale in this city of gracious parks and woods, Reuter explained, was sacrilege to a Berliner. Rather than desecrate their woodlands, they would settle for 120,000 cubic meters and be proud each time they shivered.

In a city as devastated as Carthage, it was incredible that life could go on, yet five newspapers went to press nightly by candlelight, and forty-two cinemas and theaters played to packed houses. On weekends people still flocked to Berlin's famous zoo, though it now had few attractions aside from three lions, two bears, and a hippopotamus. In Reinickendorf a wiry calisthenics teacher, Ilse von Metnitz, ran twenty-eight classes a week for all who still had energy.

Despite the cold some still recall the blockade as a time of warm camaraderie. In her Tiergarten apartment, Cornelia Herstatt always opened the window if her radio was

132

working—so that all passing along the street could share the program. The police, by tacit consent, halted their black-market raids. It was recognized that many must either trade illegally or starve.

There were many human encounters that would never be forgotten. For the Salvation Army's Major William Fenwick, it was the night he stood in as guest preacher at a Spandau church. No sooner had he reached the pulpit than a power cut plunged the nave into darkness. Fumbling for his notes, Fenwick and his interpreter were helpless—until suddenly lights flickered and danced in every pew as the congregation brought forth hoarded candles. Flinging his notes aside, Fenwick spoke like a true Salvationist from the heart. "What we have seen tonight," he told his congregation, "is what Berlin needs! Not a tawdry blaze of neon, but the light of individual Christian endeavor—Christian lights in a dark world."

To Flight Sergeant George Leigh it was the dark-haired teenage girl who beckoned him one night on the steps of a canteen in Reichskanzler Platz. Instinctively Leigh knew this was no pick-up: Her features were sensitive and finely drawn. Would Leigh, she asked, come home and meet her mother? She led the way to a tumbledown block and upstairs to a sixth-floor apartment.

The room was cold and dimly lit; only sacking covered the shattered windows. Crouched beside a potbellied stove was an old woman in black shawls, her face gray and witchlike. Beside her was a large family Bible, and as they talked she tore pages from it, two at a time, fueling the stove. Now Leigh realized the girl's message; they were freezing and starving to death.

Suddenly the door burst open and a gaunt young man rushed in. It was the girl's brother, who had found a source of food. He led them to a bombed-out cellar where a shabby man sold them six frost-nipped apples, and, as Leigh watched, the family tore into them like animals.

Before he left Leigh told the girl to meet him outside the canteen the next morning. The urgency in her face was touching. Bidding her wait, Leigh entered and piled two large plates with sandwiches, pies, and cakes. Then after stuffing the food under his battledress, he rejoined the girl. Thanking him profusely, she crammed the food into a container before hurrying away.

That day Leigh was unexpectedly posted to England and never saw the girl again. Irrationally, he felt guilty of betrayal. Did she return to the canteen steps? Did she, too, feel betrayed? It was to haunt him for the rest of his life.

Perhaps most remarkable, under such adverse circumstances, was that Berlin's Free University was not only becoming an established reality—it was flourishing. All over the American sector, in dimly lit drill halls and armories and converted villas, more than 2,100 students were preparing for their matriculation, tutored by no fewer than 128 professors. Many had defected from the East, willingly leaving everything behind in the cause of freedom.

All that winter there were shortages. In many classrooms the only light came from a candle on the professor's desk. In lecture halls too dark to take notes, students struggled to retain the facts, making ready to scribble frantically once the lecture ended.

Space was still at a premium—so scarce that one professor conducted oral examinations in a *bierstube,* then clapped the graduates on the back and bought them a beef tea. Commuting was a problem for many, and only Ernst Reuter's gift of a streetcar to carry venereology students between West End and Britz-Sud hospitals made their studies possible.

But to one law student, Paul Michael von Broecker, the first day of the semester was bliss incarnate. All night he had stirred restlessly in his lodgings, cold and hungry, but at 8:00 A.M. came the day's first lecture—in the underground American Cinema in the U-Bahn station at Onkel Toms Hütte. Von Broecker took one look at the furnishings, the most sumptuous he had seen in all his eighteen years, and blinked: deep fauteuils upholstered in velvet, pile carpeting, the grateful all-enveloping warmth of central heating.

He sank back into an armchair, notebook poised on his knee, but within ten minutes the lecturer's voice had gone very far away. The notebook slipped to the floor unheeded, and von Broecker slept.

In his Wiesbaden office Tunner reached a painful decision. It cost him many sleepless nights, for his crewmen's lives were at stake, but so, too, were the lives of 2,500,000 Berliners. The city had less than fifty days' coal supply, and on November 13 the worst fog in years blanketed central Europe. Thus, when Lieutenant Colonel Nicholas Chavasse, commanding the 2105th Weather Group, warned that the fog might last for weeks, Tunner, in concert with LeMay's recent successor, Lieutenant General John Cannon, gave the only order that could save Berlin: "From now on we fly zero-zero."

Not every pilot relished the solution. Initially, a pilot was supposed to see four runway lights—a quarter of a mile visibility—before take-off. Tunner told Chavasse, "If the ceiling's below 2,500 feet, I'll space them to five minutes apart. If it drops below 250, they'll sit on the runway, engines running." But in practice many operations officers, to keep the lift going, permitted no safety margins. At Rhein-Main, Lieutenant Edward Weber and his crew had the news in classic army fashion from the base commander: "Well, fellows, you just volunteered to fly zero-zero." Groping to the plane, Weber had first to position the nose above a white line, then taxi blindly into nothingness. Once the air-speed indicator showed 100 mph, the plane fought into the solid overcast to fly on instruments all the way to Berlin.

All through November the fog persisted, an ice-cold saffron blanket 1,000 feet thick muffling the three and three-quarter-million square miles of Europe. Thus challenged, Chavasse pioneered a new innovation: observation stations, at the far end of each runway, to report a pilot's eye-view. Often planes took off from Rhein-Main when no buses ran in Frankfurt's streets, through gloom so impenetrable a man could barely see a flashlight before his eyes. To keep them loaded was a problem in itself. At Biebrich, on the Rhine River, eighteen miles from the air base, 1,000 Germans, working in shifts, formed a chain from coal barges to trucks, passing sacks from hand to hand, left foot lodged against the next man's heel to maintain contact. Then, at walking pace, the trucks moved off, each driver sighting on the red taillight ahead, guided by a man with a flashlight groping ahead of the convoy. Often it was an eight-hour journey—but every few minutes a plane took off.

There were many perilous moments. Navy Lieutenant Richard Gerszewski, setting his plane down on a Rhein-Main runway, was told: "Turn left, then right again to the hardstanding area." But sudden instinct stopped Gerszewski dead and he sent Ensign Bernald Smith to investigate. It was just in time; they had halted seven feet from the nose of a giant C-75 Globemaster.

Yet night and day the lift continued, the pilots rising to this fresh challenge as they had risen to every other. At Wunsdorf, near Hanover, Squadron Leader David Bevan-John of No. 51 Squadron stood in one night as tower control officer, intent on bringing all his planes in if humanly possible. The criteria were firmly laid down—200 feet ceiling and 400 yards visibility—and any man not registering these minimums must be diverted to an alternate base. No runway lights were visible, yet to his astonishment every man joining the circuit reported as if by rote: "Two hundred feet—four hundred yards." As the last man touched down, Bevan-John summoned them to the bar for a drink, then challenged them: "You lied to me, didn't you? How much could you see of the true conditions?" It was New Zealander Les Gow, replying for all, who embodied the spirit that would see the airlift through: "We couldn't even see the bleeding runway."

By November 30 the airlift had touched bottom. On that day only ten planes reached the city. Even the Tegel airfield, which the Berliners had completed two months ahead of schedule, lay silent under a creeping canopy of fog.

Slowly food stocks were dwindling, and many small traders faced a dilemma. In mid-October the Berliners' rations had been increased to ensure that all survived: one daily ounce of fat, two ounces of Spam or powdered egg, three ounces of dehydrated potato or flour, two ounces of cereal, one ounce of sugar, seventeen-and-a-half ounces of bread. But now the traders often could not honor the ration coupons even of long-standing customers.

Most did their best to make amends. If supplies arrived late, greengrocers stayed open until midnight, selling dehydrated cabbage by candlelight to families who would have gone to bed hungry. In some boroughs customers lined up outside butcher shops as early as four o'clock in the morning for bowls of hot broth made from boiled bones.

How many Berliners died from hunger may never be known for certain, but in Steglitz, Dahlem, and Lichterfelde firemen were called to scores of houses where the old and friendless had starved to death. Among the living hunger bred fierce suspicions of inequity. In Charlottenburg, Margret Unruh, a laborer's wife, noted that though dinner was always the same—semolina soup and a slice of dried bread—everyone in the family gave sidelong glances, checking that nobody's slice was bigger. Grocer Robert Gottfried noted the same sad phenomenon. If there were five in a family, five came to shop—and hoarded their rations in separate drawers at home.

Many found their reactions growing painfully slow. Accountants became baffled over simple columns of figures; elementary addition and subtraction seemed like advanced calculus. Opticians could barely muster the concentration to make a correct change of eyeglasses for their customers. Pupils like fifteen-year-old Renate Helbig, at Wannsee's Dreilinden Secondary School, found the simplest facts impossible to retain; often she slumped at her desk, half sleeping while Fräulein Klatte tried over and over to hammer home the basics of English syntax.

Outlandish recipes abounded for any mush that would assuage the hunger pangs. The cookery column of *Telegraf* featured such stomach-stretchers as jam made from rotting apples and cinnamon, or black bread fried in candle grease, then spinkled with powdered onion to disguise the taste. Flavor was now of small account. Herta Jungtow, an engineer's wife, bound a pancake mixture of minced potato peel with flour and powdered egg, then fried the cakes in the engine oil her husband brought home from work.

The privations drove some to petty thefts they would have

shrunk from even in wartime. Inga Michaelsen, a schoolteacher's widow, was so distressed by the hunger of her children,
Uta, aged fifteen, and Stefan, thirteen, that one morning around
three o'clock she crept from her apartment near the zoo, heart
thumping wildly, and hurried along Fasanen Strasse into the
whispering shadows of the Tiergarten. Days earlier she had
spied a turnip plot, and she had determined that for the first
time in years the children would taste fresh vegetables.

But as she hacked at the frozen earth she glanced up and a
black-lettered notice threatened: "Theft Will Be Punished by
Death." In truth, it was the Free University's plot, and the
warning was a bluff, but Inga did not know that. Her heart
bursting, she fled back to her apartment, the turnips in her
rucksack. At five o'clock that morning her children were
breakfasting with gusto on mashed boiled turnips. Fear had
robbed Inga of appetite; she could eat nothing.

Pilfering at Berlin's three air bases reached epic proportions.
Not all were black-market thefts—merely the desperate attempts of famished Berliners to pit their wits against the
security guards and appease their hunger. Those without
familes to feed ate on the spot and escaped detection. At
Tempelhof, one loader, Horst Miehe, once devoured three
kilos of Spam in a night. But to get past the guards at the main
gates called for true subtlety. Gatow leader Eberhard Leu, with
only four ounces of coffee, was one of many who didn't make
it. Upbringing had convinced him that one portion of a man's
anatomy was sacrosanct from search, but the RAF Regiment
was less squeamish. Sadly, the jobless Leu told his friends.
"The sergeant didn't believe that any German could be so
masculine."

The pilots, too, were suffering privations, gradually suc-
cumbing to an overwhelming fatigue. Few men had ever flown
under such taxing conditions—and now the strain began to tell.

Most often the enemy that sapped the pilots' strength was
fog, but they battled against the terrors of ice as well. On one
take-off from Celle, 160 miles west of Berlin, aerial engineer
John Dundas recalls ice forming even as the pilot gave the
plane full throttle, so fast and inexorably that the top-heavy

ship refused to lift. Then the flight deck became a frantic ballet of darting hands, working the deicer boots on props and wings until the plane, clearing the runway's end, lifted a few feet into the air. Painfully climbing at 200 feet per mile, they fought their way to Berlin.

Ice brought scores of men to the brink of death. One freezing night, way below minimums, Lieutenant Vernon Hamman, circling Tempelhof, had been told to return to Rhein-Main forthwith when absolute silence fell: All four engines had iced up as one. From 200 feet Hamman began a deadly glide toward eternity—then, miraculously, hit the deck in St. Thomas Cemetery, on the eastern perimeter, so hard that he bounced clean out of it, landing on the main runway without even blowing a tire.

All the pilots hated their cargoes. The tankers' couplings weeped Diesel oil, and the control columns were tacky with it; it impregnated the men's boots, inflaming the soles of their feet. In heavy rains the fifteen feet between cockpit and unloading door often became "one big gob of flour paste." Coal dust seeped everywhere, choking control columns, irritating eyes and nostrils, eroding switches and contact points; from every coal carrier sweepers removed nine tons of dust a day. Some pilots flew straight to Copenhagen for a steam bath when their leave came up.

But whatever the hazards or discomforts, they all added up to one invincible enemy: fatigue. Off duty, men slept fifteen hours at a stretch, then awoke not knowing where they were. Back on the tarmac in line for take-off they dozed again. It was so bad that Lieutenant Tom Cates, VR-6 operations officer, kept a fishing pole in the alert shack to awake dead-beat pilots by pounding a tattoo on the fuselage. In the air it was tempting to set the auto-pilot and sleep some more; one crew, thus tempted, didn't awaken until they reached the English Channel, 350 miles west.

Men tried every trick they could devise to beat the fatigue. One RAF crew of No. 51 Squadron played a nonstop game of bridge. Lieutenant Bob Stemmler knitted socks—one foot up the corridor, one foot down. Lieutenant Victor Wieback sucked dry Alka-Seltzer tablets. None hit on a solution as

139

intriguing as a newlywed RAF pilot of No. 46 Squadron: He browsed through a sex instruction manual.

Yet it was a battle of attrition few could win—and the crashes mounted. Circling Rhein-Main one icy night, Captain Jack Olin Bennett, in his DC-3, could clearly see the runway below and the plane ahead of him—when a sudden blizzard swept in from the Taunus Mountains. As flakes hit his windshield "like machine-gun bullets," the veteran Bennett, wary of snowstorm vertigo, snapped off his landing lights and ducked his gaze to the instrument panel. Unfortunately, the pilot ahead, also blinded by whirling snowflakes, had no such skills and his plane hit the ground like a fiery skidding projectile, ripping itself apart.

On many nights the controllers listened helplessly to men in mortal distress. At Gatow, Flight Lieutenant George Gilbert eavesdropped on the last interchange of two C-54 pilots above the forests between Frohnau and Dannenberg. "I'm trying to hold her," one man cried. "I think I can." While the other was urging, "Get out—get *out!*" Then the stricken pilot gasped, "I'm down to five hundred," before the second voice pronounced his epitaph, "God, he's *down!*"

Some were luckier. Captain Franklin Crawford and his co-pilot, Charles Weaver, were barely airborne from Celle when the number-one engine cut, followed by the number two. Suddenly the duty controllers heard their frantic, "Celle Tower, this is 218. We just lost our number three." Then the tower heard no more as 218 lost height by the second, sustained by one coughing engine, until it was shearing the branches from the pine trees, scattering wreckage for miles. As the Skymaster ripped into the forest, 20,000 pounds of coal took fire and Crawford saw Weaver slump forward, his skull fractured by the impact. The heat was so intense he could not unfasten his co-pilot's belt, so with unimaginable strength Crawford tore him to safety, still strapped to his seat, through the broken window.

The crashes led many to believe sabotage was rife. Rumors reached Tunner that some planes had crashed because Soviet agents had seeded the coal with dynamite. Another alert from an SED double agent reported that eighty saboteurs would be infiltrated into Tempelhof and Gatow to impregnate sacks with sodium chlorate, combustible in midair. How true this was Tunner never knew, but Lieutenant Thomas Diab unearthed positive proof of one such attempt at Wiesbaden. Checking on his parachute, he found the silk sliced away, replaced by GI blankets—and a check of other chutes in the 60th Troop Carrier Group revealed the same condition.

As nerves grew frayed, bitterness against the Russians mounted sharply and in defiance of orders the pilots began hitting back. Nightly, Squadron Leader Ernest Moody's No. 46 Squadron, determined to rob the Russians of sleep, zoomed at zero feet above the barracks at Dalgow. From Fassberg, other pilots harassed the Russian target-towing planes, swooping in to give them a four-engine prop wash, exulting when the plane spun heavily away.

But the Russians had no intention of giving up. Even now, in an effort to close the lift down forever, they were planning a campaign of harassment more intense than anything the Allies had yet faced.

Though he yearned to defy the Russians, Boy George Lea was powerless. Why they were detaining him, Lea could not divine, but day and night he dreamed of escape. He studied the windows. The vertical bars were cemented firmly into the wall, but the horizontal bars were secured loosely—with wire. They had given him a knife, fork, and spoon for his meals, and Lea worked with the knife all through one night to pry the wire loose. When he awoke at noon, he saw that it had been firmly secured. They must have worked through the morning while he slept, within sight of his bed. Yet he had heard no sound.

One day, without warning, they moved Lea from the Big House to The Barracks. It was a large building with a yard housing a motor transport pool, ringed with barbed wire, lit at night by arc lights and twenty minutes' drive away from the village of Sakrow. Trucks groaned in and out through its high gates day and night. In a smaller room that was his new prison, Lea began to ponder fresh ways of escape.

At one side of his small room a nailed-up door intrigued him. The Russians still fed him white bread, and using the knife, he

141

began dislodging the nails, kneading the bread into tiny pellets to plug up the holes. Slowly the door was yielding enough for him to see that beyond it, high up on a wall, was a window without bars. Nobody seemed to notice his activity, but next day, while removing one more nail, he realized again they were ahead of him. He had heard nothing—but overnight the window had been bricked up.

Each day one of the noncoms took him for exercise in the yard along a corridor, past a barrack room smelling of wet sheepskin coats, soap, and sweat, through an office thick with stale *makhorka* tobacco, and into the yard. Lea fell to studying the doors. He noticed that unlike English doors none of them had tumbler locks. The aluminum keys were made to fit the lock face. So one key, filed to the shape of the lock, would fit any door.

On the third day after this observation, Lea took the risk. The corporal was a step ahead, and in the office door was an unguarded key. Heart throbbing, he slid it from the lock and into his pocket. The exercise period over, Lea stowed it carefully under a frayed corner of the thick brown linoleum covering the floor of his room.

Now he waited. How long before they removed it? Two days? A week? But ten days passed and each time he checked the key was there. This time Lea was in no hurry. He, too, was growing sly, perfecting the game of cat-and-mouse.

The Berliners, too, remained unrepentantly defiant of the Russians.

Sunday, December 5, was the date of the mayoral election. But the Communists, with their prestige at low ebb, could not afford another free election, and Sokolovsky announced there would be no balloting in the Soviet sector.

Even in the Western sectors the Communists had gone to sinister lengths to scare off voters from the ballot booths. Black-lettered pamphlets littered the Soviet-controlled S-Bahn trains: "Stay away from the polls. Don't endanger your future." And wall posters near the Brandenburger Tor threatened, "Those who vote will be duly noted." Such threats could seriously affect hundreds of little men, part-time party workers and shop stewards whose lives were at risk each time they spoke up for democracy.

Howley, standing in during one of Clay's absences in Frankfurt, did his best to rally the timorous. Alerted that gangs of Red musclemen were to march in and disrupt the voting, he had warned the Soviet sector in a RIAS broadcast: "Attempts to use force will be met by force. If anyone marches into our sector he won't run into a handful of frightened unarmed Germans but into the United States Army." At dawn on December 5, 6,500 Allied troops would stand by on readiness alert, further reinforced by 4,500 German police.

Even so, Clay insisted that he himself must get back to Berlin by dawn. Despite the fact that fog had socked in every available air base, he persuaded a reluctant Tunner to fly with him. "We must," he stressed, "let the flag be seen." Finally, with a hand-picked crew under Captain Norman Robinson, Clay and his party clambered aboard—after signing waivers absolving the Air Force of all responsibility.

Over Berlin, damp yellow fog blocked off all visibility, and at Gatow the tower flatly refused to accept the plane. It was the same at Tempelhof, until Clay, invading the cockpit and grasping the mike, sharply overruled the duty controller. With 100 feet of ceiling and 100 feet of visibility, the sweating Robinson brought his VIP cargo to earth.

In fact, Clay's anxiety had been groundless: Again the Berliners were showing their mettle. All over the city they flocked in droves to the 1,500 polling sites—in bombed-out basements, in beer halls and schoolrooms—to record their votes. In Zehlendorf one aging man limped forty steps at a time toward the polling station, collapsed onto a camp stool carried by his sons, then, his breath recovered, once more limped on. Even hospital patients were included. To ensure privacy, they marked their ballots behind a towel held by two nurses.

Communist plans for disruption fell down almost everywhere. All told, police grabbed seventy activists. At first the 150,000 Western sector residents with jobs in the East had been dismayed, for they had orders to report at eight in the morning—when the polls opened—for a working Sunday on behalf of the Hennecke movement—the German equivalent of the Russians' Stakhanovite speed-up. But the transport workers resolved their dilemma. By striking from six to ten o'clock that morning, they gave the West Berliners a chance to vote before clocking in.

Only once—at a polling booth in the British zone near Staaken—did the Russians intervene directly, when two drunken noncoms attempted to seize the ballot box. But Major Ronald de Havilland, of the Provost Marshal's office, detailed by General Herbert, hastening to the spot, drove one man off at pistol point, shanghaied the other into a jeep ride that left him sober and stranded miles from the polling station.

Thus when the ballots were counted Clay learned that more than 86 percent of West Berliners had courageously cast their vote. Reuter's Social Democrats had gained a two-thirds majority, with the Christian Democrats edging over the right-wing Liberal Democrats for second place. That same day a motion came before the City Assembly that Reuter finally be confirmed in his post.

In his second-floor office at the Assembly's new meeting place, Schöneberg City Hall, Reuter heard this news with quiet satisfaction. For the foreseeable future, a three-party coalition would rule, but he could not deny that he was gratified. This morning the airlift had operated for 164 days and still his people were staunch.

As proudly as if it had been Paris or London or Washington, Reuter told his assembled staff: "Now I am Lord Mayor of rubble."

9

"Gentlemen,
There Is No More Problem"

DECEMBER 6, 1948–MAY 12, 1949

At Tegel Field, in the French sector, there was an air of subdued excitement. At 9:00 A.M. on December 16, 100 gendarmes had suddenly materialized and were turning back all but essential traffic from the perimeter roads. Below the tall towers of Soviet-controlled Radio Berlin, rising almost 400 feet above the field, a team of French engineers worked in busy silence.

At 10:45 A.M. near Tegel's runway, a Diesel mechanic, Günter Michaelis, was chatting idly with one of the gendarmes. Suddenly a devastating explosion shook the field. Speechless, the two watched as the Soviet towers trembled ominously, then with a rending crash collapsed in a mushroom of dust. Almost aggrievedly, the gendarme told Michaelis: "They never told me that they were going to do that!"

The Soviet towers had long constituted a navigational hazard. As far back as November 20, Ganeval had given Kotikov and Radio Berlin's director fair warning: If the towers were not transferred elsewhere, he would demolish them on December 16.

The dust had barely settled when Kotikov stormed into

145

General Ganeval's office of French GHQ in nearby Frohnau. "How could you do that?" Kotikov bawled at the top of his lungs. Smiling urbanely, Ganeval chose to take him literally: "From the base—with dynamite."

Kotikov was so consumed with rage that Ganeval, knowing the Russian's heart condition, was alarmed he might drop dead on the spot. Angrily he bunched his fists. "This airfield," he warned, "may well cost you French dear." And with that, he departed.

Kotikov proved true to his word. In an all-out effort to close down the airlift for good, the Russians stepped up the harassment with everything they had. Pilots airborne from Rhein-Main heard an eerie whining noise in their headphones that sent the radio compass out of kilter, as the Russians began jamming the beacons. Barrage balloons drifted perilously in the planes' flight paths. At Gatow, a Red artillery unit fired streams of incendiary bullets between the incoming planes. Russian searchlights blinded incoming flights, and many pilots adopted a veteran's technique when landing against the sun: Ducking their heads, they went in on instruments.

Each day, Russian planes moved in closer until often they were less than a hundred feet away. Ensign Bernald Smith had twenty-two Yaks on his tail at one time, feinting at him like a swarm of vicious wasps. At night, Russian fighters swooped from the darkness to switch on their landing lights. Lieutenant Edward Weber felt his plane shake all over as a Yak, flying nose to nose with him, turned and slid under his belly. Some of the persecution came close to acts of war: MIGs harassing planes out of Fassberg swung what looked like a wrecker's steel ball on a whirling length of chain.

Tunner called for freshly minted pilots, but the replacements, though willing enough, were no match for the old-timers. Many veterans were wartime bomber men, steeled to hold formation in the face of flak or fighters. The Russians might irk them but they would never swerve from course. Newcomers often could be bullied from the corridors.

Check pilots, briefed to create emergency situations such as engine cut-outs and radio failures and correct latent faults, found their pupils' lack of reaction unnerving. Captain Joe

146

Tytus, flying with one novice over Tempelhof, was peering ahead for the landing lights: Amber marked the left of the runway, red the right. Just in time he saw red to the left of him, banked in steep and pushed hard over. The new pilot, off course, had almost sideswiped the apartment building.

"Many of the replacements coming in were no-nos," recalls Captain John Lawler, check pilot for the 60th Troop Carrier Group, "violators of every rule in the book." Check pilots inclined to tolerance came swiftly to regret it. Flying with new pilots from Wunsdorf, Squadron Leader David Bevan-John's attitude was: Don't interfere or impair confidence; just sit back and relax. Too late, he realized one night that the rookie at the controls hadn't checked in over Frohnau Beacon. There was a thunderclap of sound and the York glowed with greenish light, rocking like a truck out of control. "Jesus," someone shouted, "it's flak! We're over the Russian zone." All tolerance gone, Bevan-John seized the controls, bringing the plane back on course, to reach Gatow at the tail of the wave.

By mid-December, the stresses had become too much for many. Some Tempelhof officers were sent back to the States after refusing point-blank to fly. Drinking jags became routine, particularly among charter pilots. At Wunsdorf one crew drank for three hours solid, then sobered up for the cockpit with alternating hot and cold showers. Some British charter pilots, out on a binge, took a welding kit to Hamburg's streetcar tracks and were summarily returned to England. And then there was the group of fliers armed with shovels who hijacked the Lübeck-Stockholm Express to take them back to their airfield. It was a particular problem for Wing Commander Hugh Johnson, Flight Refueling's Chief of Operations, in his efforts to keep the "wet lift" going. To ensure thirty-two sober pilots per day, Johnson signed 150 men on his payroll.

In stark contrast, Donald Bennett's crews continued to live as austerely as monks. Yet, despite his asceticism, Bennett worried some airlift planners. How could a man fly twice-nightly sorties, work with two crew members on an engine change, a task for five RAF fitters, and still retain his health? Like a good-natured schoolmaster, Bennett would reply, "Physical endurance is mainly mental, after all."

In the small hours of December 8, however, Bennett's burden was increased to breaking point.

For two months Bennett had flown every Airflight night sortie, adhering to a precise timetable. That day, though, he had entrusted Captain Clement Utting, his tall, dashing chief pilot, with his first night flight. At 2:20 A.M. Utting headed across the tarmac for the lone Tudor, followed by Radio Officer John Kilburn and the first officer. At that moment a Bedford truck, driving without lights, came out of the darkness, heading straight for Utting. The pilot went down like a slaughtered animal. The truck raced on.

At Utting's bedside, Bennett waited in silence, listening to the quick, shallow breathing of a mortally injured man. It was 9:20 A.M. when Utting came awake and focused on his chief. "Did I crash on my first flight?" he asked. Bennett gripped his shoulder and said, "No, Clem, you did all right," and Utting smiled, closed his eyes, and died.

Why had it happened? Bennett did not know, but one factor was plain: No truck had been due on the hardstanding at that hour—and the driver had ample leeway to swerve from one lone pedestrian. It was also plain that for two months on end only one man had crossed that stretch of tarmac with his habitual stopwatch precision at exactly 2:20 A.M., the man who personified the airlift's pile-driving thrust, Donald Bennett.

Had the Soviets hired a hit man to stop him in his tracks? Sick with anger at the death, Bennett was powerless to pursue the mystery further. Now, as the sole Airflight pilot cleared for night operations, he must fly on for five more months like a latter-day Flying Dutchman—proving the Tudor, proving himself.

At dusk on the day Utting died, G-AKBY once more rolled up Wundsdorf's runway, leading the evening wave. In the last orange light of the day, Bennett was in there, fighting again.

Christmas came as Christmas should, with a white bandage of snow wrapping trees and tenements, turning ugly piles of rubble into sparkling mountains. In thousands of shattered windows, candles wavered beside fir trees—the cherished *Tannenbaum.*

It was a hungry Christmas, and in most families there were few enough gifts to place beneath the tree. Yet there was a special warmth to it. Waitress Elisabeth Hiller recalls it as "truly a Christmas of love, because we made everything ourselves—bed socks from old sweaters, purses out of old shoes."

All Christmas day the lift rolled on. At 6:00 A.M., Flying Officer John Beddoes flew the 50,000th sortie into Gatow, with three tons of coal. To his surprise and delight, he was met by the *Schornsteinfeger* (chimney sweeps) Club, arrayed in their traditional high silk hats and black frock coats, crowding around the Dakota to make him an honorary member. Tunner, too, was on the job without cease. His Christmas Day was spent guiding Secretary of the Air Force Stuart Symington on a step-by-step tour of Rhein-Main, stressing the still crucial shortages of supplies and accommodation.

That night officers and GIs packed out Tempelhof's main hangar to watch Bob Hope's "Christmas Caravan," with Jinx Falkenburg and Irving Berlin. The pilots reveled in Hope's crack about the fog—"Soup I can take—but this stuff has noodles in it"—but the hit of the show was the airlift anthem composed in their honor by Irving Berlin.

As the words drifted out across the snowy field, the airlift already seemed a part of history:

> Operation Vittles,
> We'll soon be on our way
> with coal and wheat and hay
> and everything's okay,
>
> Operation Vittles,
> as in the sky we go
> we won't forget to blow
> a kiss to Uncle Joe . . .

Looking back, Frank Howley saw the first two weeks of January as crucial. Food stores were adequate—a thirty-one-day supply—but coal stocks were dwindling at an alarming rate. Within a week, or at most ten days, they would be exhausted. Then Berlin would begin to die.

Praying for a break in the weather, Howley, in concert with Herbert and Ganeval, put into effect the most stringent energy cuts of the blockade. Though often the thermometer showed 10 below zero, gas and electricity supplies were reduced to a new low. Trolley cars meant to carry a maximum of 124 persons were packed to suffocation with 175. Within days coal stocks were back to the twenty-day level, and the worst of the fuel crisis was over.

But the commandants took other steps to lighten Berlin's burden. More than 50,000 adults and 17,000 children were flown out to Western zones by the RAF. Each plane carried out twenty fewer mouths to feed—and at Herbert's request the nervous got top priority. "If they're windy they can infect a hundred others," Herbert urged. "Let them go."

Meanwhile, time was working in the Allies' favor. Counter-restrictions on the shipment of critical materials to Soviet-controlled areas were slowly starving the Russian zone of vital West German products such as Ruhr coal and steel and machine parts. All supply trucks bound for the Russian zone were turned back. The bitter economic blockade was now pinching harder in the East than in the West.

Mayor Ernst Reuter was optimistic. On January 31, he was lunching with his old friend Drew Middleton of *The New York Times*. Suddenly, as if a vision had just been granted him, he turned to Middleton and announced, "It's over." The Russians know they can't get Berlin by blockade. Soon they will start to find a way out."

Almost 4,000 miles away in Washington, D.C., the same thought occurred to Dean Gooderham Acheson, Truman's new Secretary of State. It struck him that the Soviets might be seeking a face-saver.

The first intimations of a Russian thaw had come in Stalin's answer to a series of questions submitted in writing by Kingsbury Smith, European general manager of Hearst's International News Service. One question was of special interest: Would the U.S.S.R. be likely to lift the blockade if the Allies postponed the West German state, pending a meeting of the Council of Foreign Ministers? Stalin replied that he saw no difficulty, providing the counterblockade was lifted at the same time. Curiously, he made no reference to the currency dispute—all along cited as the blockade's *raison d'être.* Was this accidental or deliberate?

At the United Nations temporary headquarters outside New York, all this fell into the lap of Philip Jessup, a lanky, tweed-suited college professor, often regarded as America's most unorthodox diplomat. As U.S. representative to the United Nations, Jessup had long enjoyed cordial relations with his Russian counterpart, the blond, back-slapping Jacob Malik. On February 15, in what one State Department official termed "probably the most carefully planned casual meeting in history," Jessup ran into Malik in the delegates' lounge. The two men chatted idly about the weather. Then Jessup asked whether Stalin's omission of the currency dispute had been accidental.

As Jessup recalls it, Malik froze completely, afraid of being trapped into an indiscreet remark. Cautiously, he replied, "I have no information on the subject."

"Well, if you do get any," Jessup stressed, "perhaps you would let me know. I should be interested."

On March 15, Jessup was invited to Malik's office in the Soviet Mission's New York headquarters. They traded pleasantries, then Malik said evenly, "I have been in touch with Moscow regarding your question. I am informed that Marshal Stalin's omission of any reference to the currency question was not accidental." Jessup nodded quietly. In this moment he knew for certain that Moscow had "seen the red light."

Will Tunner wasn't taking any chances. Calling in his cargo officer, Colonel Edward Guilbert, he asked, "Gil, how can we achieve the mostest?"

Guilbert had long pondered this question. Early in the lift he and his staff, sketching a diagram of a clock face, had divided the day into 1,440 minutes and dreamed an airlifter's dream: to lay down ten tons a minute. "If conditions were right," Guilbert told Tunner, "we'd shift 14,000 tons in a day."

"Gil," Tunner announced, "we're going to do just that—and if you don't do it, watch out."

151

Plans now moved swiftly. A survey of the fifty analytical charts flanking Tunner's conference room showed that optimum conditions would pertain on the twenty-four-hour period between noon on Saturday, April 16, and Easter Sunday, April 17. The weather was set fair, and almost 225 C-54s would be in service. A stockpile of over 10,000 tons of coal and other supplies was ready for hauling—50 percent more than they had ever lifted in one day. "It'll be an Easter Parade," Tunner decided. "An Easter present for the people of Berlin."

Until the last, there was total secrecy. For if word got out and the massive effort failed, Soviet propagandists would have a field day.

At noon on the 16th, when the quotas were tacked up on the Howgozit boards, there was mounting excitement: This was to be no ordinary day. At Celle, Lieutenant Eugene Wiedle noted that the 41st Troop Carrier Squadron's quota had been almost doubled to 1,000 tons. "We're going to be really under the gun," he said in astonishment.

As the first crews sprinted for their planes, they shared Wiedle's premonition: Today, as never before, the airlifters were on their mettle. On the flight line of the 1st Troop Carrier Squadron, Captain Joe Wroblewski rallied to the slogan that would mark the day's endeavor: "It's tons for Tunner—let's go!"

On every base the tempo mounted by the minute; the sky became a sounding board, giving back the thunder of the engines. Dimly heard above the roar of planes were other sounds: the cannonball rumble of coal down the chutes . . . harsh cries of *"Schnell, schnell"* (faster) . . . the groaning of heavy ten-ton trucks and the clanging of fire tenders.

The planes streamed across the sky, spaced as close as ninety seconds apart, a glittering conveyor belt of aircraft. There had never been a mercy armada like it. Most planes were piled to the hatches with coal, but others carried every conceivable item that a blockaded city could utilize: cocoa, sausages and rolled oats, hogsheads of tobacco, an entire planeload of manhole covers, a snow-white billygoat (the regimental mascot of the Royal Welch Fusiliers), prophylactics, frogs' legs for a French banquet, dried banana flakes for sick children, 2,000 rubber hot-water bottles for Berlin's hospitals, ping-pong balls, cuckoo clocks, dried apricots and noodles, even a load of loudspeaker magnets, demagnetized lest they affect the pilot's compass, to be remagnetized in Berlin.

As the vast defile of carriers increased, earphones crackled with the nonstop radio chatter: "Baker Easy 34, this is Jigsaw, your final controller, how do you receive?" . . . "Over the Red Barn, men, at 500 feet." . . . "This is your controller Digger O'Dell—you are two miles away from home and hotcakes." . . . "Tegel Approach, this is Halifax HY—over Frohnau at one point five." . . . "Gatow Control, I have lost one engine—am on three." . . . "Bring it on in, chum—we'll give you a Purple Heart." One near-deafened pilot sarcastically rebuked the others: "How about shutting up? Some of us up here is trying to get some sleep."

On the ground, the excitement rose to fever pitch. Each time Staff Sergeant Kitty Dillon left Tunner's office, a horde of clerks bearded her, avid for details: "Hey, Sarge, what's the tonnage now?" A corporal on his honeymoon called her all the way from Italy to check statistics he'd heard on the radio. And though no orders had been issued, word swiftly spread among the German base workers that this was *Der Tag*.

At Tempelhof, the frenetic pace of the ramp crews reminded Major John Gordon of "an old-time Keystone Cops movie"—and Colonel Theodore Ross Milton, Tunner's chief of staff, almost fell victim to their zeal. In the darkness an eager crew had seized him up, preparing to toss him bodily onto the truck along with the coal sacks.

No man refused to fly, no matter what the state of his plane. Colonel Stanley Wray, commanding 7497th Airlift Wing, flew out of Rhein-Main in a plane that didn't even have an oil pressure reading. Lieutenant John Nordstrom flew one round trip in a cockpit swirling with smoke from a faulty hydraulic system.

The parade's inexorable rhythm astonished even the veterans. At Tempelhof, Ensign Bernald Smith saw a plane overshoot, cartwheel onto its back and break in half—yet even as the shaken crew scrambled clear, loaders were racing to the scene to retrieve the coal.

153

It was tough on the controllers, too. At Wiesbaden, traffic officers opted to work through the twenty-four-hour period, taking time out to sleep only between 3:00 A.M. and 6:00 A.M. But day and night the picture of the long-range radar scopes remained constant: tiny close-packed blobs of light boring toward Berlin in two ragged antlike columns, a third column moving as purposefully away.

All day Tunner was in his element, shuttling from base to base heartened by a message from Clay: "I don't know what it is you're trying to do but keep doing it."

Already, Tunner believed, the parade had marked the blockade's turning point, but until the very last there must be no slackening of effort. Arriving at Fassberg long after midnight, he was greeted by the base commander, Colonel John Coulter, who announced jubilantly that Fassberg was running 10 percent ahead of its quota.

"That's fine," Tunner replied, "but of course it's not up to what they're doing at Celle. They're really on the ball over there."

The smile vanished from Coulter's face as he hurried back to the flight line to speed the loading. In fact, Celle was no more than 2 percent ahead of Fassberg, but the rivalry between the two bases would up the tonnage still further in the twelve hours yet to come.

It was dawn when Tunner finally reached his bunk. Later that day he would learn the triumphant totals: In 1,398 flights, Allied planes had hauled in 12,941 tons of coal and supplies, more than double the record for a single day. But Tunner already grasped the significance of this effort: The Russians' land blockade had failed ignominiously. Within minutes he was asleep.

Jessup and Malik met again on Tuesday, April 27. Jessup read a statement drafted with Truman's approval. All restrictions must be lifted in Berlin simultaneously. Later in May the Council of Foreign Ministers would meet in Paris to discuss all questions affecting Germany, including currency. Meanwhile, preparations for a West German government would go ahead as planned.

Malik seemed resigned. No mention had been made of

Tunner's Easter Parade, but the point, Jessup guessed, had not been lost on Moscow. "Then," Malik volunteered quietly, "it remains only for us to issue a four-power communiqué . . ."

Rudolf-Günter Wagner, in his RIAS jeep, had never had such an audience. As far as he could see the Kurfürstendamm was black with people, waiting for him to read the news. Now Wagner began:

> *Agreement has been reached between the three Western Powers and the Soviets regarding raising the Berlin Blockade and the holding of a meeting of the Council of Foreign Ministers. All communications, transportation and trade restrictions imposed by both sides . . . and between Berlin and the Eastern zones will be removed on May 12 . . .*

Wagner doubted whether the crowd heard more. Suddenly the city had gone wild. *"Hurra! Wir leben Noch!"* (Hurrah! We're still alive!) The rallying cries of liberated Berlin echoed through the streets. A proud people had won, and from the back seat of his Horch, Frank Howley, who had done much to sustain their courage, summed up Berlin's victory: "It was their Valley Forge. They bought their right as a people willing to suffer and die for democracy."

Promptly at 12:01 A.M. on the 12th, in the harsh white glare of floodlights, the Russian barriers went up on the *autobahn* at Helmstedt, and the first convoy of British trucks, speeding supplies to the city poured through. Ahead of them streaked a gray Ford convertible driven by the United Press's Walter Rundle. At 1:46 A.M., as Rundle's car, the first to reach Berlin for eleven months, jounced off the *autobahn* at Zehlendorf, thousands of Berliners surged to greet him, crowning him with a chaplet of red roses.

It was a night to do all the things that had been so long denied. Families flocked from room to room like children, switching the electric lights on and off for the sheer pleasure of it. Others solemnly donned evening dress and drove to the *autobahn* exit to dance on the sidewalks by the light of their headlights.

In Grunewald, housemaid Anna Suess, who had hoarded the cyanide capsule bequeathed her by her father, handed it to her British employer. "I know the Allies will never move out," she explained. "I won't need to use it now." It was even a night to repent. In West End, one black marketeer, belatedly stricken by conscience, smashed a thousand eggs in his cellar—emerging plastered with yolk but morally purged.

Marlena Eberhardt ended the blockade as she had begun it: as a survivor. In a beer garden beside the Olympic Stadium, Marlena had marked May 11 by stealing one of the proprietor's chickens—luring it to a clump of bushes with a bread-and-milk bait, scooping it up into a rug she had filched from the saloon floor. A neighborhood poulterer offered sixty marks for the bird, and the deal was clinched. The money guaranteed weeks of survival. It covered food for her daughter and rent besides.

The next day, when Marlena went shopping, she could hardly believe her eyes. The provision shops were crammed with food unseen in years: joints of pork, cream cakes, butter, crusty bread, strings of sausages. Some housewives, noses pressed to the window glass, were weeping in sheer disbelief.

Farther along the street Marlena ran into the poulterer. His greeting was that of a man acknowledging an operator who could outsmart him every turn of the way. "And just where," he asked blandly, "did you get that beautiful sixty-mark chicken? I ate it myself—but I had to boil the bloody thing for five hours."

The news of the blockade's end had not reached Boy George Lea, but he was ready. It had taken Lea weeks to work on the stolen key, honing it on the stone windowsill, shaping the edges to fit the bevels of the lock. One night he slipped it gingerly into the lock of his door. It fitted perfectly.

Now only one factor was essential for the breakout: courage. Ironically, the airlift provided it. All through May 11, the noise of the planes was louder than he could ever remember as the Yorks thundered into Gatow. The thunder of the engines surged like adrenalin in Lea's veins, willing him to defy his oppressors.

By midnight he was ready. Dressed in an old Russian uniform (his own had fallen to tatters), his hair long and matted and his beard beginning to form, he looked like a ragged Russian foot soldier.

As he turned the key, the lock seemed to click very loudly. His nerves were taut, but he made himself move cautiously— out the door of his small cell, down the unguarded corridor of the larger room to the lavatory, and out the window to the asphalt six feet below.

Then he was tearing across the yard, ducking through shadows, and sprinting through the unguarded wicket gate. Pausing for breath, he noted the Yorks overhead. They would be his compass. Using their flight path, he would find his way back to Gatow.

Suddenly in the moonlight ahead loomed a Russian sentry. Drymouthed, Lea advanced toward him. *"Dobraye utra"* (Good morning), he ventured, the standard greeting he had heard so often before. Automatically, the man snapped to the "Present," and Lea moved on.

More Yorks droned through the sky, and Lea saw their flight path crossed a plowed field, heading north and east along the narrow strip of land dividing the Sakrower See from the Havel See. It was sandy soil he stumbled through, dry and parched like his mouth. He had been going for more than an hour and was still inside the Russian zone.

Then the field petered out. Scrambling up a bank, Lea saw a dirt road that he recognized plainly: the crossroads by Spandauer Strasse, a southerly spur of the road leading to Gatow Field. One mile ahead lay Kladow village and Montgomery Barracks.

Now Lea trudged on lightheartedly. For the first time he wondered how the Worcesters had viewed his absence. He had arrived just in time. On May 16 the regiment was moving out to Göttingen.

As the familiar sprawl of the barracks came in view, a kilted Highlander was doing sentry duty at the guardhouse. Outraged by the jaunty approach of a mud-smeared Russian ragamuffin, the sentry swung his rifle barrel up. "Piss off, you Russian bastard," he challenged the intruder.

157

The response nearly floored him. "Drop dead, Jock," said Boy Lea.

Though many crews were leaving, the airlift was by no means over. Despite the lifting of the blockade, the Allies were determined to ensure a stockpile. Not until September 30, when Captain Perry Immel, on the 276,926th flight, took in the last planeload of coal, did the lift grind to a halt. By then, the sheer statistics defied the imagination. Altogether 689 planes—441 American, 147 RAF, 101 British charter—flew more than 124 million miles, hauling over 300,000 tons of supplies. It had cost some $350,000,000 and sixty-five lives. As twentieth-century battles go, it had been cheaply won.

Tunner was alone in his Wiesbaden office. He felt proud— and with reason. Many complex factors lay behind the blockade's end, but paramount among them was the part his men had played—in all weathers, against all odds. He had been lucky to command men like these. All Europe could take courage from the rescue of Berlin.

Those who were staying on had few illusions as to the future. The airlift, the North Atlantic Pact, the emergence of a strong West German state—all these would contribute to Russian intransigence and insecurity. The war of nerves would continue. At a four-power meeting to discuss the question of future access to Berlin, Russia's Vladimir Semeneov did nothing to allay the Allies' concern. "Gentlemen, the roads, rails and canals are all open and functioning," he said genially, "so there is no more problem. Why don't we just forget it?"

Few men were more aware of the latent Russian threat than Ernst Reuter. On the day the blockade ended, Reuter was engaged in a friendly discussion with Carl J. Friedrich, Clay's special adviser on government affairs. Friedrich was in an optimistic mood. He thought that most probably Berlin's crisis was solved for good and that the future held only peace.

Reuter smiled gently, as if Europe, so old in conflict and cynicism, must make due allowance for the untutored innocence of the New World. "I don't really believe it will," Reuter confessed, "but we are going to act as if it will."

By 11 o'clock on the morning of May 12, the streets surrounding Schöneberg City Hall were thick with people. In the sunlit square 300,000 Berliners had come to pay tribute and bid farewell to the man who had led them through 328 days of stress and privation: General Lucius Clay.

Until the end, he had maintained his outward calm. Now, flanked by many who had supported him through the stormy months—Robertson, Koenig, Howley, Reuter—Clay mounted the speaker's dais on City Hall's balcony. There were, he told the massed Berliners, two kinds of airlift heroes. First, there were the pilots who had flown the planes to Berlin in every kind of weather. But no less important was the city's population, which, having chosen precious freedom, had made the sacrifices needed to achieve it.

Then a vast cheer rose up to greet him, and as Clay stood there, bereft of words, his interpreter, Robert Lochner, saw that the mask had slipped and tears were streaming down his face. But there was no need for Clay to say more. The cheering redoubled, saying it for him. It rang like a paean over the whole city of Berlin.

Afterword

The Berlin Airlift directly affected the lives of three million men and women. It is impossible to do more than tell the story of a relatively small number of those who were caught up in this historic confrontation. Thus, this book could not present all the factual information that involved people who have not been named in this account.

Yet there remains a list of basic questions about the airlift, mostly about the statistics and logistics of the incredible bridge across the sky. Here are some of those questions and some of the answers.

What was the airlift's time span?

It began on June 26, 1948, when the first C-47s of the 61st Transport Group ferried eighty tons of milk, flour, and medicine to Tempelhof before nightfall. The Soviets lifted the blockade on May 12, 1949, but the airlift continued, to ensure a stockpile, until September 30, when Captain Perry Immel—on the 276,926th flight—flew in a planeload of coal. The British pulled out a trifle earlier, the civil lift terminating on August 16, the RAF on September 23, when Dakota KN 652 left Lübeck for Gatow at 18:30 hours. For the record, the plane bore the inscription: POSITIVELY THE LAST LOAD FROM LÜBECK—73,705 TONS—PSALM 21, VERSE 11. *For they intended evil against thee: they imagined a mischievous device which they are not able to perform.*

For the purposes of dramatic unity my own time span does not extend beyond the official lifting of the blockade.

How many planes took part?

American sources detail 441 planes, comprising 309 C-54s, 105 C-47s, 21 R-5Ds, 5 C-82s, and 1 C-97. (Of the C-54s only 203 were normally assigned to corridor flights.) RAF figures show 147 planes, approximately one-third Dakotas, with a final total of 101 operating at the lift's end: 40 Dakotas, 35 Yorks, 26 Hastings. Figures for the British civil lift show a total of 104 planes with 41 operational in the final stages.

What was the tonnage hauled?

All told, 2,323,067 tons were flown to Berlin, according to American sources. British figures, by contrast, show the combined effort hauling 2,325,809 tons. Contrary to widespread belief, only 30 percent of the cargoes were edible. Three out of every five tons carried was coal. Combined total costs for U.S. loads came to $57.48 per ton: maintenance costs $36 per ton, flying costs 15 cents a mile, base cost $9.41 per ton, supply cost (transporting cargo) $12.11 per ton. Toward the lift's end, for every 260 tons of raw material flown in daily, 100 tons of manufactured goods were flown out.

The biggest haul, the "Easter Parade" of April 16, 1949, landed 12,940.9 tons, 10,905 tons by the U.S. The all-time low: November 30, 1948, when the British made seven trips, totaling 62 tons, the Americans landed just one ten-ton load.

How many personnel were involved?

Here figures are no more than approximate, since contemporary calculations failed to take into account maintenance workers located as far apart as Honington, Suffolk, England, and Moffett Naval Air Station, California. E.J. Kahn, Jr., surveying the close of the airlift for *The New Yorker* in May 1949, estimated roughly 75,000 people were involved on the Continent alone: 45,000 German cargo-loaders and airfield workers, 12,000 members of the United States Air Force, 8,000 British Army and RAF personnel, including fliers from Australia, New Zealand, and South Africa, 3,000 Baltic DPs, 2,000 members of the United States Army Airlift Support Command, 800 men from the air arm of the United States Navy, several hundred American, British, and French civilians in military government agencies.

Which aircraft took part?

Principal planes handling the bulk of the cargoes were the Douglas Skymaster C-54 (9–10 tons loading capacity), responsible for one-third of the lift, and the Douglas Dakota C-47 (3 tons), the latter used not only by the USAFE but by the RAF and British charter firms. Also involved: the Fairchild Packet C-82, dubbed "The Flying Boxcar" (5.5 tons), valuable for ferrying ambulances, dump trucks, and steam rollers; the Avro York (9 tons); the Handley Page Hastings (8.5 tons), then the RAF's biggest transport plane; the Bristol Freighter and Wayfarer (3.7 tons), transferred to handle bulky loads from the Lympne–Le Touquet car ferry service; the Handley Page Halton (6 tons), developed from the Halifax bomber and used as both transport plane and tanker; the Avro Lancastrian and the Avro Tudor (5.5 tons), both latterly used as tankers; the Short Sunderland hydroplane (9 tons), used from Hamburg to Havel See from July–December 1948; the Globemaster C-74 (25 tons), used only from July to August 1948; the Boeing Stratocruiser C-97, brought in for test flights at the end of the lift in May 1949.

Featured briefly in the lift: two converted bombers, the Liberator, used by Scottish Airlines from August 4–14, 1948, and the Lincoln, part of Air Vice Marshal Bennett's Air Flight tanker fleet from June 24 to July 12, 1949.

What was the extent of the British civil lift?

In all, 104 planes were contributed by 25 contractors, some pitifully brave little outfits possessing only one mortgaged airplane. Among the companies: Air Contractors; Air Flight Ltd; Airwork; Air Transport (Channel Islands); Aquila Airways; British American Air Services; British Nederland Air Services; British South American Airways; British Overseas Airways Corporation; Bond Air Services; Ciros Aviation; Eagle Aviation; Flight Refuelling; Hornton Airways; Kearsley Airways; Lancashire Aircraft Corporation; Scottish Airlines; Silver City Airways; Sivewright Airways; Skyflight; Skyways Ltd; Transworld Charter; Trent Valley Aviation; World Air Freight; Westminster Airways.

All told, from August 1948 to August 1949, they flew 59,796.37 hours, carried 146,980.2 tons of cargo.

What was the degree of harassment?

These figures are necessarily approximate, since the British maintained no figures on corridor incidents. But U.S. pilots, between August 1948 and August 1949, reported no less than 733 instances of harassment, made up as follows: Searchlights (103), Close Flying (96), Radio Interference (82), Buzzing (77), Flares (59), Ground Fire (55), Flak and Chemical Laying (54 apiece), Air-to-Ground Fire (42), Ground Explosions (39), Bombing (36), Air-to-Air Fire (14), Balloons (11), Unidentified Objects (7), Rockets (4).

Fatalities of the airlift totaled 65 whose names are enshrined at the base of Berlin's Luftbrücke Memorial: 31 Americans, 18 RAF, 11 charter personnel, 5 Germans. Whether any of these deaths were directly or indirectly due to in-flight harassment remains unknown.

What was the mileage flown?

Between them, the men of the airlift flew 124,420,813 miles—as early as May 1949, according to the statisticians, they had equaled 133 round trips to the moon or 4,000 times around the world. Total sorties were estimated as 277,804: 189,963 U.S., 65,857 RAF, 21,984 British charter pilots.

What did the servicing involve?

Experts estimated that for every hour flown by a C-54, 20 man hours of maintenance were needed. All airlift planes underwent 50-, 100-, and 150-hour checks at their home bases—the 100-hour check involving a change of spark plugs and oil. American 200-hour inspections involved a six-phase system based on Burtonwood, Lancashire—(1) washing and cleaning; (2) Engine run-up; (3) work on pipes, engines, ignition; (4) electrical, instruments, cable and rigging; (5) inspection of hydraulics system, plus wheels, brakes, tires; (6) preflight check and final clearance. For checks of 1,000 hours and upward, planes were returned to the United States. RAF servicing was carried out by Transport Command's Major Servicing Unit at Honington, Suffolk, which through its "Plumber Flight," an airborne delivery service, also supplied spare parts and wheels to RAF units in Germany.

What did the airlift cost?

Again, such figures as have been released must be treated with caution. Lieutenant General William H. Tunner, quoting the official estimate of $300,000,000 for the American contribution alone, protests that this is too high—more than a probability, since *The Air Force Blue Book*, Vol. II, of 1960 estimates the U.S. and British governments between them spent out no more than $200,000,000. Some idea of the scale of expenditure is given through official figures supplied to E. J. Kahn just prior to May 1949: The American share was then said to total $500,000 a day, with the British contribution fluctuating between $50,000 and $100,000 daily. But as General Lucius Clay remarked at the time: "There is no expenditure currently being made for training and for national defense that, dollar for dollar, gives a better return."

What did people say?

There are no imaginary conversations in this book. Apart

from contemporary accounts and intelligence reports, such dialogue as is quoted represents a genuine effort by one or more individuals to remember what he or she said at the time.

When did various events occur?

Official papers *do* confirm that the total blockade of Berlin began at midnight on June 23, 1948, and that the first train to mark the blockade's end reached Berlin–Charlottenburg at 5:32 A.M. on May 12, 1949. In between, though, there are wide discrepancies. Every time given in the text follows an existing report or logbook, but in the mounting tension of the blockade days often elapsed before reports were made up. For example, Major Otschkin's peremptory summons of Frau Schröder and Dr. Friedensburg to the City Hall on June 23 is timed at 11:00 P.M. by *The New York Times*, at around 10:00 P.M. on that day by Jackson Bennett, at 9:00 P.M. on June 22 by *Die Städtischen Körperschaften in der Berliner Krise*, a collection of documents published by the City Assembly in 1949.

Every care was taken to check that the incidents described pertain to the right day, but the time phases at the head of each chapter are a rough guide only. Inevitably, some incidents began earlier and finished later than the compass of that chapter.

R.C.

Berlin
1944 - 1974

A Chronology

1944

SEPTEMBER   European Advisory Commission works out plan
for occupation of Berlin.

1945

MAY 2   Soviet forces occupy Berlin.

MAY 8   Capitulation of Germany announced.

MAY 17   Soviet Command creates Greater Berlin City
Assembly with overwhelming Communist majority.

JULY 3   American and British forces occupy their sectors of Berlin.

1946

OCTOBER 20   Elections held for Berlin City Assembly.
Communist-sponsored SED Party receives only
26 seats out of 130.

1947

JUNE 24   Soviet veto in Allied Control Council annuls election of Ernst Reuter as Lord Mayor of Berlin.

1948

MARCH 20   Marshal Sokolovsky walks out of Allied Control Council.

APRIL 1   Soviets state that permits will be required for Allied troop movements through the Russian zone.

APRIL 5   Fatal collision of B.E.A. Viking and Yak fighter over Gatow.

JUNE 18   All movements of passenger trains, automobiles, and pedestrians between Berlin and the Western zones of Germany prohibited by Soviets.

JUNE 24   Blockade commences.

(For Blockade and Airlift Chronology, see pages 175–187)

1949

MAY 12   Blockade ends.

OCTOBER 7   German Democratic Republic (DDR) proclaimed in East Berlin.

1950

MARCH 14   Federal Republic proclaims state of economic emergency in West Berlin. Necessary conditions thus created for financial help to restore West Berlin economy.

OCTOBER 1   Constitution of Berlin comes into force. Article One defines Berlin as both a *Land* of the Federal Republic and a German city.

1951

JANUARY 18   Ernst Reuter re-elected as Lord Mayor.

1952

JANUARY 4   3rd "Transfer Law" of German Bundestag incorporates West Berlin into financial, legal, and economic systems of Federal Republic.

MAY 27   DDR breaks off telephonic communication between the zones and forbids West Berliners to enter East Berlin.

1953

JANUARY 15   DDR suspends all bus and tram traffic between two zones. Only U-Bahn and S-Bahn continue to function.

JUNE 17   Soviet troops suppress uprising of East Berliners.

SEPTEMBER 29   Death of Ernst Reuter.

1954

FEBRUARY 18   Conference of Foreign Ministers, sitting alternately in East and West Berlin since January 25, achieve no positive solution to Berlin problem.

OCTOBER 3   The three Western Powers issue a declaration of guarantee for Berlin in London. This is endorsed three weeks later by all members of NATO.

1955

JANUARY 11   Dr. Otto Suhr elected Lord Mayor.

JANUARY 19   Bundestag holds first three-day session in Berlin.

1956

MAY 3   First section of U-Bahn to be built since war becomes operative.

1957

JUNE 4   Death of Frau Louise Schröder.

AUGUST 30   Death of Otto Suhr.

OCTOBER 3   Willy Brandt elected Lord Mayor.

DECEMBER 19   DDR issues sharper regulations concerning escapes from its territory.

1958

NOVEMBER 27   Soviets demand that Berlin be transformed into a "Free City" within six months.

1959

AUGUST 5   Big Four Foreign Ministers adjourn conference in Geneva, after debating without result the reunification of Germany and the question of Berlin.

1960

SEPTEMBER 9 DDR relaxes restrictions on West Germans entering East Berlin, subject to entry permits.

1961

MARCH 13 Willy Brandt received by President Kennedy at the White House. Kennedy reaffirms American determination to maintain the freedom of West Berlin.

AUGUST 13 DDR begins erection of barbed-wire barriers between Eastern and Western zones, followed by the building of "The Berlin Wall." Through traffic by U-Bahn and S-Bahn suspended. Approximately 60,000 East Berliners are forbidden to travel to their employment in the West. The escape routes of thousands are blocked off.

AUGUST 19 Vice President Lyndon B. Johnson visits Berlin to renew the American guarantee.

AUGUST 23 Citizens of West Berlin are forbidden to enter East Berlin.

SEPTEMBER 20 Communists begin forcible evacuation of houses adjoining the frontier.

FEBRUARY 22 The American Attorney General, Robert F. Kennedy, declares in Berlin that an attack on the city will be regarded as equivalent to an attack on New York, London, or Paris.

AUGUST 17   An 18-year-old East Berliner, Peter Fechter, is shot by frontier guards attempting to scale the wall. Violent protest demonstrations ensue in West Berlin.

1963

FEBRUARY 17   Willy Brandt reconfirmed as Lord Mayor.

JUNE 26   President John F. Kennedy visits Berlin. Declaring *"Ich bin ein Berliner"* in front of City Hall, he condemns the Berlin Wall as "an offense to history and an offense to humanity."

DECEMBER 17   For the first time in 28 months, West Berliners are permitted to visit close relatives in East Berlin over Christmas and New Year's. More than one million make the journey.

1964

NOVEMBER 2   DDR citizens above retirement age now permitted to visit West Berlin for up to four weeks a year.

1965

MAY 27   Queen Elizabeth II and the Duke of Edinburgh visit Berlin.

1966

MARCH 7   West Berliners given permission to visit relatives in East Berlin over Easter and Whitsun.

DECEMBER 1   Willy Brandt retires as Lord Mayor.

1967

OCTOBER 19   Klaus Schutz elected Lord Mayor.

1969

FEBRUARY   President Richard M. Nixon visits Berlin during
27   tour of Europe.

1970

MARCH 26   Four Power talks on Berlin begin at ambassado-
              rial level in former Allied Control Council build-
              ing.

1971

JANUARY 31   Telephonic communication restored between
              the zones.

DECEMBER   Following an agreement in Bonn between the
20   Federal Republic and the DDR, concerning the
              transit of civilians and goods between the Fed-
              eral Republic and West Berlin, another agree-
              ment is signed in East Berlin, aimed at easing
              and improving travel conditions and settling
              frontier problems.

1972

MARCH 29   DDR issues decree enabling Berliners to visit
              East Berlin during Easter and Whitsun holidays,
              following Big Four agreement on the city.

MAY 26   General treaty to improve travel between the
              two Germanies signed in East Berlin.

SEPTEMBER 3	First direct flight between Frankfurt and Leipzig.
NOVEMBER 9	United States, Great Britain, France, and Soviet Union release declaration signed in Berlin paving way to United Nations membership for both German states.
DECEMBER 21	Basic "good neighbor" treaty between East and West Germany signed in East Berlin.

1973

JULY 8	Angry West Berliners storm Berlin Wall after East German guards fire on escapees.
OCTOBER 9	East Germans tighten control for escapees after seizing 12.

1974

FEBRUARY 3	East Germans tighten control of escapees still further.
AUGUST 20	Soviets reject joint protest by United States, Great Britain, and France over Communist interference with road traffic.

The Berlin Blockade and Airlift

A Chronology

1948

JUNE

11 All Allied and German railroad freight traffic between the Western zones and Berlin suspended by the Russians for two days.

12 Resumption of railroad traffic. Elbe Bridge over *autobahn* near Magdeburg blocked to traffic by Russians, allegedly on account of needed repairs.

15 Russians issue new regulations for interzonal passenger traffic.

16 Soviets walk out of Allied *Kommandatura* meeting, Berlin.

18 Currency reform for Western sectors of Berlin announced. Russia protests and refuses to join scheme.

22	Big Four Berlin meeting fails to produce agreement. Russians announce new separate currency reform.
23	Berlin City Councilors abused and manhandled outside City Hall after supporting Western currency reform measures.
24	Russians halt all freight, passenger, and water traffic to Berlin.
25	Russians serve notice they will not supply food to Western sectors of Berlin. First 8 aircraft of RAF arrive at Wunsdorf in British sector to commence airlift operations.
26	Airlift begins. 32 flights of C-47s carry 80 tons of supplies from Wiesbaden Air Force Base to Tempelhof AFB, Berlin. USAFE have approximately 100 C-47s available.
28	First 35 C-54s en route from Alaska, Hawaii, and Caribbean to join lift. Brigadier General Joseph Smith, commanding Wiesbaden Military Post, assigned command of Berlin Airlift by Lieutenant General Curtis LeMay, commanding USAFE.
30	Wiesbaden joins lift in major effort, using 80 planes. First C-54s arrive 9:30 A.M., leave for Berlin 7:36 P.M.

JULY

1	Russians withdraw from Berlin *Kommandatura*.
5	Two squadrons of RAF Sunderland flying boats join lift, operating from Finkenwerder (Hamburg).
7	First coal flown to Berlin in barracks bags as airlift exceeds 1,000 tons in 24 hours.

176

9   First fatal accident on airlift near Wiesbaden results in death of 2 pilots and Department of Army civilian employee.

12   New runway started at Tempelhof.

17   RAF Gatow complete 2,000-yard concrete runway.

19   To eliminate congestion, RAF move all C-47s from Wunsdorf to Fassberg.

20   General Lucius D. Clay flies to Washington to discuss the situation with President Truman. Aircraft strength reaches 54 C-54s and 105 C-47s. British planes, aside from flying boats, total 40 RAF Yorks and 50 C-47s (Dakotas). Maximum daily tonnage to date: 1,500 tons (U.S.) and 750 tons (British).

23   HQ USAF directs MATS to establish provisional Task Force Headquarters, plus maintenance facilities and traffic personnel for 8 additional squadrons of 9 C-54s. Major General William H. Tunner, MATS deputy commander for Air Transport, to direct, under the control of HQ, USAFE.

25   Second fatal airlift crash. C-47 crashes into Berlin apartment house in Friedenau borough. Two killed.

26   West Germans agree to form a government. Berlin police split between East and West.

27   Russians threaten to fly in 20-mile-wide corridor to Berlin. General Tunner and advance party leave for Wiesbaden with first 2 squadrons. First British civil aircraft, 3 Lancastrians of Flight Refuelling, commence tanker operations.

29   General Tunner and Advance party arrive in Wiesbaden.

30	2 additional squadrons of C-54s arrive. New airlift daily record: 1,918 tons flown by U.S. planes.
31	Western envoys discuss blockade situation with Foreign Minister Molotov in Moscow. In 339 flights, lift hauls exactly 2,027 tons.

AUGUST

1	RAF reach decision to operate C-47s from Lübeck, British zone.
2	Western envoys have long talk with Stalin.
3	2 further MATS squadrons leave for U.S. for airlift.
4	New record for U.S. planes: 2,104 tons. 11 British planes join civil lift: 9 C-47s (Fassberg), 2 Hythe flying boats (Finkenwerder), 1 Halton, 1 Liberator (Wunsdorf).
5	Oberpfaffenhofen Air Force Base, in U.S. zone, converted to Maintenance Department for the purpose of performing 200-hour inspections on airlift planes. First manufactured goods leave Berlin for Western zones. First sod cut on site of new airfield at Tegel, in French sector of Berlin.
7	Combined airlift sets new record with 666 flights, delivering 3,800 tons.
8	Third flight of 2 MATS squadrons leaves U.S. for Germany.
10	Remaining flight of 2 squadrons, ex-Japan and Hawaii, leave for Germany. New record lift: 2,437 tons, 346 flights.
12	In 707 flights U.S. and RAF deliver 4,742 tons, first above daily average of 4,500 tons estimated necessary to keep Berlin fed and warm.

13   Airlift's 50th day. After hazardous stacking conditions over Tempelhof, General Tunner demands a revised flight pattern and the dispatch of experienced traffic controllers from the U.S.

14   First Douglas C-74 Globemaster arrives from U.S., carrying 18 C-54 engines, weighing 38,000 pounds.

15   First 10-ton cargo of newsprint since blockade's inception reaches Berlin.

17   C-74 makes first internal airlift flight, hauling 20 tons of flour to Berlin—twice normal C-54 payload.

21   3 squadrons of C-54s shift to Fassberg, British zone, to move coal to Berlin.

24   4 U.S. airmen killed in midair crash of 2 C-47s during fog over Ravolzhausen. New U.S. record: 3,030 tons delivered on 395 flights.

26   Total tonnage delivered to Berlin by U.S. planes passes 100,000 mark.

27   RAF C-47s operational from Lübeck.

28   All civil aircraft based at Fassberg moved to Lübeck.

31   Four military governors meet in Berlin to work out a Moscow decision aimed at giving Russia the right to issue a single Berlin currency and to discuss technical procedure on lifting the blockade. Talks fail. New daily record: 3,124 tons carried by U.S. planes.

September

1   Work begins at Burtonwood, Lancashire, England, to replace Oberpfaffenhofen as Maintenance Department. Construction workers at

179

Tegel now total 19,000 German civilians, including women.

2   First 20 civilian traffic controllers demanded by General Tunner recalled to USAFE service in Germany.

6   Councilors surrender City Hall to mobs of German Communists and retreat to British sector. 19 Western sector policemen arrested trying to protect them.

8   Further 19 Western sector policemen kidnapped by Russian police after leaving City Hall under Russian safe-conduct guarantee.

9   Thousands of Germans hold protest demonstration before Berlin Reichstag. U.S. planes haul record 3,392 tons.

10   New U.S. record: 3,527 tons.

13   Three twin-engined "Flying Boxcars," C-82s, arrive at Wiesbaden to supplement lift.

14   81st day of airlift.

15   Work begins on 1,800-yard runway at Celle, British zone.

18   USAFE celebrates Air Force Day by hauling combined record load of 6,987.7 tons to Berlin. Special coal bonus distributed to people of Western Berlin. 15,000 German guests visit Rhein-Main and Wiesbaden.

19   First fatal British crash: 5 airmen killed when 4-engined York crashes on take-off at Wunsdorf.

21   50 South African pilots depart for Germany for airlift duties with RAF.

24   C-74 makes last of 24 flights to Berlin to deliver a total tonnage of 428.6.

26	British Tudors of civil lift begin test flights to Berlin with Diesel oil.
30	All USAFE C-47s withdrawn from lift.

OCTOBER

1	1st Lt. John Finn, of Jackson, Michigan, is first man to complete 100 missions. Pilot training camp, designed to train pilots to substitute on the airlift, established at Great Falls, Montana.
2	Fire truck collides with C-54 at Rhein-Main. 1 killed.
4	United Nations Security Council begins discussing dispute.
5	All British civilian planes based at Lübeck moved to Fuhlsbüttel, Hamburg.
7	Felling of trees for fuel commenced in Berlin.
12	RAF decide to use Schleswigland, British zone, for 2 squadrons of Hastings plus civilian tankers.
14	British and American airlift efforts combined under one operational headquarters. Major General William H. Tunner appointed Commanding General of Combined Airlift Task Force, with Air Commodore John Merer, RAF, as Deputy. 1,000th C-54 flight out of Wiesbaden.
15	Lieutenant General John K. Cannon takes over as Commanding General of USAFE.
18	First fatal C-54 crash: 3 airmen die in dense forest area 4 miles from Rhein-Main. USAF recalls 10,000 former pilots, radio operators, and flight engineers for active airlift duty in Western Europe.

21   President Truman directs USAF to augment lift with up to 66 more C-54s after White House conference with General Clay.

26   Russia rejects UN Security Council resolution to terminate blockade.

28   Stalin accuses West of deliberately refusing to abide by August 30 "agreement" in Moscow.

29   Tegel Air Force Base dedicated in ceremonies to mark opening of Berlin's 3rd airlift terminal.

NOVEMBER

2   RAF Hastings begin operations from Schleswigland.

5   Operations begin at Tegel. 300,000th ton flown into Berlin by 1st Lt. Donald G. Bidwell from Dayton, Ohio.

8   First 3 of 24 Navy R-5Ds (C-54s) arrive for airlift duty. Free University opens at Dahlem, in U.S. sector of Berlin.

15   Final shipment by air of maintenance airmen from Oberpfaffenhofen to Burtonwood, to begin regular C-54 maintenance by Nov. 18.

16   Airlift passes first test against winter weather, continuing normal operations despite heavy fog.

17   USAF radar team departs Westover AFB, Mass., to commence installation of CPS-5 radar device for use on airlift.

18   RAF C-47 crashes in Russian zone near Lübeck. 3 killed instantly; 1 survivor dies later in hospital.

23   British Lancastrian tanker crashes at Thruxton, England, killing 7.

26   Foggy weather continues to hinder airlift. Extensive use of radar assistance GCA for landings; Gatow records 1,316 in one month. Backlog of one month's food stocks in Berlin. All civilian C-47s withdrawn from lift.

30   Russian-sponsored groups set up rump City Council under Friedrich Ebert.

December

1   East-West split of Berlin complete as Western liaison officers transfer offices from City Hall. Weather reconnaissance unit organized to make observation flights over North Atlantic and through the corridors.

5   Elections held for City Council in three Western sectors. Ernst Reuter unanimously elected Lord Mayor. Construction of second (2,300-yard) runway begins at Tegel.

6   C-54 crashes after take-off at Fassberg. 3 killed.

7   Airlift back to normal as fog lifts.

9   Lift delivers 6,133 tons, second high mark.

11   Navy R-5D with 6 aboard crashes in Taunus Mountains. Crew chief killed.

13   Airlift passes 171st-day mark. Total tonnage delivered: 640,284. U.S. tonnage: 460,501. British tonnage: 179,783.

15   317th Troop Carrier Group moves from Wiesbaden to Celle, opening second U.S. airlift terminal in British zone. All RAF and civil flying boats withdrawn from lift.

16   French Army engineers blow up transmitting towers of Communist-controlled broadcasting

station in immediate vicinity of Tegel Air Force Base. 5,000th landing of British civil aircraft made by York of Skyways. USAF announce that airlift C-54s will be increased to 225 by December's end.

20   Fassberg's "Operation Santa Claus" flies in gifts for 10,000 Berlin children.

24   Vice President Elect Alben C. Barkley, Secretary of the Air Force W. Stuart Symington and Bob Hope with "Christmas Caravan" troupe start entertainment tour of airlift bases.

26   700,172.7 tons lifted to Berlin in 96,640 flights during 6 months.

31   Airlift completes 100,000 flights to Berlin since operation began.

1949

JANUARY

2   Rotation for USAFE airlift personnel becomes a reality as first 12 aircrew members depart for original home bases.

7   C-54 crashes north of Burtonwood, England, killing 6.

13   Airlift establishes record second only to Air Force Day by flying 6,678.9 tons to Berlin in 755 flights.

14   C-54 crashes near Rhein-Main; 3 killed.

15   Tegel Air Force Base opened to civil aircraft.

17   Set weekly record of 41,540 tons.

18   C-54 crashes 10 miles east of Fassberg. Pilot killed.

24   RAF C-47 crashes in Russian zone near Lübeck. Wireless operator and 7 German passengers killed. 250,000th ton of coal arrives at Tegel from Fassberg.

31   January records shatter all others with 171,960 tons. Stalin, answering first set of questions submitted to him by Kingsbury Smith of International News Service, makes no mention of West German currency problem.

FEBRUARY

15   Dr. Philip C. Jessup, U.S. delegate to the UN, confers with Jacob Malik, Soviet delegate, on significance of Stalin's omission.

18   1,000,000th ton of supplies reaches Berlin.

20   Weather reduces lift to 205.5 tons in 22 flights. 200th day of British civil lift.

22   New record: 7,513 tons in 876 flights.

23   7,897 tons in 905 flights.

26   8,025 tons in 902 flights for all-time airlift tonnage record. Top weekly tonnage record of 44,612 tons.

MARCH

5   British Prime Minister Clement Attlee inspects Berlin Airlift installations.

12   New weekly tonnage record of 45,644 tons.

15   British civilian York crashes near Gatow; 3 killed.

16   USAFE reveal that from July 1, 1948, to March

1, 1949, U.S. planes have accomplished 36,797 GCA landings.

21   Malik tells Jessup blockade can be lifted in advance of a Foreign Ministers' meeting. British civilian Halton crashes near Schleswigland; 3 British killed.

22   RAF C-47 crashes in Russian territory near Lübeck; 3 killed.

31   New monthly record of 196,160.7 tons. 61st Maintenance Squadron, Rhein-Main, claims new Air Force record for 154 engines, rebuilt during March. Navy squadron VR-8 sets all-time record of 155 percent efficiency—with hourly utilization of 12.2 hours per aircraft.

APRIL

7   Tempelhof GCA crew handles plane every 4 minutes over a period of $6^{1}/_{2}$ hours to set a new high in sustained operation. 102 planes are handled. A Fassberg C-54 completes entire round trip to Berlin in 1 hour 57 minutes. Turnaround time: 15 minutes, 30 seconds.

11   New tonnage figures of 8,246.1 tons in 922 flights for 24-hour period.

16   General Tunner's "Easter Parade" flies 12,940 tons of coal, food, and other supplies in 1,398 flights to raise 24-hour operation record to new high. Lift planes fly 78,954,500 miles. 3,946 landings and take-offs are made, plus 39,640 radio contacts—one every 4 seconds during the 24-hour period. 80% of all aircraft are in commission, with many groups maintaining 100% utilization during most of the period.

21   300th day of blockade. 927 planes carry 6,393.8 tons of goods to the city. Work begins on third runway at RAF Gatow.

22	Supplies hauled during a 5-day period have more than equaled Berlin's normal incoming supplies by rail prior to blockade.
23	Third-high single-day tonnage: 8,774.3 tons in 974 flights. New weekly tonnage figure: 58,155.8 tons in 6,437 flights.
25	Tass news agency reveals Russian willingness to lift blockade. New second-high figure: 8,939.1 tons in 1,011 flights.
26	U.S. State Department reveals Jessup–Malik talks and says "way appears clear" for lifting blockade.
27	Another second-high record: 9,119.9 tons in 1,022 flights.
30	New monthly high of 232,263.7 tons set. This marks a daily average of 7,845.5 tons during the month. New weekly record of 60,774.2 tons of food and supplies. British civilian Halton crashes north of Tegel in the Russian Zone; 4 killed.

MAY

2	First Boeing C-97 transport joins the airlift at Rhein-Main.
4	Big Four delegates announce Berlin blockade will be lifted and a Foreign Ministers' council will be held May 23. C-97 carries its first 10-ton load to Tempelhof.
7	British Foreign Secretary Ernest Bevin arrives in Berlin to inspect airlift installations.
10	9,257 tons carried in 1,019 flights to establish new second high.
12	Rail lines and highways to Berlin reopened. Blockade ends.

The Eyewitnesses

and what they do today

The 453 men and women listed below provided the hard core of facts on which this book is based. While some furnished contemporary letters and diaries or specially written accounts, most of them submitted themselves patiently to question-and-answer interviews. To avoid confusion, ranks, and in some cases names are those which pertained during the specific period which he or she described.

Occupations listed are as at time of going to press. Where a name is placed within brackets, it indicates that a contributor has died since this list was compiled. While not all eyewitnesses are mentioned in the narrative, their contributions to the story of the Berlin blockade and airlift have been invaluable.

THE AMERICANS

Alger, 1st Lt. Robert, 54th Troop Carrier Squadron, Fassberg. *Lt. Col., ret'd; Executive Vice-President, Command Airways, Wappinger Falls, N.Y.*

Amman, Lt. Cmdr. Bernard, USN, Squadron VR 6, Rhein-Main. *Cmdr., ret'd; schoolteacher, Newport, R.I.*

Arata, Sgt. John, 559th Medium Automotive Maintenance Co., Rhein-Main. *Auto mechanic, Watertown, Mass.*

Barrette, Sgt. Rudolph, 7296th Maintenance Squadron, Oberpfaffen-hofen. *Aircraft electrician, Jacksonville, Fla.*

Bass, 1st Lt. Robert, 9th Air Transport Squadron, Wiesbaden–Fassberg. *Col., ret'd; county development commissioner, Punta Gorda, Fla.*

Beachmer, 1st Lt. Carlton, 331st Troop Carrier Squadron, Rhein-Main. *Maj., ret'd; Tampa, Fla.*

Bedette, 1st Lt. Ellsworth, 60th Troop Carrier Group, Rhein-Main. *Lt. Col., ret'd; farmer, Palmyra, N.Y.*

Benedick, Capt. Beatrice, WAC, H.Q. Eucom, Frankfurt-am-Main. *Legal secretary, New York, N.Y.*

Bennett, Capt. Jack Olin, American Overseas Airlines, Rhein-Main. *Consultant engineer, North American Rockwell Corporation, Berlin, Germany.*

Bennett, Jackson, Financial Adviser, HQ, OMGUS, Berlin. *Ret'd. Chapel Hill, N.C.*

Bettinger, Lt. Col. Sterling, HQ, Combined Airlift Task Force, Wiesbaden. *Brig. Gen. ret'd; Colorado Springs, Colo.*

Biel, Capt. Ulrich, Berlin *Kommandatura*: Political Affairs Division. *Lawyer, Berlin, Germany.*

Blake, Capt. Harry, 330th Troop Carrier Squadron, Rhein-Main. *Col., ret'd., El Cajon, Calif.*

Boyd, Lt. Cmdr. Joseph, USN, Squadron VR-8, Rhein-Main. *Men's clothing store, Glendale, Ariz.*

Brundage, S/Sgt Frank, HQ, Combined Airlift Task Force, Wiesbaden. *Civil servant, Carmel, Calif.*

Calabrese, Airman Anthony, 60th Troop Carrier Group, Wiesbaden. *Aircraft maintenance instructor, Baldwin, N.Y.*

Caputo, S/Sgt Joseph, 330th Troop Carrier Squadron, Rhein-Main. *Engineer-mechanic, Pratt & Whitney, East Hartford, Conn.*

Carlucci, Raymond, Director, Criminal Investigation Division, Dept. of the Army, Berlin. *Fish market proprietor, Budd Lake, N.J.*

Caruso, S/Sgt. Joseph, 53rd Troop Carrier Squadron, Rhein-Main. *Bank employee, Elmira, N.Y.*

Casey, Capt. William, 7807 Transportation Truck Bn., Berlin. *Production planning dept., Beech Aircraft Corp., Wichita, Kans.*

Cates, Ens. Thomas, USN, Squadron VR 6, Rhein-Main. *Cmdr., ret'd; Federal Aviation Administration, Washington, D.C.*

Chavasse, Lt. Col. Nicholas, O.C., 2105th Weather Group, Wiesbaden. *Col., ret'd; Camp Springs, Md.*

Cheever, T/Sgt C.E., 317th Troop Carrier Wing, Celle. *Postal delivery superintendent, Austin, Tex.*

Clark, Sgt. Reginald, 759th Military Police Detachment, Berlin. *Truck driver, Chicago, Ill.*

Clay, Gen. Lucius D., Military Governor and Commander-in-Chief, U.S. Forces in Europe, HQ, OMGUS, Berlin, 1947–49. *Honorary Chairman of the Board, Continental Can Co., New York, N.Y.*

Clifford, Clark, Special Counsel to the President of the United States, 1948–49. *Attorney, Washington, D.C.*

Colligan, S/Sgt. Bernard, 40th Troop Carrier Squadron, Wiesbaden–Celle. *Special-delivery messenger, Riverside, Calif.*

Cooke, S/Sgt. Philip, 7350th Air Base Group, Tempelhof. *Telephone maintenance man, Commerce, Ga.*

Costi, 1st Lt. George, 14th Troop Carrier Squadron, Rhein-Main. *Col., ret'd; Grapeview, Wash.*

Coulter, Col. John, O.C., Fassberg Air Base. *Brig Gen., ret'd; Southampton, N.Y.*

Crawford, Lt. Col. John, HQ, Airways and Air Communications Service, Washington, D.C. *Col., ret'd; Tacoma, Wash.*

Crowley, Sgt. John, Jr., 60th Troop Carrier Group, Fassberg. *Defense materiel inspector, Columbus, Ohio.*

Cummings, Capt. Clarence, 252nd Engineer Construction Bn., Berlin. *Maj., ret'd; county sanitation engineer, Anaheim, Calif.*

Daniels, Capt. Courtney, 60th Troop Carrier Group, Wiesbaden. *Lt. Col., ret'd; carpenter, Salt Lake City, Utah.*

DaVania, Col. Richard, O.C., 61st Troop Carrier Group, Rhein-Main. *Chemicals leasing facility, Sacramento, Calif.*

Diab, 1st Lt. Thomas, 60th Troop Carrier Group, Wiesbaden. *Realtor, Boston, Mass.*

Dillon, S/Sgt. Katharine, HQ, Combined Airlift Task Force, Wiesbaden. *Historical researcher, Arlington, Va.*

Dinsmore, Capt. Dwight, 333rd Troop Carrier Squadron, Wiesbaden. *Col., ret'd; public-relations manager, LTV Aerospace, Washington, D.C.*

Donnan, Capt. Edloe, ADC to Military Governor and Commander-in-Chief, HQ, OMGUS, Berlin, 1947–49. *Account Manager, Continental Can Co., St. Louis, Mo.*

Donnan, Margaret, Berlin-Dahlem. *Housewife, St. Louis, Mo.*

Dorr, Col. Henry, O.C., Tempelhof Air Force Base. *Ret'd; Washington, D.C.*

Downs, Kenneth, Berlin *Kommandatura*: Information Division. *Public-relations consultant, Washington, D.C.*

[Draper, William H., Jr., Under Secretary of the Army, Washington,

D.C. *Honorary Chairman, Population Crisis Committee, Washington, D.C.*]

Dubiel, Pfc John, 1113rd Transport Squadron, Wiesbaden. *Unemployed, Mesa, Ariz.*

Dundas, Pfc John, 40th Troop Carrier Squadron, Celle. *Truck driver, Graniteville, Mass.*

Earley, T/Sgt. Vernon, 12th Troop Carrier Squadron, Wiesbaden. *Art gallery employee, Montclair, Calif.*

Edghill, Gloria, U.S. Office of Military Government, Frankfurt-am-Main. *Housewife, La Grangeville, N.Y.*

Enoch, 1st Lt. Donald, 60th Troop Carrier Group, Wiesbaden. *Maj., ret'd; charter-boat skipper, Englewood, Fla.*

Ettel, 2nd Lt. Calvin, 313th Troop Carrier Group, Fassberg. *Pilot, Ozark Airlines, Florissant, Mo.*

Farrar, Lt. Col. J. Montgomery, H.Q., C.A.L.T.F., Wiesbaden. *Construction magazine editor, Richmond, Va.*

Fernandez, Lt. Col. Manuel, HQ, Combined Airlift Task Force, Wiesbaden. *Col., ret'd; Greenville, S.C.*

Ferrell, Lt. Col. James, O.C., 14th Troop Carrier Squadron, Rhein-Main. *Personnel officer, State Liquor Control Board, Olympia, Wash.*

Finn, 1st Lt. John, 54th Troop Carrier Squadron, Rhein-Main–Fassberg. *Realtor, Tucson, Ariz.*

Flemming, Sgt. James, 317th Field Maintenance Squadron, Celle. *Office machine repairs, Hastings, Neb.*

Frederick, T/Sgt. Vincent, Jr., 333rd Troop Carrier Squadron, Wiesbaden. *Ret'd., Melbourne, Fla.*

Garges, Capt. Eugene, Jr., 330th Troop Carrier Squadron, Rhein-Main. *Pilot, Eastern Airlines, New York, N.Y.*

Gerald, Capt. Robert, 317th Troop Carrier Group, Celle. *Instructor, American Airlines Flight Academy, Fort Worth, Tex.*

Gibson, Catherine, H.Q., Combined Airlift Task Force, Wiesbaden. *Ret'd; Chesterfield, Mo.*

Gilbert, Ellen "Pat," H.Q., Combined Airlift Task Force, Wiesbaden, *Lt.-Col., ret'd; Lebanon, Ill.*

Glaeser, CPO F.W., USN, Squadron VR 8, Rhein-Main. *Cmdr., ret'd; Gulf Breeze, Fla.*

Glatiotis, Pfc William, 513th Supply Squadron, Fassberg. *Disabled, Denver, Colo.*

Gordon, Maj. John, 61st Troop Carrier Wing, Rhein-Main. *Mortgage banker, Sumter, S.C.*

Granger, Cpl. Norman, 60th Troop Carrier Group, Wiesbaden. *Assistant maintenance manager, School Dept. Beverly Hills, Calif.*

Gratton, Cpl. Roland, 7798th Traffic Regulating Detachment, Berlin. *Mail carrier, Ware, Mass.*

Greenwood, 1st Lt. Gene, 14th Troop Carrier Squadron, Rhein-Main. *Col., ret'd; Assistant Dean, Florida Institute of Technology, Jensen Beach, Fla.*

Greno, S/Sgt. John, 779th Traffic Regulating Unit, Rhein-Main. *Truck fleet manager, Kenosha, Wis.*

Gruber, 1st Lt. Robert, 7350th Air Base Group, Tempelhof Air Force Base. *Realtor, Dallas, Tex.*

Guilbert, Maj. Edward. HQ, Combined Airlift Task Force, Wiesbaden. *Col., ret'd; President, Transportation Data Coordinating Committee, Washington, D.C.*

Gullette, Walter, Supt., Aircraft Shops, UK Air Materiel Area, Burtonwood, England. *Engineer, ret'd; San Antonio, Tex.*

Gustafson, 1st Lt. John, 61st Troop Carrier Group, Rhein-Main. *Missile engineer, Redland, Calif.*

Haigler, Capt. Claude, 1st Air Transport Squadron, Fassberg. *Lt. Col. ret'd; insurance salesman, Ann Arbor, Mich.*

Hallas, 1st Lt. Gerald, 12th Troop Carrier Squadron, Rhein-Main–Wiesbaden. *Col., ret'd; Oxford, Ohio.*

Halvorsen, 1st Lt. Gail, 17th Troop Carrier Squadron, Rhein-Main. *Col., ret'd; guidance counselor, Brigham Young University, Provo, Utah.*

Hamman, 1st Lt. Vernon, 53rd Air Transport Squadron, Rhein-Main. *Lt. Col., ret'd; pilot, United Air Lines, Denver, Colo.*

Harris, Capt. Clifford, 313th Troop Carrier Group, Fassberg. *Pilot, American Airlines, Hamilton, Mass.*

Hays, Maj. Gen. George, Deputy Military Governor and Commander-in-Chief, HQ, OMGUS, Berlin. *Ret'd; Pinehurst, N.C.*

Hedges, T/Sgt. Emery, 48th Troop Carrier Squadron, Rhein-Main. *Business machines company, Huntington, Ind.*

Heimlich, William, Berlin *Kommandatura*: Radio in the American Sector. *Vice-President, Association of National Advertisers, Washington, D.C.*

Hennessey, 1st Lt. Richard, 54th Troop Carrier Squadron, Rhein-Main–Fassberg. *Major, ret'd; insurance, Hartford, Conn.*

Hogg, Capt. Robert, HQ, Combined Airlift Task Force, Wiesbaden. *Executive, Hughes Air West, Long Beach, Calif.*

Holly, Pvt. Kenneth, 7350th Air Base Group, Tempelhof Air Force Base. *Home improvement store, Otsego, Mich.*

Horn, Kurt, 2nd Air Transport Group, Fairfield Suisun Air Force Base, Calif. *Civil servant, Military Airlift Command, Honolulu, Hawaii.*

Hovde, St. Karl, 317th Motor Vehicle Squadron, Celle. *Unemployed, Westby, Wisc.*

Hovik, Maj. Clifford, 12th Troop Carrier Squadron, Rhein-Main. *Real-estate salesman, Lomita, Calif.*

Howley, Col. (later Brig. Gen.) Frank, Director, American Military Government, Berlin Sector, 1947–49. *Public-relations consultant, Madison, N.J.*

Humphrey, Capt. Ivan, attd. 158th AACS Squadron, Berlin. *Lt. Col., ret'd; Aerospace and Communications Division, Ford, Washington, D.C.*

Huston, Capt. Lewis, 14th Troop Carrier Squadron, Rhein-Main. *Tourist promotion, El Cajon, Calif.*

Jessup, Philip, U.S. Representative to UN General Assembly, 1948–52; Ambassador at Large, 1949–53. *Judge, ret'd; Honorary Member, governing council, International Institute for Unification of Pvt Law, 1967–; Norfolk, Conn.*

Job, Cpl. Raymond, HQ, Airlift Wing (Provisional), Rhein-Main. *Farmer, Ipswich, N. Dakota.*

Jones, Lt. Col. Curran "Jack," O.C. 47th Troop Carrier Squadron, Fassberg. *Clothing store, Salado, Tex.*

Kaeser, 1st Lt. Joseph, 53rd Troop Carrier Squadron, Rhein-Main. *Program developer, Westford, Mass.*

Kay Irene, Allied Control Authority, Berlin: Allied Liaison and Protocol Section. *Ret'd; Hempstead, N.Y.*

Kennedy, Capt. Francis, 7100th HQ Support Wing, Wiesbaden. *Lt. Col., ret'd; county administrative analyst, Riverside, Calif.*

Kennedy, Maj. Robert, 85th Vehicle Repair Squadron, Weinheim. *Stockbroker, Kansas City, Mo.*

King, M/Sgt. William, 60th Air Police Squadron, Kaufbüren. *Ret'd; Whiteriver, Ariz.*

Kinser, 1st Lt. George, 15th Troop Carrier Squadron, Rhein-Main. *Tour guide, Kennedy Space Center, Cape Canaveral, Fla.*

Kissner, Brig. Gen. August, Chief of Staff, HQ, United States Air Forces in Europe, Wiesbaden. *Maj. Gen. ret'd; Sarasota, Fla.*

Kottner, S/Sgt. Louis, 60th Troop Carrier Group, Wiesbaden. *Aircraft mechanic, Greenbush, Mich.*

Krenek, S/Sgt. Lawrence, HQ, USAFE, Wiesbaden. *Account office manager, Houston, Tex.*

Larotonda, 2nd Lt. Robert, 29th Troop Carrier Squadron, Fassberg. *Electrical inspector, Lima, Ohio.*

Lawler, Capt. John, 60th Troop Carrier Group, Wiesbaden. *Pilot, American Airlines, Dallas, Tex.*

LeMay, Lt. Gen. Curtis E., Commander-in-Chief, United States Air

Forces in Europe, Wiesbaden, 1947–48. *Gen., ret'd; Vice Chief Staff, HQ, USAF, 1957–61; Chief of Staff, 1961–65; Chairman of the Board, Networks Electronic Co., Newport Beach, Calif.*

Lochner, Robert, Control Officer, Radio Frankfurt. *American Chamber of Commerce, Berlin.*

Lother, M/Sgt. Clyde, HQ, C.A.L.T.F., Wiesbaden. *Capt., ret'd; Army security officer, Burlington, Ia.*

Lovett, Robert, Under Secretary of State, Washington, D.C. *General partner, Brown Brothers, Harriman, N.Y.*

Madison, Dorothy, Berlin-Lankwitz. *Housewife, Gary, Ind.*

Madison, S/M James, 16th Constabulary Squadron, Berlin. *Maj., ret'd; Dept. of Labor, Gary, Ind.*

Malzan, Cpl. Edwin, 7350th Air Base Group, Tempelhof Air Force Base. *Insurance claims adjuster, Buffalo, N.Y.*

Mantor, Sgt. Edward, 133rd Labor Supervision Co., Berlin-Lichterfelde-West. *Subcontroller, Capitol Cadillac, Washington, D.C.*

Martin, Capt. Robert, 313th Troop Carrier Group, Fassberg. *Pilot, American Airlines, Dallas, Tex.*

Mautner, Maj. Karl, Berlin *Kommandatura*: City Hall Liaison. *Office of International Affairs, Washington, D.C.*

McKinney, 1st Lt. Elwyn, 17th Troop Carrier Squadron, Rhein-Main. *Executive director, Chamber of Commerce, Perry, Ga.*

Meredik, Pvt. Donald, 7798th Traffic Regulating Detachment, Berlin. *Disabled, Scranton, Pa.*

Metz, Capt. Michael, 7798th Traffic Regulating Detachment, Berlin. *Zone enforcement officer, Upper Saddle River, N.J.*

Michaels, M/Sgt. Valentine, 12th Troop Carrier Squadron, Tempelhof. *Bartender, Murfreesboro, Tenn.*

Michaud, 1st Lt. Clarence, 332nd Troop Carrier Squadron, Rhein-Main. Lt. Col., ret'd; flight instructor, United Airlines, Denver, Colo.

Milton, Col. Theodore Ross, Chief of Staff, HQ, Combined Airlift Task Force, Wiesbaden. *Gen., ret'd; Colorado Springs, Colo.*

Miner, Harold, Information Services Division, OMGUS, Berlin. *Ret'd, Damascus, Md.*

Murphy, Robert. Political Adviser to U.S. Military Governor and Commander-in-Chief, HQ, OMGUS, Berlin. *Honorary Chairman of the Board, Corning International Corporation, New York, N.Y.*

Nordstrom, 1st Lt. John, 313th Troop Carrier Group, Fassberg. *Lt. Col., ret'd; Loda, Ill.*

O'Donnell, James P., Berlin-Zehlendorf: *New York Daily News, Saturday Evening Post. Newsweek, Berlin, Germany.*

Olds, 1st Lt. John, 317th Troop Carrier Group, Celle. *Auto salesman, Elkhart, Ind.*

Panak, T/Sgt. A.J. "Tony," HQ, C.A.L.T.F., Wiesbaden. *Newspaperman, Minersville, Pa.*

Parsons, Barbara, Berlin-Wannsee. *Housewife, Oyster Bay, N.Y.*

Parsons, David, American Overseas Airlines, Berlin. *Ret'd, Oyster Bay, N.Y.*

Patterson, Capt. Neill, 12th Air Transport Squadron, Rhein-Main. *Col., ret'd; Waynesville, N.C.*

Pope, T/Sgt. Roy, 22nd Air Transport Squadron, Rhein-Main. *Exhibit technician, Oklahoma Historical Society, Midwest City, Okla.*

Powell, T/Sgt. Milton, 317th Troop Carrier Group, Wiesbaden-Celle. *Automobile mechanic, Palacios, Tex.*

Prevost, Maj. Jules, HQ, Combined Airlift Task Force, Wiesbaden. *Col., ret'd; W. Danville, Vt.*

Pucher, Sgt. Cecilia, WAC, Berlin Military Post. *Housewife, Walnut Creek, Calif.*

Richardson, Capt. Howard. HQ, Department of the Army, Washington, D.C. *Col., ret'd; Jackson, Miss.*

Robbins, Irvin, Berlin *Kommandatura*: Legal Division. *Assistant State's Attorney, Chicago, ILl.*

Roberts, Cpl. Raymond, 47th Troop Carrier Squadron, Fassberg. *Maj., ret'd; auto dealer, Christiansburg, Va.*

Rodenbaugh, Tom, American Overseas Airlines, Frankfurt-am-Main. *Ret'd, Miami, Fla.*

Roellig, Capt. Howard, 146th AACS Squadron, Berlin. *Lt. Col., ret'd; electronics engineer, Fairbarn, Ohio.*

Rylander, Cpl. Roland, 317th Troop Carrier Wing, Celle. *C/M/Sgt., ret'd; Sacramento, Calif.*

Sabey, T/5 Walter, 16th Constabulary Squadron, Berlin. *Helicopter pilot, Toms River, N.J.*

Saldonik, T/Sgt. Robert, 53rd Troop Carrier Squadron, Rhein-Main. *Auto supply dealer, Duluth, Minn.*

Sandmeier, 1st Lt. Warren, 61st Troop Carrier Group, Rhein-Main. *Lt. Col., ret'd; Knoxville, Ia.*

Schmick, Sgt. Albert, HQ Combined Airlift Task Force, Wiesbaden. *Radio network president, Staunton, Va.*

Schmidt, Pfc Russell, 7111th Motor Vehicle Squadron, Wiesbaden. *Auto Stores, Gibson City, Ill.*

Schuffert, T/Sgt. John "Jake," HQ, Combined Airlift Task Force,

Wiesbaden. *Audio-Visual Service, Bolling AFB, Washington, D.C.*

Schwarz, Dr. Eugene, Berlin *Kommandatura*: Public Health Division. *Consultant physician, New York, N.Y.*

Shack, 1st Lt. Edward, Fassberg—HQ Combined Airlift Task Force, Wiesbaden. *Speechwriter, Dept. of Commerce, Washington, D.C.*

Sims, Capt. Harold, HQ Combined Airlift Task Force, Wiesbaden. *Col., ret'd; artist, San Antonio, Tex.*

Skoog, Cpl. Kenneth, 14th Troop Carrier Squadron, Rhein-Main. *Railroad brakeman, Wahpeton, N. Dakota.*

Smith, Ens. Bernald, USN, Squadron VR 8, Rhein-Main. *Pilot, United Airlines, San Francisco, Calif.*

Smith, Brig. Gen. Joseph, Commanding General, Berlin Airlift Task Force, Wiesbaden, June–July, 1948. *Lt. Gen. ret'd; Washington, D.C.*

Smith, 1st Lt. Lewis, 7360th Air Base Group, Tullin, Vienna-Wiesbaden. *Col. ret'd; Austin, Tex.*

Smith, Capt. Tom Warren, attd. AACS Detachment 133-1, Frankfurt-am-Main. *Federal Aviation Administration, Atlanta, Ga.*

Snyder, Sgt. Henry, attd. 60th Troop Carrier Group, Wiesbaden. *Service-station attendant, Pine Grove, Pa.*

Steber, 1st Lt. Russell, 60th Troop Carrier Group, Wiesbaden. *Ret'd; Crystal River, Fla.*

Steele, 1st Lt. James, 40th Troop Carrier Squadron, Celle. *Sales Division, Westinghouse Communications, Severna Park, Md.*

Stevens, Col. Ronald, HQ, United States Air Forces in Europe. *Ret'd; Meriden, Conn.*

Stork, M/Sgt. Joseph, 514th Materiel Squadron, Wiesbaden. *Ret'd; Minneapolis, Minn.*

Symington, W. Stuart, Under Secretary for Air, Washington, D.C. *Senator from Missouri, 1952–, Washington, D.C.*

Taylor, Thayle, McDonnell Douglas Corporation, Santa Monica, Calif. *Senior Project Engineer, Douglas Aircraft Company, Long Beach, Calif.*

Thomason, M/Sgt. Galen, 313th Troop Carrier Headquarters, Fassberg. *Rehabilitation counselor, Alamosa, Colo.*

Thompson, 1st Lt. William, HQ, Combined Airlift Task Force, Wiesbaden *McDonnell Douglas Corporation, Huntington Beach, Calif.*

Tilton, Lt. Col. Charles, HQ, C.A.L.T.F., Wiesbaden. *Ret'd; Arlington, Va.*

Towne, Capt. Raymond, HQ Combined Airlift Task Force, Wiesbaden. *Col., ret'd; Director, External Relations, McDonnell Douglas Corporation, Long Beach, Calif.*

Trudeau, Brig. Gen. Arthur, O.C., 1st Constabulary Brigade Wiesbaden. *Lt. Gen., ret'd; management consultant, Chevy Chase, Md.*

Tully, 2nd Lt. Randolph, 39th Troop Carrier Squadron, Wiesbaden. *Auto Stores, Rantoul, Ill.*

Tunner, Maj. Gen. William, Commanding General, HQ Combined Airlift Task Force, Wiesbaden. *Lt. Gen., ret'd; Deputy Commander of Operations, Military Air Transport Service, 1949–50; C-in-C, Combat Cargo Command, 1950–51; C-in-C, United States Air Forces in Europe, 1953–57; C-in-C, Military Air Transport Service, 1958–60; Ware Neck, Va.*

Tytus, 1st Lt. Joe, 12th Troop Carrier Squadron, Rhein-Main. *Realtor, Napa, Calif.*

Vallier, Pfc Earl, 1807th Airways and Air communications Group, Wiesbaden. *Storekeeper, Keene State College, N.H.*

Vaughn, Sgt. Chester, 47th Troop Carrier Squadron, Fassberg. *Maintenance division, United Airlines, San Francisco, Calif.*

Vollmer, Ens. C.R., USN, Squadron VR 8, Rhein-Main. *Capt., ret'd; Annandale, Va.*

Waag, S/Sgt. Bernard, 60th Troop Carrier Group, Wiesbaden. *Draftsman, Grumman Aircraft Corporation, Levittown, N.Y.*

Walsh, Maj. Gen. Robert, G-2, HQ, OMGUS, Berlin. *Ret'd; Washington, D.C.*

Ward, 1st Lt. Harry, 331st Troop Carrier Squadron, Rhein-Main. *Maj., ret'd; school principal, Baton Rouge, La.*

Waters, 1st Lt. Don, 12th Troop Carrier Squadron, Kaufbüren-Wiesbaden. *Aircraft research and development, San Diego, Calif.*

Weber, 1st Lt. Edward, 61st Troop Carrier Group, Rhein-Main. *Electrical design engineer, Piedmont, Calif.*

Wedemeyer, Lt. Gen. Albert, Director of Plans and Operations, U.S. Army, Washington, D.C. *Gen. of the Army, ret'd; Boyds, Md.*

Wenk, 1st Lt. James, 53rd Troop Carrier Squadron, Rhein-Main. *Pilot, United Airlines, La Grangeville, N.Y.*

Whearty, 1st Lt. Everett, 10th Troop Carrier Squadron, Fassberg-41st Troop Carrier Squadron, Celle. *Beech Aircraft Corporation, Wichita, Kans.*

Whelan, Capt. Joseph, 29th Troop Carrier Squadron, Fassberg. *Chiropractor, Minneapolis, Minn.*

White, S/Sgt. Marvin, 317th Air Police Squadron, Celle. *Printer's deliveryman, Cocoa, Fla.*

Wiedle, 1st Lt. Eugene, 41st Troop Carrier Squadron, Celle. *Lt. Col., ret'd; artist, Long Beach, Calif.*

Wilkinson, Lawrence, Director, Economics Division, HQ, OMGUS, Berlin. *Consultant, Phelps-Dodge Corporation, New York, N.Y.*

Wray, Col. Stanley, O.C. 7497th Airlift Wing, Rhein-Main. *Maj. Gen., ret'd; Shalimar, Fla.*

Wroblewski, Capt. Joseph, 1st Troop Carrier Squadron, Fassberg. *Lt. Col., ret'd; pilot, State Aviation Dept., Atlanta, Ga.*

Zagorsky, 1st Lt. Stanley, 60th Troop Carrier Group, Wiesbaden. *Lt. Col., ret'd; schoolteacher, Brookhaven, N.Y.*

Zozolo, Sgt. Peter, 317th Communications Squadron, Celle. *Engineering supervisor, Fairchild Republic Company, Farmingdale, N.Y.*

THE BRITISH

Abrahams, First Officer Gerald, Airwork Ltd., Fuhlsbüttel. *Garage proprietor, Birchington, Kent.*

Adams, Sgt. Cyril, 11th (Prince Albert's Own) Hussars, Berlin-Grunewald. *Sheet rubber worker, Deal, Kent.*

Adams, Eileen, Berlin-Grunewald. *Housewife, Deal, Kent.*

Aikman, Barrie, Aquila Airways, Finkenwerder. *Travel agent, Kensington, South London.*

Alabaster, Capt. Robert, British South American Airways, Wunsdorf. *Pilot, Gulf Air, Bahrein.*

Anderson, G/Capt. Leslie, O.C., RAF Wunsdorf, Jan. 1949–. *Ret'd; Henley-on-Thames, Oxon.*

Armstrong, L.A.C. Charles, York Servicing Flight, RAF Wunsdorf. *Proofreader, "News of the World," London.*

Ashley, First Officer Clifford, Airflight Ltd., Wunsdorf. *Pilot, British Caledonian Airways, Henfield, Sussex.*

Aspden, Flight Engineer Ronald, Silver City Airways—Bond Air Services, Fuhlsbüttel. *Engineering division Superintendent, British Caledonian Airways, Horsham, Sussex.*

Atkinson, Robin, Civil Airlift Operations Officer, Fassberg. *Operation Planning Superintendent, Tristar, British Airways.*

Bacon, William Edward, Sivewright Airways, Barton Aerodrome, Manchester. *Director, Sivewright, Manchester.*

Bailey, Donald, Senior Traffic Manager, British European Airways, Berlin. *Operations Division Manager, British Airways, London Airport.*

Baker, Air Marshal Sir Brian, AOC-in-C, RAF Transport Command, Bushey Park, Middlesex. *Ret'd; RAF Benevolent Fund, Edinburgh.*

Bamberg, Harold, Eagle Aviation Ltd, Bovington, Herts. *Company chairman, Sunninghill, Berks.*

Banfield, Lt.-Col. Ralph. Bezirk Resident Officer, Berlin–Wilmersdorf Tiergarten. *Ret'd; Bournemouth, Hants.*

Barden, Signaller I Peter, No. 206 Squadron, RAF, Wunsdorf. *Builder, Hastings, Sussex.*

Batt, Robert, Chief Inspector, Aviation Traders Ltd. *Director, Aviation Traders, Southend-on-Sea, Essex.*

Beevers, First Officer Stewart, Skyways Ltd., Wunsdorf. *Pilot, British Airways, Churt, Surrey.*

Bennett, Air Vice Marshal Donald, Airflight Ltd., Wunsdorf. *Company chairman, Blackbushe Airport, Camberley, Surrey.*

Benson, Brigadier Edward, Deputy Commandant, British Element, *Kommandatura*, and Deputy Director Military Government, Berlin. *Maj.-Gen., ret'd; Aldermaston, Berks.*

Benson, Isolda. Berlin–Charlottenburg. *Housewife, Aldermaston, Berks.*

Best, S/Ldr Eric, O.C., No. 59 Squadron, RAF Wunsdorf. *Bank employee, Huntingdon, Cambs.*

Bevan-John, S/Ldr David, O.C., No. 51 Squadron, RAF Wunsdorf, Dec. 1948–Mar. 1949. *G/Capt., ret'd; managing director, timber importers, Newport, Gwent.*

Biggar, G/Capt. A.J. "Wally," O.C., RAF Stations, Fassberg, 1948; Lübeck (from Feb. 1949). *Ret'd; Aldeburgh, Suffolk.*

Billman, W/Cdr Sydney, O.C., Technical Wing, RAF Station, Celle. *Ret'd; Ivybridge, Devon.*

Bingham, Flight Engineer V.F., World Air Freight Ltd., Wunsdorf–Fuhlsbüttel. *British Airways, Basingstoke, Hants.*

Bowen, Capt. T.C. "Bill," M.C., 1st Bn, The Worcestershire Regt., Berlin-Kladow. *Colonel-in-Chief, The Worcestershire and Sherwood Foresters Regt.; Steward, Worcester Cathedral.*

Brinkely, Major William, 1st Bn, The Norfolk Regt, Berlin–Spandau. *Lt. Col., ret'd; Royal Military School of Music, Twickenham, Middx.*

Brooke-Johnson, Capt. St. John, MBE, 1st Bn, The Worcestershire Regt., Berlin-Kladow. *Serjeant-at-Arms, Mansion House, London.*

Brownlie, S/Ldr Ian, O.C., No. 297 Squadron, RAF Schleswigland. *Executive, Guest, Keen and Nettlefold, London.*

Buchanan-Dunlop, Lt.-Col. Archibald, O.C., 2nd Bn, The Royal Scots Fusiliers, Berlin-Spandau. *Brigadier, ret'd; Edinburgh.*

Bullock, W/Cdr Philip, Bezirk Resident Officer, Berlin-Spandau. *Ret'd; Lymington, Hants.*

Burton-Gyles, Maj. Richard, Flight Refueling Ltd., Tarrant Rushton–Wunsdorf–Fuhlsbüttel. *Ret'd; Sunningdale, Berks.*

Carter, Gilbert "Nick," Civil Airlift Operations Officer, Fuhlsbüttel. *Ret'd; Exminster, Devon.*

Cattle, F/O Frank, No 230 Squadron, RAF, Finkenwerder. *W/Cdr, HQ RAF Training Command, Brampton, Cambs.*

Cawthray, Dorothy, RAF Wunsdorf. *Secretary, Leeds, Yorks.*

Chippindale, Maj. Martin, 1st Bn, The Worcestershire Regt., Berlin-Kladow. *Remedial teacher, Rye, Sussex.*

Churcher, S/Ldr Thomas, O.C., No. 10 Squadron, RAF, Fassberg. *Baby linen shop, Brandon, Suffolk.*

Clark, Flight Engineer Joe, Eagle Aviation Ltd., Wunsdorf. *Chief Engineer, Dan Air Services, Gatwick, W. Sussex.*

Clark, First Officer Noel, British European Airways, Fuhlsbüttel. *Pilot, British Airways, Beaconsfield, Bucks.*

Coates, A.C.1 Alan, No. 4 G.C.A. Unit, RAF Wunsdorf. *Gas Board employee, Sheffield, S. Yorks.*

Collis, Harry, British European Airways, Berlin. *General Manager, Sales Development, British Airways, London.*

Coslett, Sgt. Edmund, 1st Bn, The Worcestershire Regt., Berlin-Kladow. *Senior storekeeper, Worcester.*

Coverdale, Major Terence, Military Assistant to the Military Governor and Commander-in-Chief: Bad Oeynhausen–Berlin. *Lt.-Col, ret'd; wine merchant, Middlesbrough, Cleveland.*

Craig, Major John, R.A.S.C., Forward Air Supply Officer, Schleswigland. *Lt.-Col., ret'd; Basingstoke, Hants.*

Crompton, Lt. John, 1st Bn, The Worcestershire Regt., Berlin–Kladow. *Lt.-Col., Ministry of Defence, London.*

Crosbie, W/Cdr John, O.C., RAF Flying Boat Detachment, Finkenwerder. *G/Capt. ret'd; near Ipswich, Suffolk.*

Cross, G/Capt. Kenneth, HQ, British Air Force of Occupation, Buckeburg. *Air Chief Marshal, ret'd. KCB(1959); London Co-ordinator, the British Red Cross Society.*

201

Cullingworth, Trooper Walter, 11th (P.A.O.) Hussars, attd. 76th Air Freight Co., R.A.S.C., Celle-Wunsdorf. *Photographer's assistant, Leeds, W. Yorks.*

Cushen, Sgt. Jimmie, 1st Bn, The Worcestershire Regt., Berlin-Kladow. *Grocer, Worcester.*

Duckworth, Capt. Alan, Eagle Aviation Ltd., Wunsdorf. *Pilot, British Airways, Manchester.*

Durrant, Capt. L.S. "Bob," 1st Bn, The Worcestershire Regt., Berlin-Kladow. *Executive, Morganite Crucible Ltd., Worcester.*

Durrant, Ruth. Berlin-Kladow. *Housewife, Worcester.*

East, Lt.-Col. Lancelot, O.C., 1st Bn, The Queen's Own Regt., Berlin-Spandau, June–Oct., 1948. *Col., ret'd; near Woking, Surrey.*

Fenwick, Maj. William, Salvation Army, Berlin-Spandau. *Col., Salvation Army Internationl HQ, London.*

Finlayson, S/Ldr Peter, O.C., No. 47 Squadron, Schleswigland. *W/Cdr HQ, RAF Training Command, Brampton, Cambs.*

Firth, Brigadier Charles, Deputy Commander, British Troops, Berlin. *Maj.-Gen., ret'd; near Marlborough, Wilts.*

Florey, Radio Officer William, Flight Refuelling Ltd., Wunsdorf. *British Caledonian Airways, Crawley, W. Sussex.*

Foster, Gerry, Civil Airlift Operations Officer, Wunsdorf-Gatow. *Area Sales Manager, British Airways, Birmingham.*

Franks, Sir Oliver, KCB(1946), British Ambassador at Washington, 1948–52. *The Rt. Hon. Lord Franks of Headington (cr. 1962); Provost, Worcester College, Oxford.*

Freeman-Taylor, Lt.-Col. Richards, O.C., 1st Bn, The Norfolk Regt., 1948–49, Berlin-Spandau. *Col., ret'd; Aldeburgh, Suffolk.*

Gilbert, F/Lt. George, Air Traffic Control, RAF, Gatow. *Management Accountant, British Airways, Germany.*

Greensted, Capt. Bryan, Skyways Ltd., Wunsdorf, *Company secretary, consultant engineers, London.*

Hagues, Capt. Cyril, Skyways Ltd., Wunsdorf. *Pilot, British Airways, London Airport.*

Hagyard, Capt. Ken, Airflight Ltd., Wunsdorf. *Pilot, British Airways, Newbury, Berks.*

Hallett, Capt. John, 1st Bn, The Norfolk Regt., Berlin-Spandau. *Television executive, Norwich, Norfolk.*

Hallett, Pat, Berlin-Spandau. *Housewife, Lyng, Norfolk.*

Hardman, Air Vice-Marshal Donald, Air Ministry, London: Assistant Chief of Air Staff (Ops). *Air Chief Marshal, ret'd, KCB(1952); near Winchester, Hants.*

Harkness, F/Lt. Alan, No. 230 Squadron, RAF, Finkenwerder. *G/Capt., HQ Air Cadets, Brampton, Cambs.*

Hart-Dyke, Lt.-Col. Trevor, O.C., 1st Bn, The Queen's Own Regt., Berlin-Spandau, Oct. 1948–Jan. 1950. *Brigadier, ret'd; near Sheffield, Yorks.*

Haslehust, Capt. Desmond, 1st Bn, The Worcestershire Regt., Berlin-Kladow. *Canon, Diocese of Plymouth, Exmouth, Devon.*

Hepburn, Capt. James, Eagle Aviation Ltd., Wunsdorf. *Occupation unknown, North London.*

Herbert, Maj.-Gen. Otway, Commandant, Allied *Kommandatura* (British Element) & G.O.C., British Troops, Berlin, 1947–49. *Lt.-Gen., ret'd, KBE(1955); Brinsiencyn, Gwynedd.*

Hodges, Col. Alexander, Chief, Allied Liaison and Protocol, Control Commission, British Element. *Ret'd; near Sherborne, Dorset.*

Hood, S/Ldr Edward, British American Air Services, Fuhlsbüttel. *Executive, Decca Engineering, London.*

Hope, G/Capt. Sir Archibald, Bt., Airwork Ltd., Blackbushe Airport, Camberley, Surrey. *Group Treasurer, General Electricity Co., London.*

Horner, S/Ldr Denys, O.C., No. 201 Squadron, RAF, Finkenwerder. *Ministry of Defence, Southampton, Hants.*

Horton, Capt. John, 1st Bn, The Worcestershire Regt., Berlin-Kladow. *Maj., ret'd; Brixham, Devon.*

Howarth, S/S/M Herbert "Sam," 11th (Prince Albert's Own) Hussars, Berlin-Grunewald. *Caretaker, ret'd; Andover, Hants.*

Hughes, Maj. Ronald, Assistant Provost Marshal (Special Investigation Branch), Berlin-Charlottenburg. *Security consultant, North London.*

Hurry, S/Ldr John, O.C., No. 51 Squadron, RAF, Wunsdorf. *G/Capt. ret'd; Ministry of Defence, Halton, Bucks.*

Jenkins, P/O Roy, No. 24 Squadron, RAF, Wunsdorf. *G/Capt. HQ, RAF, Germany.*

[Johnson, W/Cdr Hugh, Chief of Operations, Flight Refuelling Ltd., Tarrant Rushton-Wunsdorf-Fuhlsbüttel. *Ret'd; Wimborne Minster, Dorset.*]

Johnstone, S/Ldr Andrew, O.C., No. 30 Squadron, RAF, Wunsdorf-Fassberg, Lübeck. *HQ Air Cadets, Brampton, Cambs.*

Jones, Harold B., Operations Officer, British Overseas Airways Corporation, Fuhlsbüttel. *Statistician, International Aviation Services, Gatwick, W. Sussex.*

Jones, Pte Llewellyn, R.A.S.C. Supply Dept., Lübeck. *Stocking factory supervisor, Millom, Cumbria.*

Joslin, Brigadier Stanley, Director of Mechanical Engineering, HQ, British Army of the Rhine, Bad Oeynhausen. *Maj.-Gen., ret'd; Uckfield, Sussex.*

Kilburn, Radio Officer John, Airflight Ltd., Wunsdorf. *Senior Air Traffic Controller, Blackpool Airport, Lancs.*

Knox, R.S.M. Harold "Knocker," 1st Bn, The Worcestershire Regt., Berlin-Kladow. *Maj., ret'd: Secretary, the Worcestershire Regiments' Association, Worcester.*

Lea, Boy George, 1st Bn, The Worcestershire Regt., Berlin-Kladow/Sakrow. *Metalworker, Worcester.*

Leigh, Pilot 1 George, No. 51 Squadron, RAF, Wunsdorf. *Pilot, Ghana Airways, Accra.*

Leman, Lt. Richard, 1st Bn, The Worcestershire Regt., Berlin-Kladow. *Lt.-Col., HQ School of Infantry, Warminster, Wilts.*

Lennan, Elizabeth, Berlin-Spandau. *Housewife, Cranbrook, Kent.*

Lennan, Maj. Niall, 1st Bn, The Queen's Own Regt., Berlin-Spandau. *Ret'd; near Cranbrook, Kent.*

Lynch-Staunton, Maj. Anthony, 1st Bn, The Queen's Own Regt., Berlin-Spandau. *Building society executive, Bristol, Avon.*

McArthur, Capt. Arthur, 1st Bn, The Norfolk Regt., Berlin-Spandau. *Occupation unknown, West London.*

Macer, L/Cpl. John, R.A.S.C., RAF, Schleswigland. *Traveling representative, Harlow, Essex.*

Mahoney, Capt. George, Westminster Airways, Fuhlsbüttel-Schleswigland. *Pilot, British Airways, Hillingdon, Middx.*

Manning, F/Lt. Jim, No. 30 Squadron, RAF, Wunsdorf-Lübeck. *Schoolteacher, Blandford Forum, Dorset.*

Marsden, Maj. Norman, 1st Bn, The Queen's Own Regt., Berlin-Spandau. *Ret'd; near Bath, Avon.*

Milward, Anthony, General Manager, British European Airways, Continental Division. *Kt. (1966); chairman, London Tourist Board.*

Moody, S/Ldr Ernest, O.C., No. 206 Squadron, RAF, Wunsdorf. *Inland Revenue valuation officer, Guildford, Surrey.*

Murrell, Flight Engineer Charles, British South American Airways, Wunsdorf. *Technical Director, Aviation Traders, Southend-on-Sea, Essex.*

O'Day, Sgt. Terry, 76th Air Freight Co., Wunsdorf. *Professor of Palmistry, Brighton, Sussex.*

Ormerod, First Officer Dennis, Ciros Aviation, Fuhlsbüttel–Flight Refuelling Ltd., Wunsdorf. *Pilot, British West Indian Airways, Port-of-Spain, Trinidad.*

Pascall, Cpl. Eric, RAF, Fassberg. *Electronics engineer, Watford, Herts.*

Patrickson, Capt. Dennis, 1st Bn, The Worcestershire Regt., Berlin-Kladow. *Col., ret'd; Ministry of Defence, Chessington, Surrey.*

Payn, S/Ldr Tony, O.C., No. 230 Squadron, RAF, Finkenwerder. *Bank employee, Aldwick, Sussex.*

Pettit, First Officer John, Westminster Airways, Fassberg-Lübeck-Fuhlsbüttel-Schleswigland. *Pilot, British Airways, Marlow, Bucks.*

[Piper, W/Cdr Tim, RAF, Gatow. *Air Marshal, ret'd, KBE (1968); near Devizes, Wilts.*]

Pitman, Maj. Tommy, O.C. 11th (Prince Albert's Own) Hussars, Berlin-Grunewald. *Managing director, Malt roasting company, Masham, N. Yorks.*

Rainsford, G/Capt. Frederick, Air Ministry, London; Deputy Director Transport Operations. *A/Cdre, ret'd; RAF Benevolent Fund, London.*

Reynolds, Capt. John, 1st Bn, The Worcestershire Regt., Berlin-Kladow. *School bursar, Bromsgrove, Herefs & Worcs.*

Robertson, Lady (Edith), Ostenvalde; Berlin-Grunewald. *Far Oakridge, Glos.*

Rowland, Sgt. Henry, R.A.S.C., Celle-Fassberg-Gatow. *Occupation unknown, Northampton, Northants.*

Salter, S/Ldr Arthur "Pop," O.C., No. 46 Squadron, RAF, Wunsdorf-Fassberg-Lübeck. *Textile executive, Croydon, Surrey.*

Samson, G/Capt. Bryan, Senior Technical Staff Officer, No. 46 Group (Advanced) HQ, Buckeburg. *Ret'd; near Dorking, Surrey.*

Sheldon, Maj. Laurence, 1st Bn, The Queen's Own Regt., Berlin-Spandau. *Lt.-Col., ret'd; near Yeovil, Somerset.*

Smith, S/Ldr George, O.C., No. 511 Squadron, RAF, Wunsdorf. *W/Cdr ret'd; bank employee, Brixham, Devon.*

Smith, S/Ldr Thurston, Chief Operations Officer, Kearsley Airways, Stansted, Essex. *Ret'd; Richmond, Surrey.*

Stapleton, Signaller II John, No. 10 Squadron, RAF, Wunsdorf. *Films Division, British Council, London.*

Stephenson, G/Capt. John, O.C., RAF Station, Celle. *Air Vice-Marshal, ret'd; Dymock. Glos.*

Stratton, Maj.-Gen. William, Chief of Staff, HQ, British Army of the Rhine, Bad Oeynhausen. *Lt.-Gen. ret'd, KCB (1957); Midhurst, Sussex.*

Swan, Maj.-Gen. Dennis, Chief Engineer, HQ, British Army of the Rhine, Bad Oeynhausen. *Ret'd; Chichester, Sussex.*

Tetlow, Edwin, "The Daily Telegraph," Berlin-Dahlem. *Author, Alligerville, N.Y.*

Tetlow, Kay, "The Star," Berlin-Dahlem. *Housewife, Alligerville, N.Y.*

Thickins, Reg, International Voluntary Service for Peace, Berlin-Grunewald. *Social worker, ret'd; West London.*

Tremarco, A.C.1. Danny, No. 54 Rifle Squadron, RAF Regt., Gatow. *Unemployed, Liverpool, Merseyside.*

Turner-Cain, Lt.-Col. George, O.C., 1st Bn, The Norfolk Regt., Berlin-Spandau, 1947–48. *Maj.-Gen., ret'd; chairman, maltsters, Stiffkey, Norfolk.*

[Waite, A/Cdre Reginald, Berlin-Charlottenburg: Commander, Airlift HQ. *Ret'd; near Southampton, Hants.*]

Walmsley, Acting Air Marshal Hugh, Air Ministry, London: Deputy Chief of Air Staff. *Air Marshal, ret'd, KCB (1952); Lymington, Hants.*

Whalin, L.A.C. David, York Servicing Flight, RAF, Wunsdorf. *Blacksmith, Horsmonden, Kent.*

Wharton, Lt.-Col. George, Head, British European Airways Charter Section, London. *Executive, Diners Club, London.*

Whitefoord, Lt.-Col. Penry, Berlin: Magistrat-Liaison. *Col., ret'd; Exmouth, Devon.*

Wilson, Lt. Edward, 1st Bn, The Worcestershire Regt., Berlin-Kladow. *Col., ret'd; Military Adviser, Emirate of Abu Dhabi, U.A.R.*

Woodroffe, Station Supt. William, British European Airways, Gatow, Jan. 1949–. *Photo-journalist, Hale, Cheshire.*

Wright, Mary, British European Airways, Gatow. *Housewife, near Leatherhead, Surrey.*

Yarde, G/Capt. Brian, O.C., RAF Station, Gatow. *Air Vice-Marshal, ret'd; near Andover, Hants.*

THE BERLINERS

Alker, Edith. Tempelhof: Inneres Mission. *Social worker.*

Arnold, Ella. Neukölln. *Pensioner.*

Arnold, Kurt. Gatow. *Wine merchant.*

Bach, Otto. Lankwitz. *Senator, ret'd.*

Baillieu, Werner. Tegel-Lübars-Tempelhof. *Engine locksmith.*
Balczau, Hans. Neukölln. *Civil servant, ret'd.*
Bartsch, Elsa. Tempelhof. *Occupation unknown.*
Blös, Dr. Dietrich. Public health officer, Reinickendorf. *President, German Red Cross, West Berlin.*
Böhme, Herbert. Mitte. *Savings bank director, ret'd.*
Borries, Siegfried. Charlottenburg. *Concertmaster.*
Brandt, Katharina. City Hall Liaison, U.S. Military Govt. *Secretary.*
Brauner, Arthur. Dahlem. *Film producer.*
Brickwell-Graeber, Marie-Luise. Lichterfelde. *Lawyer.*
von Broecker, Paul Michael. Dahlem: Free University. *Lawyer.*
Coper, Helmut. Dahlem: Free University. *Professor of Pharmacology.*
Derigs, Margot. Charlottenburg. *Broadcaster.*
Dürr, Hans-Jochen. Frohnau. *Accountant.*
Englebrecht, Eva. Dahlem. *Translator, Supreme Restitution Court.*
Ettlich, Gerhard. Schöneberg. *Florist.*
Felgentreff, Kurt. Tegel-Tempelhof. *Journalist.*
Fentrosz, Dora. Zehlendorf: Zinnowald Hospital. *Nurse.*
Fischer, Eva. Sachsenhausen. *Police official.*
Flatow, Curth. Wilmersdorf. *Dramatist.*
Foljanty, Klaus. Grünau-Steglitz. *Executive, confectionery manufacturers.*
Friedrich, Dr. B.A. Westend Hospital. *Surgeon.*
Fritz. Bruno. Wilmersdorf. *Actor.*
Ganz, Hildegard. RAF Gatow. *Housewife.*
Gatz Bailey, Gisela. Kladow. *Lecturer, Slough, England.*
Gottfried, Robert. Lankwitz. *Grocer.*
Graf, Jurgen. Schöneberg. *Executive, RIAS.*
Gross, Walter. Grunewald. *Actor.*
Grund, Wolfgang. Lichterfelde. *Manager, British Airways.*
Grünewald, Käthe. Kladow. *Secretary.*
Haarmann, Gudrun. Wilmersdorf. *Ret'd.*
Hahn, Anneliese. Gatow. *Motor rally driver.*
Hahn, Hans-Joachim. Tempelhof. *Mortician.*
Harder, Rudolf. Steglitz. *Fireman.*
Hartwich, Horst. Dahlem: Free University. *University official.*
Hartwich, Klaus. Wilmersdorf. *Boardinghouse proprietor.*
Hauck, Heinz. Tegel. *Air traffic controller.*
Heim, Dr. Wilhelm. Wedding: Rudolf-Virchow Hospital. *Surgeon.*
Helbig, Renate. Wannsee. *Vocational teacher.*
Herstatt, Cornelia. Tiergarten. *Editor.*

Hess, Otto. Dahlem: Free University. *Publisher.*
Hesse, Eberhard. Wannsee. *Ret'd.*
Hiller, Elisabeth. Siemenstadt. *Curtain maker, Pudsey, England.*
Jeschke, Ewald. Steglitz. *Greengrocer.*
Jungtow, Herta. Wittenau. *Housewife.*
Karge, Walter. Lichterfelde. *Bank manager.*
Kästner, Else. Tegel. *Pensioner.*
Kay, Ella. Prenzlauer Berg-Schöneberg. *Senator, ret'd.*
Keilbach, Richard. Frohnau. *Nursing-home proprietor.*
Kersten, Hans Ulrich. Charlottenburg. *Journalist.*
Keul, Heinrich. Grünau-Charlottenburg. *Senator, ret'd.*
Knade, Harry. Charlottenburg. *Plumber.*
Knorr, Herbert. Tempelhof. *Occupation unknown.*
Kotowski, Georg, Dahlem: Free University. *Professor of Philosophy.*
Krappe, Edith. Mitte. *Party secretary, SPD.*
Kressmann, Willy. Kreuzberg. *Mayor, ret'd.*
Kruger, Helmut Otto. Mitte. *Chief Postmaster, ret'd.*
Kubicky, Carol. Dahlem: Free University. *Professor of Neurology.*
Kuhnohl, Martin. Steglitz. *Jeweler.*
Kunse, Carl. Grunewald. *Butler, ret'd.*
Kunse, Maria. Halensee. *Housewife.*
Küssner, Valeska. Spandau. *Housewife.*
Lasson, Gerhard. Mitte. *Mayor, ret'd.*
Lerch, Josef. Tegel. *Policeman, ret'd.*
Leü, Eberhard. RAF Gatow. *Cabin Services Supt., British Airways, West Germany.*
Mattick, Kurt. Mitte. *Member, Federal Diet.*
Meissner, Karl-Heinz. Tempelhof. *Stonemason.*
von Metnitz, Ilse. Reinickendorf. *Calisthenics teacher.*
Meyer, Margot. Kreuzberg. *Insurance worker.*
Michaelis, Günter. Hermsdorf. *Driving instructor.*
Michaelsen, Inga. Charlottenburg. *Pensioner.*
Miehe, Horst. Tempelhof. *Police commissioner.*
Milde, Rudolf. Tempelhof. *Baker.*
Mittelstädt, Anni. Neukölln. *Pensioner.*
Mühle, Horst. Steglitz. *Confectionery manufacturer.*
Mühle, Ilse. Steglitz. *Housewife.*
Mundt, Kurt. Spandau. *Police commissioner, ret'd.*
Neumann, Johannes. Schöneberg: *Chimney sweep.*
Niensdorff, Eva-Maria. Wilmersdorf. *Housewife.*
Odrowski, Max. Wilmersdorf. *Druggist.*
Osadczuk-Korab, Dr. Bogan. Charlottenburg: Polish Military Mission. *East European Institute, Free University.*

208

Ottong, Willy. Charlottenburg. *Shoemaker.*
Pischke, Heinz. RAF Gatow. *Insurance official.*
Pizold, Herta. Wittenau. *Housewife.*
Reichert, Elisabeth. Wilmersdorf. *Apartment-house owner.*
Reinke, Gerhard. Weissensee-Charlottenburg. *Police commissioner.*
Rerup, Wilhelmina. Halensee. *Factory worker, Millom, England.*
Richter, Dr. Hans. Zehlendorf. *Industrial chemist, ret'd.*
Richter, Johann. Wilmersdorf. *Banker, ret'd.*
Rix, Hans-Jürgen. Friedrichshain. *Police commissioner.*
Rojek, Alfred. Neukölln. *Alderman, ret'd.*
Roloff, Alfons. Gatow. *Occupation unknown.*
Rymarczik, Ingeborg. Neukölln. *Housewife, Liverpool, N.Y., U.S.A.*
Schieckel, Dr. Fritz. Grunewald. *Pediatrician.*
Schieckel, Vera. Grunewald. *Housewife.*
Schilling, Carl. Wittenau. *Free-lance translator.*
Schreck, Ferdinand. Tegel. *Laundry proprietor.*
Schroth, Anneliese. Kladow. *Housewife, Hale, England.*
Schulze, Peter. Zehlendorf. *Current Affairs Director, Radio Free Berlin.*
Schwantke, Irmgard. Neukölln. *Occupation unknown.*
Schwennicke, Karl-Hubert. Pankow-Dahlem. *Executive, Siemens.*
Seepold, Gerhard. Tempelhof. *Machine toolmaker.*
Sieben, Richard. Charlottenburg. *Representative, West German Economics Ministry.*
Sonnenfeld, Hans. Tempelhof. *Newspaper proprietor.*
Sönnichsen, Helga. Fuhlsbüttel Airport, Hamburg. *Planning Superintendent, British Airways, West Germany.*
Stamm, Herbert. Wilmersdorf. *Doctor of medicine.*
Stumm, Dr. Johannes. Mitte-Kreuzberg. *Chief of Police, ret'd.*
Suhr, Susanne. Wilmersdorf. *Journalist.*
Tausch, Erika. Tempelhof. *Secretary.*
Theuner, Otto. Mitte. *Mayor of West Berlin, ret'd.*
Träger, Lenchen. Neukölln. *Buffet attendant.*
Tübke, Fritz. Kreuzberg. *Tie manufacturer.*
Ungnad, Erich. RAF Gatow. *Bank clerk.*
Unruh, Herbert. Charlottenburg. *Engineer.*
Unruh, Margret. Charlottenburg. *Housewife.*
Urban, Dr. Hans-Georg. Mitte-Kreuzberg. *Chief of Protocol, Berlin Senate.*
Vater, Gerd. Tegel. *Occupation unknown.*
Wagner, Rudolf-Günter. Wilmersdorf. *Free-lance broadcaster.*
Wallenda, Maria. Grunewald. *Ret'd, London, England.*
Wehlak, Adolf. Schmargendorf. *Hairdresser.*

Wiede, Otto. Wedding. *Welder.*
Winiarz, Luise. Tempelhof. *Butcher.*
Winkens, Maria. Nikolassee. *Actress.*
Wolff, Jeanette. Britz Sud. *President, Jewish Christian Brotherhood.*
Zellermayer, Heinz. Charlottenburg. *Secretary, Berlin Hoteliers' Guild.*
Zerndt, Leni. Wedding. *Housewife.*
Zerndt, Wilhelm. Wedding. *Town planner.*

THE FRENCH

Ganeval, General de Brigade Jean, Commandant, Allied *Kommandatura* (French Element) & G.O.C., French Troops, Berlin, 1947–49. *Général de corps d'armée, ret'd; Paris.*

Bibliography

Printed Sources

Abosch, Heinz.   *The Menace of the Miracle.* London: Colletts, 1962.

Acheson, Dean.   *Sketches from Life.* London: Hamish Hamilton, 1961.

————.   *Present at the Creation.* London: Hamish Hamilton, 1969.

Adams, Charles.   "Berlin Airlift: Transport Air Power in Action," in *Aviation Week*, New York, February 28, 1949.

Adler, Hans.   *Berlin in jenen Tagen: Berichte aus der Zeit von 1945–48.* Berlin: Kongress-Verlag, 1959.

Airlift Berlin.   Berlin: Verlags GMBH, 1949.

"Airlift to Berlin,"   in *National Geographic,* Washington, D.C., May 1, 1949.

Aldunate Phillips, Raul.   *Reportaje a Berlin.* Santiago, Chile: Zig-Zag, 1951.

Alsop, Stewart.   *The Center.* London: Hodder & Stoughton, 1968.

Ambrose, Stephen E.   *Eisenhower and Berlin, 1945: The Decision to Halt at the Elbe.* New York: W.W. Norton, 1967.

Attlee, Clement R.   *As It Happened.* London: William Heinemann, 1954.

Avro on the Airlift.   Manchester: A.V. Roe & Co., n.d.

B.A.O.R. Wife.   "Siege," in *The New Statesman and Nation,* London, August 14, 1948.

211

Barnes, C.H. *Bristol Aircraft Since 1910*. London: Putnam, 1964.

Bennett, Jackson. "The German Currency Reform," in *Annals of the American Academy of Political and Social Sciences*, Philadelphia, January 1950.

Bennett, Lowell. *Berlin Bastion*. Frankfurt: Fred Rudl, 1951.

Berger, Alfred. *Berlin, 1945–63*. Munich: Gersbach, 1964.

Berlin—ABC. Berlin: Presse-und Informationsamt, 1968.

Berlin Airlift. London: H.M. Stationery Office, 1949.

Berlin Airlift. London: Lancashire Aircraft Corporation, n.d.

Berlin, 1945–8: Contributions to the History of the City. Leipzig: VEB Edition, 1961.

Berlin: Quellen und Dokumente, 1945–51, Vol. II. Berlin: Heinz Spitzing Verlag, 1964.

Berlin Sector: A Four Year Report. Berlin: Office of U.S. Military Government, 1949.

Berlin, The City That Would Not Die. By the editors of *The Army Times*. New York: Dodd Mead, 1967.

Berliner Schicksal, 1945–52. Berlin: Büro für Gesamtberliner Fragen, 1952.

Bess, Demaree. *"American Viceroy in Germany,"* in *The Saturday Evening Post*, Philadelphia, May 3–10, 1947.

———. *"Will We Be Pushed Out of Berlin?"* in *The Saturday Evening Post*, July 31, 1948.

———. *"What Did the Airlift Really Prove?"* in *The Saturday Evening Post*, June 25, 1949.

Bird, Lt.-Col. Eugene. *The Loneliest Man in the World*. London: Secker & Warburg, 1974.

Birdwood, Lt.-Col. Lord. *The Worcestershire Regiment, 1922–50*. Aldershot: Gale & Polden, 1952.

Bishop, Jim. *F.D.R's Last Year*. London: Hart-Davis MacGibbon Ltd., 1975.

Bohlen, Charles E. *Witness to History*. London: Weidenfeld & Nicolson, 1973.

Borneman, Ernest. "Back to Berlin," in *Harper's Magazine*, New York, August 1948.

Bradley, Gen. Omar. *A Soldier's Story*. New York: Henry Holt, 1951.

Brandt, Willy (with Leo Lania). *My Road to Berlin*. London: Peter Davies, 1960.

———(with Richard Löwenthal). *Ernst Reuter*. Munich: Kindler Verlag, 1957.

Brett-Smith, Richard. *Berlin '45*. London: Macmillan, 1966.

Brodrick, Alan Houghton. *Danger Spot of Europe.* London: Hutchinson, 1951.

Burchett, Wilfred G. *The Cold War in Germany.* Melbourne: World Unity Publications, 1950.

Butler, Ewan. *City Divided:* Berlin 1955. London: Sidgwick & Jackson, 1955.

Byford-Jones, Lt.-Col. W. *Berlin Twilight.* London: Hutchinson, 1947.

Byrnes, James F. *Speaking Frankly.* New York: Harper, 1947.

Charles, Max. *Berlin Blockade.* London: Allan Wingate, 1959.

Christie, John. "Tunner Outlines Ideal Cargo Plane," in *Aviation Week,* New York, January 17, 1949.

Clark, Delbert. *Again the Goose Step.* Indianapolis: Bobbs-Merrill, 1949.

Clay, Gen. Lucius D. *Decision in Germany.* Garden City, N.Y.: Doubleday, 1950.

―――. *Germany and the Fight for Freedom.* Cambridge, Mass: Harvard University Press, 1950.

―――. *The Papers of General Lucius D. Clay,* 2 vols. (ed. Jean Edward Smith). Bloomington, Ind.: Indiana University Press, 1974.

Clemens, Diana Shaver. *Yalta.* New York: Oxford University Press, 1970.

Collicr, David, and Glaser, Kurt (ed). *Berlin and the Future of Eastern Europe.* Chicago: Henry Regnery, 1963.

Colvin, Ian. "The Concentration Camp Berlin," in *The National Review,* London, January 1949.

―――. "Berlin and Europe," in *The National Review,* August 1948.

Conin, Helmut. *Gelandet in Berlin.* Berlin: Berliner Flughafen Gesellschaft, 1974.

Conlan, William H. *Berlin beset and bedevilled.* New York: Fountainhead, 1963.

Connell, Brian. *Watcher on the Rhine.* London: Weidenfeld and Nicholson, 1957.

Cookman, Aubrey. "Life Line to Berlin," in *Popular Mechanics,* Chicago, February 1949.

Cookridge, E.H. *Gehlen, Spy of the Century.* London: Hodder & Stoughton, 1971.

Crawley, Aidan. *The Rise of Western Germany.* London: William Collins, 1973.

Daniell, Raymond. "Berlin—City of Ruins, Doubt and Fear," in *The New York Times Magazine,* April 25, 1948.

213

Davidson, Bill. "The Surprising Mr. Jessup," in *Collier's*, New York, July 30, 1949.

Davidson, Eugene. *The Death and Life of Germany*. New York: Alfred A. Knopf, 1958.

Davison, W. Phillips. *The Berlin Blockade*. Princeton, N. J.: Princeton University Press, 1958.

———. "The Human Side of the Berlin Airlift," in *The Air Force Review*, Autumn 1958.

Del Vayo, J. Alvarez. "Inside Berlin," in *The Nation*, New York, March 5, 1949.

Detzer, Karl. "Riding the Berlin Airlift," in *Forum*, New York, March 1949.

———. "Clay of Berlin," in *The Reader's Digest*, Pleasantville, N.Y. October 1948.

Djilas, Milovan. *Conversations with Stalin*. London: Rupert Hart-Davis, 1962.

Dolivet, Louis. "Berlin's Only Open Road," in *United Nations World,* New York, August 1948.

Donner, Jörn. *Report from Berlin*. Bloomington, Ind.: Indiana University Press, 1961.

Donnison, F.S.V. *Civil Affairs and Military Government: North-West Europe, 1944–46*. London: H.M. Stationery Office, 1961.

Donovan, Frank. *Bridge in the Sky.* New York: David McKay Co., 1968.

Druène, Bernard. *Français à Berlin*. Berlin: G.F.C.C., 1949.

Easum, Chester B. *Half Century of Conflict*. New York: Harper, 1952.

Ebsworth, Raymond. *Restoring Democracy in Germany: the British Contribution*. London: Stevens and Sons, 1960.

Faviell, Frances. *The Dancing Bear*. London: Rupert Hart-Davis, 1954.

Feis, Herbert. *Between War and Peace*. Princeton, N. J.: Princeton University Press, 1960.

———. *Churchill, Roosevelt and Stalin*. Princeton, N. J.: Princeton University Press, 1957.

Fisher, Paul W. "Berlin Airlift," in *The Bee Hive* (quarterly). East Hartford, Conn: United Aircraft Corporation, Fall 1948.

Fishman, Jack. *The Seven Men of Spandau*. London: W. H. Allen, 1954.

Ford, Corey. *Donovan of O.S.S.* London: Robert Hale, 1971.

The Forrestal Diaries (ed. Walter Millis Y.E.S. Duffield). New York: Viking Press, 1951.

Foster, Major R.C.G. *History of the Queen's Royal Regiment, 1924–48.* Aldershot: Gale and Polden, 1961.

Fraenkel, Heinrich. "Berlin and the Russian Zone," in *The Political Quarterly*, London, October–December 1947.

———. "Money Talks in Western Germany," in *The New Statesman and Nation*, London, September 4, 1948.

———. *A Nation Divided.* London: Dennis Yates, 1949.

France, Boyd. "French Feeble in Berlin Air Test," in *Aviation Week*, New York, July 26, 1948.

Franklin, William M. *Zonal Boundaries and Access to Berlin.* Washington, D.C.: Department of State, n.d.

Frederiksen, Oliver J. *The American Military Occupation of Germany, 1945–52.* Washington, D.C.: U.S. Army, 1953.

Frend, W.H.C. "Berlin, Autumn, 1948," in *Journal of the Queen's Royal Regiment*, November 1948.

Fricker, John E. "Feeding Berlin by Air," in *The Aeroplane*, London, July 23, 1948.

Friedensburg, Ferdinand. *Berlin—Schicksel und Aufgabe.* Berlin: Pädagogischer Verlag Berthold Schulz, 1953.

Friedmann. Wolfgang. *The Allied Military Government of Germany.* London: Stevens and Sons, 1947.

Friedrich, Carl J. *American Experience in Military Government in World War II.* New York: Rinehart & Co., 1948.

Froelich, Michael H. "Air Lift Breaks the Berlin Blockade," in *Flying*, Chicago, October 1948.

Germany, 1947–49: The Story in Documents. (Dept. of State Pubn. 3556). Washington, D.C.: Government Printing Office, 1950.

Gimbel, John. *The American Occupation of Germany.* Stanford, Cal.: Stanford University Press, 1968.

———. *A German Community under American Occupation.* Stanford, Cal.: Stanford University Press, 1961.

Gladwyn, Lord. *Memoirs.* London: Weidenfeld and Nicholson, 1972.

Glaser, Louis. "Berlin Divided," in *The Military Government Information Bulletin*, October 19, 1948.

Golay, John Ford. *The Founding of the Federal Republic of Germany.* Chicago: University of Chicago Press, 1958.

Gratke, Charles. "Yesterday We Ate," in *The Christian Science Monitor Magazine*, Boston, January 17, 1948.

Grünig, Ferdinand. *Die Westberliner Wirtschaft, 1949–51.* Berlin: Duncher and Humblot, 1952.

Habe, Hans. *Our Love Affair with Germany.* New York: G. P. Putnam, 1953.

215

Haffner, Sebastian. "The Importance of Berlin," in *World Review*, London, February, 1948.

Hageman, Otto. *Berlin the Capital*. Berlin: Arani, 1956.

Hale, William Harlan. "General Clay—On His Own," in *Harper's Magazine*, New York, December 1948.

Halle, Louis J. *The Cold War As History*. London: Chatto & Windus, 1967.

Hare-Scott, Kenneth. "Berlin," in *The Norseman*, London, May–June 1948.

Hay, Lorna. "How the Airlift Was Operated," in *Picture Post*, London, July 17, 1948.

Heidelmeyer, Wolfgang, and Hindrichs, Guenter. *Documents on Berlin, 1943–63*. Munich: R. Oldenbourg Verlag, 1963.

Heller, Deane. *The Berlin Crisis*. Derby, Conn.: Monarch Books, 1961.

Herbert, Maj.-Gen. E.O. "The Cold War in Berlin," in *Journal of the Royal United Service Institution*, London, May 1949.

Hillgruber, Andreas. *Berlin: Dokumente, 1944–61*. Darmstadt: Stephan Verlagsgesellschaft, 1961.

Hillman, William. *Mr. President*. London: Hutchinson, 1952.

Hirsch, Felix. "Lessons of the Berlin Crisis," in *Forum*, New York, October 1948.

Hofmann, Dr. Wolfgang. *West Berlin—the isolated city*, in *Journal of Contemporary History*.

Holborn, Hajo. *American Military Government: Its Organization and Policies*. Washington, D.C.: Infantry Journal Press, 1947.

Holbrook, Sabra. *Capital Without a Country*. New York: Coward McCann, 1961.

Howley, Gen. Frank. *Berlin Command*. New York: G.P. Putnam, 1950.

———. (with Collie Small). "My Six Years' War with the Reds," in *Collier's*, New York, November 5–December 3, 1949.

———. (with J.P. McEvoy) "I've Talked 1600 Hours with the Russians," in *The Reader's Digest*, New York, May 1949.

Hughes, Emmet. "Berlin Under Siege," in *Life*, New York, July 19, 1948.

Hull, Cordell. *The Memoirs of Cordell Hull*. New York: Macmillan, 1948.

Hunter, David R., and Studd, Howard R. "Post War Social Services in Berlin," in *The Social Services Review*, Chicago, June 1948.

Hynd, John, M.P. "Tension in Berlin," in *Picture Post*, London, July 10, 1948.

Jackson, A.J. *Avro Aircraft Since 1908.* London: Putnam, 1965.

Jackson, Peter. *The Sky Tramps.* London: Souvenir Press, 1965.

Jacobs, Karl E. *Berlin.* Garden City, N.Y.: Doubleday, 1962.

Jessup, Philip C. "Park Avenue Diplomacy—Ending the Berlin Blockade," in *Political Science Quarterly,* New York, September 1972.

———. "The Berlin Blockade," in *Foreign Affairs,* New York, October 1971.

Joesten, Joachim. *They Call It Intelligence.* New York: Abelard-Schumann, 1963.

Kahn, Arthur D. *Betrayal.* Warsaw: Book and Knowledge Publishers, 1961.

Kahn, E. J., Jr. "A Reporter in Germany: *Die Luftbrücke,*" in *The New Yorker,* May 14, 1949.

Kemp, Col. J.C., M.C. *History of the Royal Scots Fusiliers.* Glasgow: Robert Maclehose, 1963.

Kemp, Lt.-Cdr P.K. *History of the Royal Norfolk Regiment.* Norwich: Norfolk Regimental Association, 1953.

Kennan, George. *Memoirs.* London: Hutchinson, 1968.

Kindler, Helmut. *Berlin.* Berlin: Kindler, 1958.

King, H. F. "B.E.A. to Berlin," in *Flight,* London, September 30–October 7, 1948.

Klimov, Gregory. *The Terror Machine.* New York: Frederick A. Praeger, 1958.

Klös, Hans-Georg. *125 Jahre Zoo Berlin.* Berlin: Haude & Sperer, 1959.

Kluckhohn, Frank L. "Behind the Scenes in Berlin," in *The American Mercury,* New York, November 1948.

Kuter, Lt.-Gen. Lawrence S. *The Story of M.A.T.S.* Washington, D.C.: U.S. Govt. Printing Office, 1951.

Lampe, Albrecht. *Berlin: aus seiner Geschichte, 1945–47.* Berlin: Addressbuch-Gesellschaft, 1958.

Lang, Will. "Wind in Berlin," in *Life,* New York, May 17, 1948.

Leahy, Admiral William D. *I Was There.* New York: Whittlesey House, 1956.

LeMay, Lt. Gen. Curtis E. (with MacKinlay Kantor). *Mission with LeMay.* Garden City, N.Y.: Doubleday, 1965.

Lemmer, Ernst (ed.) *Berlin am Kreuzweg Europas.* Berlin: Haupt & Puttkamer, 1958.

Lie, Trygve. *In The Cause of Peace.* New York: Macmillan, 1954.

Leonhard, Wolfgang. *Child of the Revolution.* London: William Collins, 1957.

217

Litchfield, Edward H. *Governing Postwar Germany.* Ithaca: Cornell University Press, 1953.

Loewenheim, Francis L., Langley, Harold D., and Jonas, Manfred. *Roosevelt and Churchill: Their Secret Wartime Correspondence.* London: Barrie & Jenkins, 1975.

Logan, Andy. "Letter from Germany," in *The New Yorker,* May 8, 1949.

Ludvigsen, Sven, & Reunert, Willy. *Berlin: oen i det rode hav.* Copenhagen: Bramner and Korch, 1952.

Luftbrücke Berlin. Berlin: Arani Verlag, 1949.

McInnis, Edgar. *The Shaping of Post-War Germany.* London: J.M. Dent, 1960.

Malkin, Richard. "Two Hours to Tempelhof"; "Rhein-Main–Berlin Shuttle"; "One Short Hop, but . . ."; "From Hot War to Cold War"; "The 513th on the Go"; "This Is the 7350th," in *Air Transportation—Air Commerce,* June–December 1949.

Mander, John. *Berlin: The Eagle and the Bear.* London: Barrie and Rockcliff, 1959.

———. *Berlin: Hostage for the West.* Baltimore: Penguin Books, 1962.

Mattick, Paul. "Obsessions of Berlin," in *The Adelphi,* London, January–June, 1949.

Mee, Charles L., Jr. *Meeting at Potsdam.* London: Andre Deutsch, 1975.

Meimberg, Rudolf. *The Economic Development in West Berlin and in the Soviet Zone.* Berlin: Duncker and Humblot, 1952.

———. *The Economy of West Berlin.* Berlin: Duncker and Humblot, 1950.

Meissner, Boris. *Russland, die Westmächte und Deutschland.* Hamburg: H.H. Nolke Verlag, 1953.

Melvin, James. "Public Health—Berlin, 1946," in *The British Medical Journal,* London, September 13, 1947.

Mendelsohn, Peter. "The Berlin Plebiscite," in *The New Statesman and Nation,* London, December 4, 1948.

Merritt, Anna J., and Merritt, Richard L. *Public Opinion in Occupied Germany.* Chicago: University of Chicago Press, 1970.

Mezerik, Avraham G. *Berlin and Germany.* New York: International Review Service, 1962.

Middleton, Drew. "He Holds the Berlin Bridge," in *The New York Times Magazine,* July 4, 1948.

———. "New Courage Rises from Berlin's Ruins," in *The New York Times Magazine,* August 15, 1948.

————. "The Two Fronts in Germany," in *The New York Times Magazine*, December 12, 1948.

————. *The Struggle for Germany*. Indianapolis: Bobbs-Merrill, 1949.

Mitchell, David. "The Strain of the Airlift," in *Picture Post*, London, September 18, 1949.

Montgomery, John D. *Forced to Be Free: the Artificial Revolution in Germany and Japan*. Chicago: University of Chicago Press, 1957.

Monthly Reports of the Control Commission for Germany (British Element). Berlin: H.B. Control Commission for Germany, 1948–49.

Monthly Reports of the U.S. Military Governor. Berlin: Office of Military Government for Germany, 1948–49.

Moseley, Lt.-Col. Harry G. "Medical History of the Berlin Airlift," in *U.S. Armed Forces Medical Journal*, Washington, D.C., November 1950.

Mosely, Philip E. "Dismemberment of Germany: the Allied Negotiations from Yalta to Potsdam," in *Foreign Affairs*, New York, Vol. XXVIII, 1949–50.

————. "The Occupation of Germany: New Light on How the Zones Were Drawn," in *Foreign Affairs*, Vol. XXVIII, 1949–50.

————. *The Kremlin and World Politics*. New York: Vintage Russian Library, 1960.

Mühlen, Norbert. *The Return of Germany*. London: The Bodley Head, 1953.

Murphy, Charles. "The Berlin Airlift," in *Fortune*, New York, November 1948.

Murphy, Robert. *Diplomat Among Warriors*, London: William Collins, 1964.

Nauman, Lt. R.D., USN. "Medical Aspects of 'Operation Vittles'" in *Journal of Aviation Medicine*. St. Paul, Minn.: February 1951.

Nelson, Walter Henry. *The Berliners*. New York: David McKay Co., 1969.

Nettl, J. P. "Inside the Russian Zone, 1945–47," in *The Political Quarterly*, London, July 1948.

————. "Inside Russia's Germany: What Russia Did to Germany; Life in Russia's Germany," in *The New Republic*, New York, August 2–16, 1948.

————. *The Eastern Zone and Soviet Policy in Germany*, 1945–50. London: Oxford University Press, 1951.

Neumann, Franz. "Soviet Policy in Germany," in *Annals of the*

American Academy of Political and Social Science, Philadelphia, Vol. CCLXIII, 1949.

Nicolson, Sir Harold. *Diaries and Letters, 1945–62* (ed. Nigel Nicolson). London: Collins, 1968.

Notes on Blockade of Berlin 1948 from a British Viewpoint. Berlin: H.Q. British Troops. 1949.

Ode, Erik. *Der Kommissar und ich.* Munich: R.S. Schulz, 1972.

O'Donnell, James P. "The Mayor Russia Hates," in *The Saturday Evening Post*, Philadelphia, February 5, 1949.

von Oppen, Beate Ruhm (ed.). *Germany Under Occupation.* London: Oxford University Press, 1955.

"Orion." "The Berlin Airlift: Operation 'Plain Fare,' " in *Journal of the Royal United Service Institution,* London, February 1949.

Orton, Peter, and Scholz, Arno. *Outpost Berlin.* London: Orton Press, 1955.

Pakenham, Frank (Earl of Longford). *Born to Believe.* London: Jonathan Cape, 1953.

Pearcy, Arthur. *The Dakota.* London: Ian Allan, 1972.

Pearson, Drew. *The Drew Pearson Diaries, 1949–59* (ed. Tyler Abell). London: Jonathan Cape, 1974.

Peel, Doris. *The Inward Journey.* London: Victor Gollancz, 1954.

Plischke, Elmer. *Berlin: Development of Its Government and Administration.* Bad Godesberg-Mehlem: Office of the U.S. High Commissioner for Germany, 1952.

Pollock, J.K., Meisel, J.H., and Bretton, H.L. *Germany Under Occupation.* Ann Arbor, Mich.: George Wahr, 1949.

Prittie, Terence. *Germany Divided.* London: Hutchinson, 1961.

———. *Willy Brandt.* London: Weidenfeld and Nicolson, 1974.

Pudney, John. *The Seven Skies.* London: Putnam, 1959.

Ray, Cyril. "The Bloodless Battle," in *The Observer*, London, June 8–15, 1958.

Reuter, Ernst. "West Berlin Mayor Defies Reds," in *Life*, New York, May 15, 1950.

Reynolds, Quentin. "Toughest Cop in Berlin," in *Collier's*, New York, January 1, 1949.

———. "Rainbow Route to Berlin," in *Collier's*, September 25, 1948.

———. *Leave It to the People.* New York: Random House, 1949.

Richter, Gigi. "Berlin Letter," in *Horizon,* London, November 1948.

Riess, Curt. *Berlin! Berlin! 1945–53.* Berlin: Non-Stop-Bucherel, 1951.

220

————. *The Berlin Story.* New York: Dial Press, 1952.

van Rijn, Modestus. *Vorposten Berlin.* Berlin: Arani Verlag, 1950.

Robichon, Jacques (with J.V. Ziegelmeyer). *L'Affaire de Berlin.* Paris: Gallimard, 1959.

Robson, Charles B. (ed.). *Berlin—Pivot of German Destiny.* Chapel Hill, N.C.: University of North Carolina Press, 1960.

Rodrigo, Robert. *Berlin Airlift.* London: Cassell, 1960.

Rogge, Peter-Georg. *Die amerikanische Hilfe für Westberlin.* Tubingen: Mohr, 1959.

Ryan, Cornelius. *The Last Battle.* London: William Collins, 1966.

Sayre, Joel. "That Was Berlin," in *The New Yorker,* September 18–October 16, 1948.

Schafer, Emil. *Von Potsdam bis Bonn.* Lahr: Moritz Schauenberg Verlag, 1951.

Schatvet, Charles E. *Island in a Red Sea.* New York: Guide-Kalkhoff Burr, 1959.

Scholz, Arno. *Amerikaner in Berlin.* Berlin: Arani Verlag, 1963.

Settel, Arthur (ed.). *This Is Germany.* New York: William Sloane Associates, 1950.

Shears, David. *The Ugly Frontier.* London: Chatto & Windus, 1970.

Sherwood, Robert E. *Roosevelt and Hopkins* (2 vols). New York: Harper, 1948.

Shinwell, Emanuel. *Conflict Without Malice.* London: Odhams Press, 1955.

————. *I've Lived Through It All.* London: Gollancz, 1973.

Shirer, William. *End of a Berlin Diary.* New York: Alfred A. Knopf, 1947.

Shub, Boris. *The Choice.* New York: Duell, Sloan and Pearce, 1950.

Siepen, Howard. "Berliners Dauntless," in *The Christian Science Monitor Magazine,* Boston, November 13, 1948.

Slusser, Robert (ed.). *Soviet Economic Policy in Post-War Germany.* New York: Research Program on the U.S.S.R., 1953.

Small, Collie. "Berlin's Winter of Fear," in *Collier's,* New York, February 21, 1948.

Smith, Jean Edward. *The Defense of Berlin.* Baltimore: The Johns Hopkins University Press, 1963.

Smith, Walter Bedell. *My Three Years in Moscow.* Philadelphia: J. P. Lippincott, 1950.

Söhnker, Hans. *und kein Tag zuviel.* Hamburg: R. Gloss & Co., 1974.

The Soviet Occupation Zone of Germany, 1945–57. Bonn: Federal Ministry for All-German Affairs, 1954.

221

"A Special Study of 'Operation Vittles.'" New York: *Aviation Operations Magazine*, April 1949.

Speer, Albert. *Spandau: The Secret Diaries.* New York: Macmillan, 1976.

Speier, Hans. *Divided Berlin.* New York: Frederick Praeger, 1961.

Stahl, Walter (ed.). *The Politics of Post-War Germany.* New York: Frederick Praeger, 1963.

Stettinius, Edward. *Roosevelt and the Russians.* Garden City, N.Y.: Doubleday, 1949.

Stimson, Henry L., and Bundy, McGeorge. *On Active Service in Peace and War.* New York: Harper, 1947.

Strang, Lord. *Home and Abroad.* London: Andre Deutsch, 1956.

Stringer, Ann. "Berlin Today: One Family's Story," in *The New York Times Magazine*, January 2, 1949.

Stringer, Ann, and Berry, Lelah. "An Army Wife Lives Very Soft in Germany," in *The Saturday Evening Post*, Philadelphia, February 15, 1947.

Suhr, Susanne. *Otto Suhr.* Tubingen: J.C.B. Mohr (Paul Siebeck), 1957.

Tergit, Gabriele. "The Russians in Berlin," in *The Contemporary Review*, London, August 1948.

Tetlow, Edwin. *The United Nations.* London: Peter Owen, 1970.

Thayer, Charles. *The Unquiet Germans.* London: Michael Joseph, 1958.

Truman, Harry S. *Memoirs* (2 vols.). Garden City, N.Y.: Doubleday, 1955.

Truman, Margaret. *Harry S. Truman.* London: Hamish Hamilton, 1973.

Tumler, Franz. *Berlin: Geist und Gesicht.* Munich: Constantin-Verlag, 1953.

Tunner, Lt.-Gen. William (with Booton Herndon). *Over the Hump.* New York: Duell, Sloan and Pearce, 1964.

Ulam, Adam B. *Stalin, the Man and His Era.* London: Allen Lane, 1974.

Utley, Freda. "The Spirit of Berlin," in *The American Mercury*, March 1949.

———. *The High Cost of Vengeance.* Chicago: Henry Regnery, 1949.

Van Wagenen, R.W. "Cooperation and Controversy Among the Occupying Powers in Berlin," in *The Journal of Politics*, Gainesville, Fla., February 1948.

Wagner, Rainer. "Wenn ich noch daran denke," in *The Berliner Morgenpost*, November 4–December 1, 1973.

Walker, Alan. "Under Blockade," in *The Christian Century*, Chicago, December 8, 1948.

Wann, Marie di Mario. *Dependent Baggage.* New York: Macmillan, 1955.

"Watchdogs of Berlin," in *Picture Post*, London, August 7, 1948.

Wechsberg, Joseph. "Letter from Berlin," in *The New Yorker*, August 5, 1950.

————. "A Reporter at Large: The Lord Mayor of Berlin," in *The New Yorker*, October 7, 1950.

Weir, Sir Cecil. *Civilian Assignment.* London: Methuen, 1953.

Werth, Alexander. "The Russians and Berlin," in *The Nation*, New York, July 10, 1948.

West, Rebecca. *A Train of Powder.* New York: Viking Press, 1955.

White, Egbert. "Where Freight Cars Earned Their Wings," in *United Nations World*, New York, June 1949.

White, Theodore. *Fire in the Ashes.* New York: William Sloane Associates, 1953.

Whyte, Anne. "Quadripartite Rule in Berlin," in *International Affairs*, London, January 1947.

Williams, Francis. *A Prime Minister Remembers.* London: William Heinemann, 1961.

Williams, J. Emlyn. "Will Berlin Rise Again?," in *The Christian Science Monitor Magazine*, Boston, July 10, 1948.

Willis, Roy. *The French in Germany, 1945–49.* Stanford, Calif.: Stanford University Press.

Windsor, Philip. *City on Leave.* London: Chatto & Windus, 1963.

Zink, Harold. *The United States in Germany, 1944–55.* Princeton, N.J.: D. Van Nostrand, 1957.

————. *American Military Government in Germany.* New York: Macmillan, 1947.

Manuscript Sources

Allied Control Commission: Minutes of 82nd Meeting. (Courtesy Col. A.P. Hodges)

Atkinson, Littleton B. *Communist influence on French Rearmament.* (Maxwell AFB, Alabama, Documentary Research Studies Institute, Air University)

Attlee, Earl. *Correspondence Concerning Berlin Blockade.* (University College, Oxford)

Berlin City Assembly: Stenographic Records of Meetings, 1948. (Landesarchiv, Berlin)

Brickwell-Graeber, Marie-Luise. *Letters from Berlin, 1948–50.* (Courtesy Frau Brickwell-Graeber)

Brundage, S/Sgt. Frank. *Letters from Wiesbaden.* (Courtesy Frank Brundage)

Clifford, Clark. *American Relations with the Soviet Union: an aide-memoire for President Truman.* (Courtesy Clark Clifford)

Collins, W/Cdr W.M. *Royal Air Force, Celle: an Unpublished Study.* (Courtesy W/Cdr S.D. Billman)

Combined Airlift Task Force: Preliminary Analysis of Lessons Learned, June, 1949. (Department of the Air Force, Air Force Museum, Wright-Patterson AFB, Ohio)

Crompton, Lt. John. *A Berlin Diary, 1948–49.* (Courtesy Lt. Col. Crompton)

Dalton, Rt. Hon Hugh. *The Dalton Diaries, 1948–49.* (British Library of Political and Economic Science, London)

Draper, Maj. Gen. *Berlin Airlift Correspondence with Gen. Lucius Clay, Gen. Albert Wedemeyer and Others.* (Courtesy the late Maj. Gen. Draper)

Helbig, Renate. *Ludwig Helbig's Letters from Berlin, 1948–49.* (Courtesy Frau Renate Goedecke)

Hodges, Col. Alexander Phelps. *Unpublished Notes on the Berlin Blockade.* (Courtesy Col. Hodges)

Johnson, W/Cdr Hugh. *The Berlin Airlift: a brief account of the work carried out by Flight Refuelling Ltd.* (Courtesy W/Cdr Johnson)

Jones, H. B. *Reports from the British Overseas Airways Contingent, Sept.–Dec. 1948.* (Courtesy H.B. Jones)

Kearsley Airways: Reports from the General Manager, Oct. 1948. (Courtesy S/Ldr Thurston Smith)

Kommandatura, Berlin: Minutes of Meetings, Jan.–June, 1948 (Courtesy Maj. Gen. Edward Benson and George Foggon)

Landesarchiv, Berlin; Records of: correspondence of City Hall officials with U.S., U.K. and French Military Governments, 1948–49: files L.A.Z. 3035/12066 inclusive. (Landesarchiv, Berlin)

Madison, Dorothy. *A Berlin Diary, 1948–49.* (Courtesy Mrs. James Madison)

Operation Plainfare: Interim Report on RAF Gatow, June 1948–July 1949, with appendices. (Courtesy Air Vice Marshal Brian Yarde)

Operation Plainfare: Organisation, Responsibilities and Duties of Army Air Transport Organisation. (Courtesy Lt. Col. J.H. Craig, O.B.E.)

Operation Plainfare: a four-part study with appendices by H.Q. British Troops, Berlin. (Courtesy Mrs. R. N. Waite)

Prevost, Maj. Jules A. *Letters, reports, directives and plans of H.Q., C.A.L.T.F. Maintenance Division.* (Courtesy Col. Prevost)

Quayle, W/Cdr A.A. *The Berlin Airlift: an unpublished study.* (Courtesy Air Vice Marshal Yarde)

R.I.A.S. (Radio in the American Sector), Berlin: transcribed tape recordings of commentaries by Jurgen Graf, Peter Schulze and others, Sept. 6 and 9, 1948. (R.I.A.S. Archives)

Shack, Lt. Edward. *Fassberg Diary, 1948.* (Courtesy Edward Shack)

Smith, Brig. Gen. Joseph. *Operation Vittles: a Daily Log for July, 1948.* (Courtesy Lt. Gen. Smith)

Trudeau, Brig. Gen. *Notes on the composition and projected role of Task Force Trudeau.* (Courtesy Lt. Gen. Trudeau)

Truman, President Harry S. *Miscellaneous Airlift Memoranda.* (Truman Library, Fulton, Mo.)

Tunner, Maj. Gen. William H. *Airlift Papers.* (Courtesy Lt. Gen. Tunner)

Waite, Air Commodore Reginald. *The Berlin Airlift: a Transcribed Tape Recording.* (Courtesy Mrs. R. N. Waite)

Whitefoord, Lt. Col. H. P. *Reports to G.O.C. Berlin on meetings with City Hall officials.* (Courtesy Col. Whitefoord)

Whitfield, Edwin. *Report on the British Civil Airlift.* (Air Historical Branch, Ministry of Defence, London)

Williams, Air Marshal T. M. *H.Q. B.A.F.O. Report on Operation Plainfare: Air Ministry A.C.A.S.(Ops).* (Air Historical Branch, Ministry of Defence, London)

Acknowledgments

The principal sources of information for this book were the participants themselves—American and British pilots, maintenance and crewmen, military-government officials, and the Berliners who survived the blockade. From its beginnings in 1974, more than 520 people contributed to the book, providing written accounts and tape recordings, as well as submitting to lengthy question-and-answer interviews. Many of them supplied me with a wealth of documentation and memorabilia ranging from diaries and letters to maps and old newspaper clippings—even with ration coupons and treasured nuggets of airlift coal. I am deeply indebted to these survivors, whose names appear in the list of eyewitnesses.

Their information was fitted into a day-by-day chronology compiled from American, British, French, and German sources. Squadron and group reports, military-government records, intelligence summaries, stenographic records of meetings were supplemented by personal interviews with key figures of the period, many of whom turned over to me their own private papers. Without these vital documents, many of them still security-classified, I should have been unable to tell the story of the blockade so fully or so frankly.

First I must thank the many archivists and librarians who made my task easier throughout, most especially Dennis Bilger of the Harry S. Truman Library, Independence, Missouri, Charles G. Worman, Chief, Research Division, Department of the Air Force, Wright-Patterson Air Force Base, Ohio; James Eastman, Chief, Research Branch, Maxwell Air Force Base, Alabama; and Carol Farrar, historian, National Security Council, Washington, D.C. Their leads and suggestions invariably proved most helpful. In Berlin, Dr. Wolfgang Reichert steered me expertly through the voluminous holdings of the Landesarchiv, while Herr Herbert Pomade, Deputy Director of Archives, RIAS, rerecorded literally hours of contemporary tapes for my use. At the Ministry of Defence (Air Historical Branch), London, I received the warmest encouragement from Group Captain Edward Haslam, Chief Archivist, and his able staff, notably Mr. E. H. Turner, Mr. J. A. Spottiswoode, and Mrs. G. A. Fowles. At the British Library of Political and Economic Science (London School of Economics and Political Science) Angela Raspin guided me patiently through the maze of the Dalton diaries. Others, too, showed that nothing was too much trouble: Mrs. Patrick Collins, Acting Assistant Librarian, University College, Oxford; Anne Abley, St. Antony's College, Oxford; and Mrs. Patricia Bradford, Archivist, Churchill College, Cambridge. And Dr. Gerald Harris, Librarian of Magdalen College, Oxford, alone knows how much I am in his debt.

Since this book depended so profoundly on locating participants I must next acknowledge my gratitude to all those who smoothed my path in tracing survivors across the United States, Great Britain, and Germany. Editors Bruce Callander (*The Air Force Times*), C. V. Clines (*The Airline Pilot*), Gene Famiglitti (*The Army Times*), and Robert B. Pitman (*The American Legion Magazine*) were all kind enough to publish my appeal, which reaped a golden harvest of replies. Also instrumental in procuring leads were the Axel Springer Press, in particular Margarete Roemer of *Bild* and Peter Ritgen of *Berliner Morgenpost*, who gave my quest the widest possible publicity. As ever my good friend Tony Arnold of *The East Kent Mercury* proved a tower of strength.

Most helpful, too, were many of the airlines and manufacturers who combed dusty company records to trace airlift personnel. In particular, I must thank Ronald J. Wilson and Willi Vogler of British Airways, London and West Germany; John Leslie, Pan American; Mitchell Badler, Eastern Airlines; Steve McClure, Beech Aircraft Corporation; Peter Bush, the Boeing Company; William D. Berry, Delta Airlines; William D. Perreault, the Lockheed Aircraft Corporation; Francis L. Murphy, United Aircraft; Edward A. Cowles, Pratt & Whitney. My warmest thanks go to the McDonnell Douglas Corporation, especially to Colonel and Mrs. Raymond Towne, for their matchless hospitality in Long Beach, California.

In England, the difficult task of unearthing participants after twenty-six years was tackled with enthusiasm by Lieutenant Colonel J.D. Ricketts and Major Harold Knox of The Worcestershire Regiments' Association, Lieutenant Colonel A. Joanny of The Royal Norfolk Regiment Association, and Major F. J. Reed of The Queen's Regiment. In the United States a similar labor was cheerfully undertaken by Dorothy L. Flanagan of the Air Force Association and Colonel Dwight Dinsmore. My time in Berlin was equally made fruitful by that city's Lord Mayor, Klaus Schutz, who gave the project his blessing, and the Chief of his Press Department, Heinz Dundalski, whose introductions opened doors all over the city. Others who played a vital role were Robert Lochner of the American Chamber of Commerce, William F. Heimlich, and Karl Mautner—all of their introductions gave me a fascinating cross-section of Berlin society. And Senator Kurt Mattick, Horst Mühle, and Erika Tausch all, in their unsparing efforts to arrange meetings, showed themselves to be *Berliner mit herz*.

In all three countries I was fortunate to spend many hours talking with the men who had the formidable task of making the airlift work—on the ground no less than in the skies. General Lucius D. Clay took time out from a busy schedule to throw many new sidelights on his years as Military Governor. Brigadier General Frank Howley devoted an entire afternoon in the University Club, New York, to refighting his battles with the Soviets. Valuable slants from the topmost political level came from Clark Clifford, Robert Lovett, Robert Murphy, helpful and courteous as ever, W. Stuart Symington, and Lawrence

Wilkinson. Illuminating, too, were my detailed discussions with Brigadier General Sterling Bettinger, Ray Carlucci, Brigadier General John Coulter, Colonel Richard DaVania, Margaret and Edloe Donnan, the late Major General William H. Draper, Colonel Edward Guilbert, Colonel Gail Halvorsen, Major General George Hays, Judge Philip Jessup, Major General August Kissner, General Curtis LeMay, General Theodore Ross Milton, Lieutenant General Joseph Smith, Lieutenant General Arthur Trudeau, Major General Robert Walsh, General Albert Wedemeyer, and Major General Stanley Wray. But above all I owe a special debt to Lieutenant General William Tunner, the airlift's mastermind, and to his charming wife, Anne, for the warmth of their reception at Ware Neck, Virginia.

In England, many of the leading participants took endless pains to make themselves available for interview and to verify facts. Thus I owe a considerable debt to Air Marshal Sir Brian Baker, Major General Edward Benson, Air Chief Marshal Sir Kenneth Cross, Major General Charles Firth, Air Chief Marshal Sir Donald Hardman, Lieutenant General Sir Otway Herbert, Major General Stanley Joslin, and Sir Anthony Milward; to Air Marshal Sir Tim Piper, Lady Robertson, Air Vice Marshal John Stephenson, Lieutenant General Sir William Stratton, Major General Dennis Swan, Major General George Turner-Cain, the late Air Commodore Reginald Waite and Mrs. Waite, Air Marshal Sir Hugh Walmsley, and Air Vice Marshal Brian Yarde. My warmest thanks, too, to Bob and Ruth Durrant for their help at a crucial hour, to Wing Commander Robert Wright for his advice in the early stages, and to Roy Allen for much invaluable expertise.

Finally, how can I thank those who worked closest to me throughout? Without the help of *The Reader's Digest*, this book would never have taken shape, and I am grateful to Hobart Lewis, the *Digest's* chairman and editor-in-chief, for his initial faith in the project, to Bruce Lee, Walter Hunt, Kenneth Wilson, and Steve Frimmer for the constructive advice they offered at various stages of the research, and to Nancy Kelly for her astute editorial suggestions in the final draft. My thanks, also, to *Digest* staffers in Paris (Jacqueline Monnier), Stuttgart (Wulf C. Schwarzwäller), and Washington (Katherine

Clark, Virginia Lawton) for their unstinted efforts on my behalf.

But my greatest debt is to the researchers who worked loyally alongside me all through, above all to Hildegard Anderson, who not only located books, documents, and reports but carried out scores of meticulous interviews throughout the length and breadth of the United States. In this task she was at times supported ably by Sewell J. Whitney, Jr., and Robert Sabbag. In England, Pamela Colman tackled the pioneer research for many months unaided, though later admirably backstopped by Margaret Duff, Jean Farrer, Inga Forgan, Elisabeth Leslie, Jane McCammond, and Caitriona Smith. In Berlin, for weeks on end, I had the noble support of Eva Travers, who oversaw my schedule and interpreted at more than 100 interviews; at a later stage the threads were taken up by Franz M. Grueger, who did a masterly job in tracking down many elusive survivors. In London, many of his findings were translated from the German by Philip Wright, while Ilse Böker stood in at a vital moment with streamlined secretarial help. And I would have been lost without Joan St. George Saunders' infallible eye for the vital fact or figure or description.

Elly Beintema again solved all my photographic problems. Jill Beck's overseeing of the final typescript was a painstaking miracle of precision. Joe and Christine Garner were always there with secretarial help just when I needed them most. I am grateful, too, to my agents in London and New York, Graham Watson and John Cushman, who provided counsel and support all through. My thanks also to my London publisher, Lord Hardinge of Penshurst, for waiting patiently for the finished manuscript for many months after the contractual deadline.

But to my wife goes, as always, my deepest gratitude. Apart from interviews in England and all over the United States from Nashville, Tennessee, to Boston, Massachusetts, she oversaw the entire chronology from beginning to end, typed, translated, offered constructive criticism, kept the home (which included the daily welfare of three cats and a horse) running serenely, and was always there when I needed her most to offer her advice, support, and encouragement.

Index

233